STRUCTURES

Robert E. Sonntag

Illustrated by Julia S. Daze

PHILOMOD CORPORATION, Jacksonville, Florida

Published by Philomod Corporation
        P.O. Box 31339, Yukon Station
        Jacksonville, FL 32230

PHILOMOD is a trademark of Philomod Corporation
and Robert E. Sonntag.

Library of Congress Cataloging-in-Publication Data

Sonntag, Robert E., 1922-
    Structures.

    At head of title: Business Media Resources.
    Bibliography: p.
    Includes index.
    1. Success in business.   I. Title.
HF5386.S74   1986   650.1   86-17042
ISBN 0-938545-00-0 (pbk.)

5   4   3   2   1

First Edition

Illustrated by Julia S. Daze

Production Coordination: BMR, Mill Valley, CA
Cover and Interior Design: BMR, Mill Valley, CA
Cover Illustration: Rosiland Soloman
Back Cover Photo: Agnes J. Sonntag

*I am indebted to my son and daughter,
both of whom are gifted illustrators.*

*Thanks to my daughter,
Julia S. Daze, for her patience—
through college and then two babies—
with hundreds of trial sketches.
All the illustrations in this book are hers.*

*And to my son,
Edward J. Sonntag, happy owner
THE NED SONNTAG STUDIO,
NEW YORK CITY,
thanks for the assistance in the
visualizations and dramatizations
of many complex and abstract
economic concepts.*

Contents

Acknowledgements

Even though a project has been strung out over fourteen years such as this one has, a writer still should not forget any of the good people who provided encouragement and assistance along the way. I hope I have not overlooked anyone.

The first 76-page outline was printed in 1974 under the tentative title *The Capipod Discovery*. The friends who responded to that amateurish, ragged effort are especially appreciated. Among them were Randy Berg, Bud Smith, Carol and Bob Shircliff, Dick Suddath, George Ellis, Bill Adams, Bill Kelley, Dick Worsham, Jimmy Taylor, Libby Wood, George Stallings, Debbie Stallings, Chick Haynes, Anne and Dave Patterson, Baylor Landrum, Marilyn and Bob Oldenberg, Bill Derbins, Roger Zion, Charles McMahan, Cinder Harwick, Mark Bramlett, Ed Brady, and Judson Yerkes.

The second 45-page outline was duplicated in 1980 under the second provisional title *The Structure of Liberty* and was distributed to fellow students at the seminar on Public Policy at Grove City College, Grove City, Pennsylvania, June 15 to 20, 1980. Helpful comments, critiques, and encouragement came from Vincent J. Mooney, Jr., John East, Sarah Sanders, David Scott, Peggy Egelhoff, and Alma Textor. Also input and encouragement from Ken Dawes at about that time.

Then there were the excellent teachers at the Hillsdale College seminar, Hillsdale, Michigan, July 25-31, 1976; at the Foundation of Economic Education seminar at Irvington-on-Hudson, New York, August 7-13, 1977, and Grove City College, June, 1980. First among these fine lecturers was Hans Sennholz, followed closely by John Sparks, Russell Kirk, Leonard Read, Bob Anderson, Ed Opitz, Paul Poirot, Bettina Greaves, and Henry Hazlitt. At Hillsdale I first met Albert Zlabinger who later moved to Jacksonville as professor of Finance and Economics at Jacksonville University. Albert and his bright wife, Terry, will always be special.

Memorable also was the seminar on April 26, 1975, in St. Louis, jointly sponsored by the Institute for Humane Studies and the St. Louis Discussion Club. There the great leader of the Austrian School himself, Friedrich Hayek, was the key speaker, backed up by Henry Manne and Ben Rogge.

Finally, thanks to John O'Connell, Jr. who executed the engineering drawings for the 16-piece Philomod model, simplifying them so that manufacturing finally became feasible. Thanks to Jack Jennings and his team of professionals at Business Media Resources in San Francisco. Their skillful guidance and copy-editing was essential. And to Susanne Wedberg at the Copy Center on Edgewood Avenue, Jacksonville, and to Brick and Adele Brickman at the Graphic Arts Center on Park Street, Jacksonville, I am indebted for hundreds of reductions, enlargements, chart work, veloxes, copies, typesetting, and all the other details that go into the process of preparing a book for publication.

Introduction:
An Open Letter to the
American Entrepreneur

Dear Entrepreneur:

This book is about you ...
It is about the fundamentals of your own enterprise. *Structures* explores what makes you and your business tick. And if your business isn't ticking so well, this book might give you some insights and ideas on how to make it tick better.

This book is about the free market ...
You and your enterprise are the backbone of this nation. You have been for more than 200 years. *Structures* tells you why America is different and great and always will be. You can feel proud; you are the hero of that story. But the story goes beyond our shores. The community of free-market organizations extends to every nation in the world.

This book is more than a book ...
It is an opportunity. *Structures* is a book and a model. The mechanical drawings for the model are in the back of this book. The basic model is made of maple or birch and stands about eight inches high. As soon as the book creates a demand for the model, we will market it.

Together the book and model are the embryos of a new product line. As you will see, we are offering this line to a selected few of you to distribute. The primary age-group markets for *Structures* are ages 18, 38 and 58. We tell you why you should begin your marketing program with these groups. And if you are close to one of these ages, all the better.

Structures is written with the young person in mind. What is familiar to you is not yet so familiar to the person still in high school or college. We use many illustrations. What the youngsters may spot immediately is that *Structures* provides the first programmable database for free-market concepts.

The *Structures* product line has many opportunities for expansion. We are looking for licensees, for example, for products that are listed in the book. We also have some exciting ideas for the future.

Structures has trademarked symbols ...

Our symbols are models. Our models are unique, tangible representations of intangible politico-economic structures. The structures represent and explain enterprise, entrepreneurs, the free market, and its opposite, which we call the anti-market. It all combines to form the most powerful argument for the free market since Thomas Jefferson and Adam Smith wrote their landmark political and economic treatises in 1776.

The products are sound ...

As you will see, *Structures* is as sound as the Declaration of Independence and our Constitution. These great documents provide the politico-economic fundamentals that make the book and model work. *Structures* has been under development for years. The first Philomod prototype was manufactured in 1974. Philomod Corporation was incorporated in 1974. The model you have before you has been simplified, tested, examined, and criticized. It holds up beautifully.

There's more I could tell you. But I'd rather you get started, so you can see what I mean. Oh, yes ... if you are one of those readers who likes to skip to the last chapter "to see how the story comes out," I suggest that you don't. You will not reap the greatest benefit from the business plan, outlined in the last chapter, unless you have approached it systematically.

Whether you are an entrepreneur, a retired entrepreneur, or want to be an entrepreneur, *Structures* will, I sincerely believe, offer you excellent value.

Sincerely yours,
PHILOMOD CORPORATION

Robert E. Sonntag, President

PART I CHOICES AND MODELS

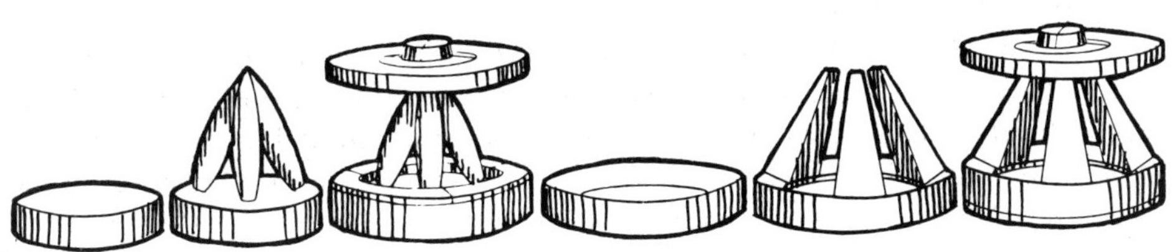

Chapter 1 — The Structure of Free Choice

Piece ① Your Freedom to Choose

If you don't do your own thinking, someone else will do it for you.
Edward de Bono

We hurry along day to day surrounded by choices.

My parents did not tell me about choices, and your parents probably did not tell you either. Nor did my schoolteachers or college professors spend any time on the subject. I wish someone had.

First, there are *choices*. Choices are a part of our environment, just like buildings, streets, trees, flowers, and mosquitoes. The difference is we can see the buildings, smell the flowers, and hear the mosquitoes and feel their sting. Our senses tell us. But unless someone convinces us that the choices are there too, just as real, just as tangible, we may not recognize it until we are twenty, forty, sixty—maybe never.

Second, there is the *freedom to choose.*
We can portray freedom to choose as a large wooden disk on which you can sit, walk, run, work, or relax.

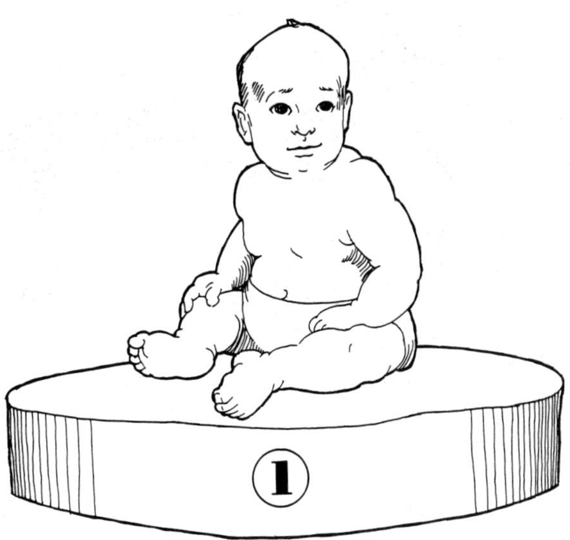

This disk was given to you at birth. It is yours and yours alone. It is under you like a flying carpet. You may use this disk well or poorly, but you cannot shake it. It is yours for life.

When you get to be ninety, you can sit and rock on it. But like choices, unless someone tells you about the disk, you may reach ninety and never know about it.

Each of us has his or her own Freedom-to-Choose disk, which we will call Piece 1.

The Freedom-to-Choose disk may be sliced into two thinner disks. The two are always the same diameter, fitting together nicely to make up the whole. When we pick up our disk and stand it on its edge like a wheel, we can see the structures of the two thinner disks.

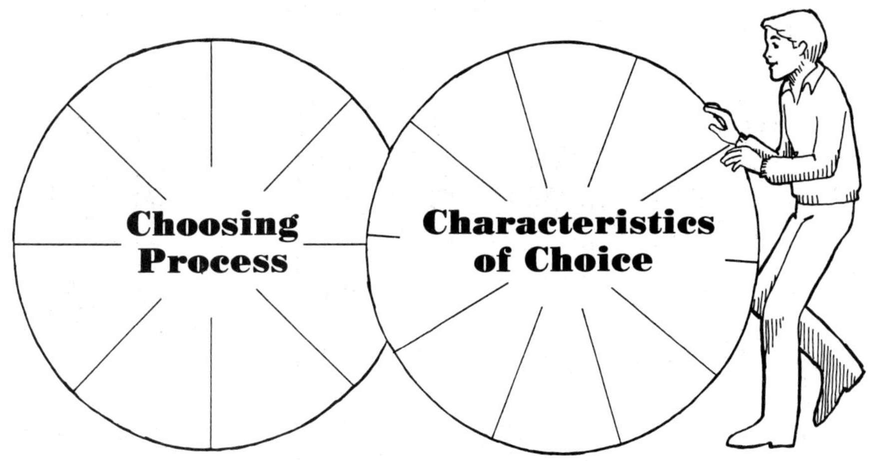

One of these structures is called the *Choosing Process.* The other is called the *Characteristics of Choice.* You will be pleased to know that either one can be on top. They are interdependent and work best when used together. A fine-quality glue named self-discipline cements the two disks together.

Each of the two disks is marked into pie-slice wedges.

The Choosing Process disk is composed of eight wedges. The Characteristics of Choice disk has ten.

Imagine walking around on top of your disk, stepping from one wedge-shaped section to the next.

The reason to step from one wedge to the next is so that when you end up at Step Eight in the Choosing Process (or Number Ten in the Characteristics of Choice), you will again be facing Step One. In other words, if you have gone through all the steps and find that you have made a poor choice, you are back at "Go," ready to try to make a better choice.

So each of us is surrounded by choices, and each of us has a lifetime base that is called the freedom to choose. And this freedom to choose is made up of ten Characteristics of Choice and a Choosing Process made up of eight steps or phases.

THE TEN CHARACTERISTICS OF CHOICE

THE CC's

All of us have a physiological range of capability, sensitivity, and productivity. Through the use of choices, we can expand our physiological range. From the easy everyday choices to the large difficult decisions a common thread runs through them all: we use choices to improve our situation as we see it at the time.

Freedom of choice is our personal servant, a pedestal upon which we stand, a gentle genie always close by to help us improve situation after situation. What are these situations? There are thousands.

The little choices such as what to have for lunch.

Should I eat heartily or try to lose weight?
Then there are some of the more important ones all of us have to deal with:

- The kind of person we want to be
- How we use our time

- How we utilize our natural talents
- How we care for our bodies
- Our moral and religious values

- Whom we will choose for lover, husband or wife
- Whom we want for long-term friends and partnerships
- Where we want to live
- As producers, how we earn our living
- As consumers, how we spend what we earn
- As investors, how best to make our savings grow
- How we rear our children
- How we use our later years

Following are descriptions of the ten Characteristics of Choice, numbered CC-1 through CC-10 for easy reference.

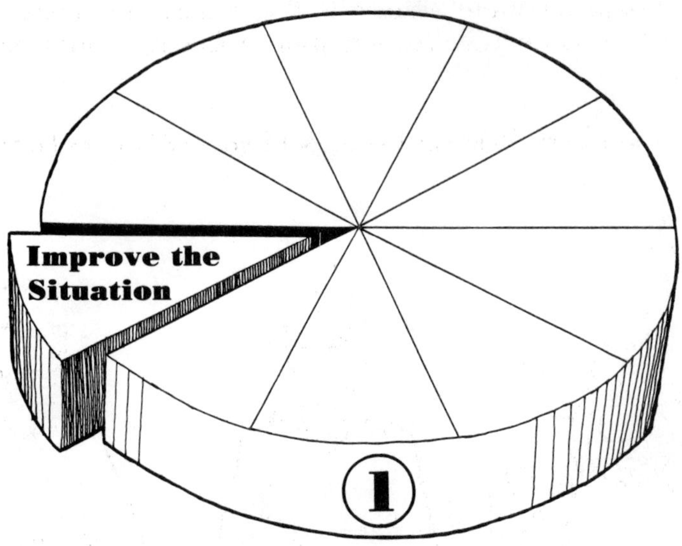

Characteristics of Choice

CC-1 Choices Have a Common Purpose: To Improve Our Situation

Economist Ludwig von Mises believed that every human action begins with "a feeling of uneasiness." In *Human Action,* he defined "felt uneasiness" as:

"The subjective feeling of discomfort, distress, or dissatisfaction with things as they are which spurs each of us on to try to improve the situation in some way.

"Man is eager to substitute a more satisfactory state of affairs for a less satisfactory. His mind imagines conditions which suit him better, and his action aims at bringing about this desired state. The incentive that impels a man to act is always some uneasiness."

If you are uneasy in your present job, you may choose to look for another. If you feel dissatisfied with the place where you live, you may choose to look for a different place. If you are dissatisfied with the slacks that hang in your closet, you may choose to buy a new pair. If you feel uneasy about the condition of your body, you may choose to eat less, drink less, and exercise more.

We do not use choices knowingly to make our situation less desirable. If a specific choice appears to result in an outcome that is less desirable, we will choose not to act, or we may select a different course of action. When we make choices that result in undesirable outcomes, we call them *mistakes.* Then we find ourselves in a new situation in which we feel uneasy, so that we must once again make new choices and take new actions.

The captain of the sailing ship reefs his sails for the approaching squall. He makes the choice he thinks best to improve the situation as he perceives it at the time. If he learns that the approaching squall is a typhoon, he may take a different course of action; for example, he may add more canvas and try to sail around the storm. The same situation at different times may call for different choices of action.

The first Characteristic of Choice is that almost all choices have a common objective, to improve our situation. A feeling of uneasiness tells us to get busy.

CC-2 Choices Come in Twos or More; A Choice of One Is Force

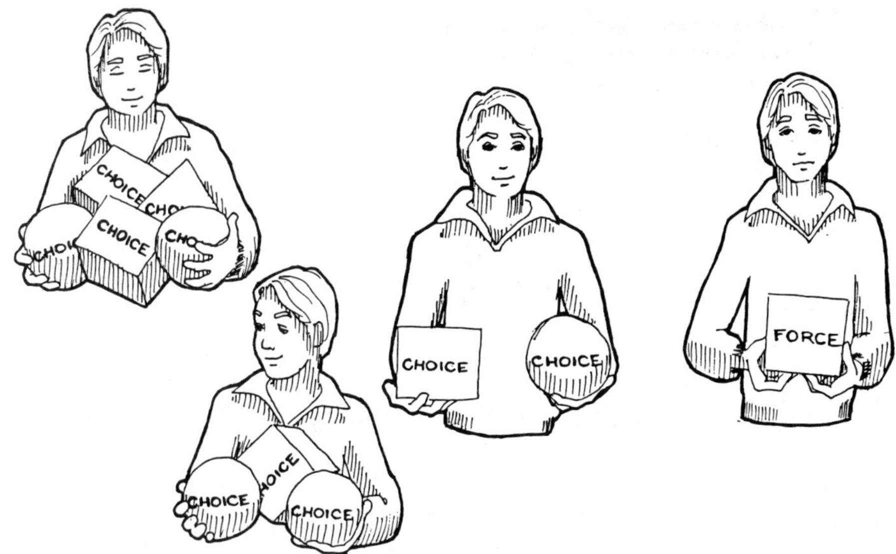

In the Soviet Union, where one political party has control, there is always only one candidate for each office—the Communist Party candidate. The citizen votes yes or no for one candidate; there is no alternative. As Mark Russell quipped, following a recent Russian election: "Leonid Brezhnev was just reelected in Russia by a landslide. In a one-man race, he came in first. They have very clean elections over there, no primary, no mudslinging, no dirty tricks, no opponent. Brezhnev watched himself making a speech on television and demanded equal time."

Choices come in twos or more. A choice of less than two options is not a choice. It may be wrapped in the cloak of choice, but it is really coercion. A choice of one implies that someone else is in charge. If you as an individual are not free to choose, you are not free. In almost any situation, it usually pays to pause and ask, "What are the alternatives to the present situation? There are other choices. It's just a matter of looking for them and finding the best one."

If you want to be your own person, want to be in charge of your own life, want to be free to improve upon your situation as you see best at the time, you will recognize the difference between choice and its opposites: force, compulsion, and coercion.

When you visit the home of a friend, she might ask, "May I get you something to drink? Coffee, tea, a lemonade?" If you choose coffee, she might follow up with "How do you like it? Cream, sugar, black?" In its simplest form choice is a courtesy. A choice of one becomes more than a discourtesy; it is at least an affront. And, as we will see further on, it may be a threat.

In our society, as we begin dating at age 18 or so, we make choices. We seek those persons who are "right" for us. In some oriental societies parents still select their child's marriage partner. It may even be someone the child has never seen. In one of life's most important decisions—the selection of a mate—these young people are not permitted to control their own situations.

The 38-year-old company purchasing agent tries to have at least three sources of supply for every material he buys. His responsibility is to compare quality, prices, and availability for delivery at a specific time. He is the shopper and buyer for his company, seeking those materials that best suit his company's needs, wants, and preferences. Only by comparison can he be reasonably sure that he is buying a known quantity at a fair price. If he purchases from only one source, that supplier would be tempted to provide lower quality, a higher price, or both. When the purchaser does not shop, he lets the seller control the situation that he should control.

Shoppers are usually winners. The 18-year-old who sets out to find a job should try to line up three different interviews before making a choice. The 38-year-old employer of part-time summer teens is wise to interview at least three applicants before making his choice. The 58-year-old CEO who is searching for a vice-president of marketing knows it is prudent to interview at least three good applicants. He who shops develops a feel for the current market. No shopping, no comparison; you have done yourself or your company a disservice. Does it happen? Four out of five Americans are in jobs that they feel are not quite right for them. Did they shop? Can they shop now?

Again and again in the following chapters we will play this tune together: Either *you* are in charge of your own situation or *someone else* is in charge. There is little or no middle ground. If you have two or more choices, you have a better chance of being free and in control. If someone hands you a choice of one—"an offer you can't refuse"—he may be a godfather.

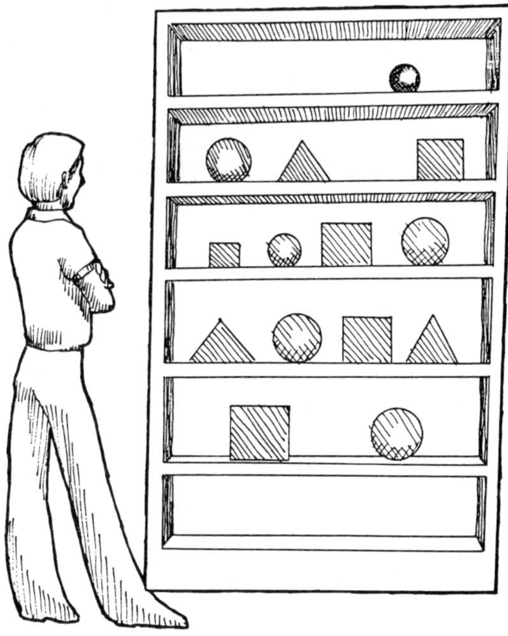

The great restauranteurs of New York, Paris, and Tokyo know about this Characteristic of Choice: to serve the best you begin with the best. The best cuts of prime aged beef. Firm, fresh vegetables. Day-old eggs. Fresh creamery butter. The first rule of Cordon Bleu chefs is the same as the third Characteristic of Choice: To get the best outcome, begin with the best ingredients. Use inferior ingredients and you will get inferior results. Computer programmers have their own way of saying it: "Garbage in, garbage out."

Perhaps the alternative on the top shelf, hidden behind other ingredients or a little high for your reach, is the one you have been looking for. Many outcomes appear satisfying at first glance. Then we are reminded of another choice that we hadn't even considered and exclaim, "Why didn't I think of that!"

So what role, if any, does this Characteristic of Choice play in our pursuit of happiness? A study by Dr. Herbert M. Greenberg of the Marketing Survey and Research Corporation showed that four out of five people are in the wrong jobs for their abilities. Other studies dealing with stress have shown that unhappiness on the job is the source of mental problems, physical illness, and alcoholism.

Have four out of five Americans made a bad job choice? Possibly. Does this mean that a young person trying to get a start has only one chance in five of landing a position in which he will be happy? Not at all.

The Labor Department's Dictionary of Occupational Titles lists 35,000 occupations, and between 4,000 and 5,000 new ones are added every few years! Even assuming that nine out of ten of these will be of no interest to you, that still leaves a list of 3,500 possibilities. Boil the list down to a tenth again. Still there are 350!

In the social sphere, people are often alarmed about our high divorce rate. In *How You Rate*, Tom Biracree tells us that half our marriages now end in divorce. Is this a record of good outcomes? Hardly. Was religion lacking? Not that frequently; four out of five marriage ceremonies, Biracree's statistics show, were religious.

Twenty-five years ago the median age at which American women married was 19. Now it is 22. During the first half of this century, according to various articles in journals of obstetrics, 50 percent of American brides were pregnant when they walked down the aisle. Half the time, therefore, people who "decided" to marry did not really decide at all. Fate dealt them a hand in which force, not choice, held all four aces.

If we choose our lifelong jobs or our mates without much attention to the quality of the input, what of our homes? How thoughtfully do we go about selecting the rose-covered cottage, the ostensible American dream? Quite carefully, it appears. According to a 1985 study, we inspect an average of thirteen possible homes before we make a purchase. Still, every year 40 million of us change our home addresses!

With more freedom of choice than any other group of individuals in the world, how far has the average American progressed toward making choice his obedient lifetime servant? Not an impressive distance. Our guess is that if you practice the principles in this book, you will have a decided advantage over 99.5 percent of your fellow citizens.

Thomas Edison said, "If we did all the things we are capable of doing, we would literally astound ourselves."

And yet our cumulative progress is undoubtedly better than that of almost any other nation, past or present. High on the list of reasons why we became number one is that we saved and invested wisely. We plowed back our savings into our farms, our businesses, our industries, and our other private institutions. We became the nation (Japan is now very close) with the highest amount of invested capital per worker. This meant higher productivity, which begat less scarcity, which begat our excellent wages and high standard of living.

To get the best outcome, start by including the best alternatives among your input-options.

We will leave the third Characteristic of Choice with the following quote by Rex Brown et. al., from their book *Decision Analysis, An Overview:* "The difference between good and bad decisions (as opposed to good and bad outcomes) lies partly in the selection of appropriate basic inputs .... The best decision cannot be made unless the best option is among those that are being considered."

In other words, the question you should ask yourself is: Before I start the choosing process, have I included all the best options?

Freedom of choice means that no one interferes as we assemble our alternatives. No one interferes as we sweat through our decisions. And no one interferes with the outcome that is the result of our thought processes.

CC-4 Every Choice Has a Cost

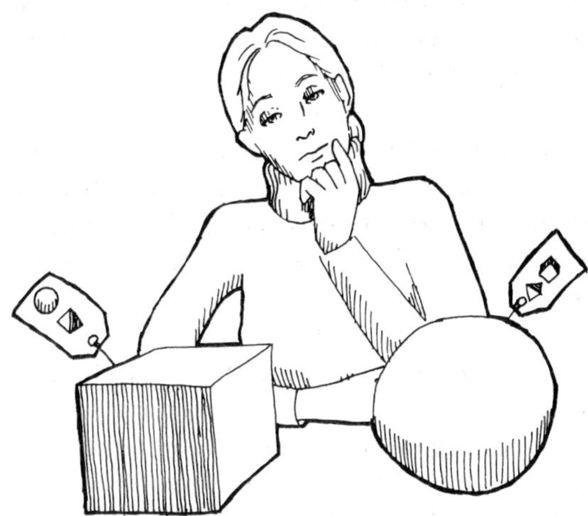

Friedrich A. Hayek, who was awarded the Nobel prize in economics in 1974, has commented that one of the reasons why economists feel compelled to express themselves about political, social, and moral problems is that each of these involves choices, and economists are trained to use certain tools when evaluating choices. One of these tools is called "opportunity cost." When we choose one course of action, the "cost" is that we deny ourselves, at least for the time being, other courses of action we might have taken. A simple example: We come home from work and have an hour to (1) walk the dog, (2) watch the last two innings of a ballgame, and (3) take a nap.

The "cost" of walking the dog is that we forgo the ballgame and the nap. The "cost" of catching the last innings of the game is that we cannot take the nap or walk the dog. We are obliged to "pay" for the nap by forgoing the walk and the ballgame.

Opportunity costs can be measured in various ways: time, money, satisfaction, and so on. The above example deals with the use of one hour of time to our greatest satisfaction. We can "see" the hour as it approaches, we experience it, then it is gone forever. It will never be repeated. Viewed in this way, the hour was very scarce—in fact, the only one of its kind.

Most people value their time very highly. Some years ago I had an importing company. On occasion I needed to visit our local customs official in his office downtown. A sign on his desk read something to this effect: "My life is my time. If you waste my time, you are taking my life."

Opportunity costs, as measured in time, assume a greater importance and may become a little frightening as we grow older. There is not as much time left for the 58-year-old as there is for the 18-year-old. At age 18 there is time to recover from most bad choices. At 38 there is still time, but much less so at 58. Time becomes more finite, more real.

Opportunity cost is also measured in dollars and cents. A simple example: It is Sunday. You have only 75 cents. It will buy only one of the following: (1) a Sunday newspaper, (2) a double-dip ice cream cone, or (3) a bus ride to the beach and back. It cannot buy all three. Buying the paper, for example, costs us the pleasure of the cone and the beach, not to mention the hundreds of other things that seventy-five cents could buy.

Frequently, the opportunity costs of one decision can be measured in several ways. We invest $10,000 in a friend's business venture, and the deals turns sour two years later. What is the cost? The loss of $10,000 is the obvious cost of our poor choice. There is the opportunity lost to have invested $10,000 in something psychically more rewarding. There is also an opportunity cost in time: the $2,000 in interest that we might have earned if, say, we had invested the money in a money-market fund over those two years.

Suppose the price of gold coins was rather low at the time we invested in our friend's business. (We had considered gold at the time but decided not to invest in it.) Two years later the price of gold has doubled. Suppose we look at opportunity cost as the best alternative that we did not choose. The opportunity cost, then, for investing in the business venture was not $12,000 but $20,000!

Choices involve sacrifices. Every action we take means that we sacrificed an alternative action. In terms of what we sacrificed, what was the cost of our choice? Was it a waste of time? A waste of money? A waste of psychic satisfaction?

CC-5 Choices Are Subjective Value Preferences

"We buy junque. We sell antiques." So reads a sign in a weekend flea market. Meander, if you will, through the market. There among the dishes, dresses, lamps, picture frames, coins, and tools you will get a postgraduate course in the study of *value*.

"What in the world," you might ask yourself, "would anyone in his right mind want with any of this stuff!"

Each item in each stall, at some moment in the past, was perceived as having value by the person who owned it. There is no such thing as an object having intrinsic value. We attach value to an item according to what it does for us, its utility, beauty, scarcity, or other factors. The value of an object is in our mind.

Here in Stall 33, for example, is a dinner plate for sale. It has about a 10-inch diameter, with a blue border design and a hairline crack on one edge. It is tan rather than ivory, suggesting that it may be at least 100 years old. What is the value of this plate, and if it has value, why is it as valuable now, or more valuable, than it was 100 years ago?

The owner of the plate, the renter of Stall 33, paid 25 cents for it at a farm auction two months ago. He is selling it now for two dollars. Your eye passes over it quickly. It takes you less than five seconds to assess the other items in Stall 33. You walk on to Stall 34. To you the plate was without value. It did not attract your attention for even one second. It was worthless.

Your wife, however, has stopped at 33 and is examining the plate. She picks it up and turns it over. She observes that its manufacturer's mark is familiar, and she is pleased. She has eleven identical plates at home. This will round out her set.

"Just what I've been looking for," she says to the man in Stall 33. "How much?"

"Two dollars."

"But it's cracked."

"OK. Knock off a half buck."

"I'll give you a dollar."

"Sold."

There has been a meeting of minds. Both seller and buyer are a little happier than they were before. In his pursuit of happiness, the seller will make a few bucks in Stall 33 this weekend. In her pursuit of happiness your wife has completed her set of dinner plates at what she considers a good value.

Still, the dinner plate has no intrinsic value. The fact that the man in Stall 33 paid twenty-five cents for it does not establish its value. The fact that he would have gladly sold it for fifty cents establishes no value. The fact that your wife paid a dollar means only that *in her eyes* the plate had a value of a dollar. It is fair to say that at that moment that particular plate had a "market value" of one dollar.

In our pursuit of happiness our choices express our value preferences. To each of us something at each particular time is number one.

Neither properties nor events have intrinsic value. Their value is only in our minds.

Let's return to Stall 33 and set up a different scenario. The vendor is selling a set of twelve of the same dishes. Your wife has ten of this same set at home.

"How much are these," she asks him.

"The set is twenty-four dollars."

"Then two would be four dollars," she says, opening her purse.

"Can't break the set, lady."

"But I need only two."

"Pay me twenty-four dollars and you get the other ten free."

"I'll have to think about that," she says and closes her purse.

Value, like beauty, is in the eye of the beholder. To your wife the plates had value of varying degrees depending upon her situation. To *you* the plates in Stall 33 were worthless. Value is subjective.

Pancakes, for some reason, are frequently used to illustrate what is called "marginal value." To a hungry boy the thought of just one pancake, covered in butter and maple syrup, is extremely valuable. He eats ten pancakes. The value he places on the 11th pancake? Not quite so high, but still exciting. As he continues to stuff himself, he sees that the value of each additional pancake is more and more marginal. Each becomes less useful than the last (less utility). And since there seem to be plenty more where those came from (no scarcity), the twenty-fifth pancake is worthless to him.

But the boy who was hungry has a hungry friend. To make our experiment more interesting, assume that the second boy has to sit and observe his friend make a pig of himself. The friend has been forbidden to take part in the feast. What is the value of the twenty-fifth pancake to the second boy? He would kill for it!

We cannot say that any one characteristic of choice is more important than any other. All ten are interdependent, like most of the pieces in our structures. But of all ten characteristics this is probably the most personal, the most individualized, and the most subjective.

What do you value most highly? Woodrow Wilson said, "It is not men that interest or disturb me primarily; it is ideas. Ideas live; men die." Is it a person that you value? An object? A belief? A cause? An organization? Is it tangible? No? An intangible then, such as the way others feel about you?

Where would you prefer to devote your energies at this time? Not at another time—now. At another time "it" may be something different. Whatever "it" is, your mind assigns considerable value to it. More value than most other people might assign; more value than others might readily understand. Whatever "it" is, it is highest on your order of value preferences. Suppose another person or organization imposes itself between you and "it"? Suppose someone wants to take "it" away? Or destroy it? That threatens you, doesn't it?

Why is it important that you start thinking about your value preferences? Later in the book, your value preferences will form the basis of an experiment that could change your life.

CC-6 Choices Are Made with Limited Time and Information

Superstar quarterback Dan Marino has about ten seconds to make his choices. "What's best now?" he asks himself, "run, pass, or kick?" And as he huddles with his team he follows up with the next question, "Which play will be the best strategy?"

The clock on the stadium scoreboard gives him very limited time to decide. If he takes a second too long, he is penalized. The skill with which he chooses under pressure is one of the reasons he is a pro.

To those who grew up in the corporate environment of the 1950s, the words of one particular management pro, Peter F. Drucker, are appropriate:

"Most decisions have to be based on incomplete knowledge—either because the information is not available or because it would cost too much in time or money to get it."

We have already seen that we can seize upon only one choice at a particular moment, because the nature of time will not usually allow us to fit two actions into the same time-space. Another limitation on choices is that they are typically based on incomplete information because we are frequently compelled to take action within a limited window of time.

When the rescue squad arrives at the scene of an auto accident, it faces limited time and incomplete information. Life may be ebbing rapidly from some of the victims. Others may have little more than scratches. The rescuers have only seconds to sort out the serious injuries and set priorities.

The 18-year-old who is interviewing for his first job has only limited information about it. He feels as though he is the only person in the world who has faced this agony. He has so little time. School starts again in September, and he must make some money.

His jitters might be somewhat calmed if he could see twenty years into his future. When he is 38, he will look at a company he would like to buy. It is listed by the mergers-and-acquisitions specialist as a fine company worth $3.5 million. Just to make the down payment, however, he will have to mortgage his home, borrow against stocks, and hock his socks. Never before has he made an entrepreneurial decision of this magnitude. With his own money on the line! Other prospective buyers are also examining it. Pressure! He has to make a choice in limited time and based on incomplete information.

When he is 58, a headhunter invites him to consider a position as a CEO to turn around a company with annual sales of $100 million. It is going down the drain fast. But what an opportunity! He has to make a choice in limited time and based on incomplete information.

Rarely is there enough time. There is never enough information. If the information concerning the outcome of the choice were 100 percent complete and accurate, of course, it would not require a judgmental decision. Anyone could make that kind of choice, because it is no longer a choice. It has already reached the level of a sure-fire certainty!

Anthony Downs, in his fascinating study *Inside Bureaucracy*, sums up our sixth Characteristic of Choice and sets the stage for the seventh:

> *Information is costly because it takes time, effort, and sometimes money to obtain data and comprehend their meaning.*
>
> *Decision makers have only limited capabilities regarding the amount of time they can spend making decisions, the number of issues they can consider simultaneously, and the amount of data they can absorb regarding any one problem.*
>
> *Although some uncertainty can be eliminated by acquiring information, an important degree of ineradicable uncertainty is usually involved in making decisions.*

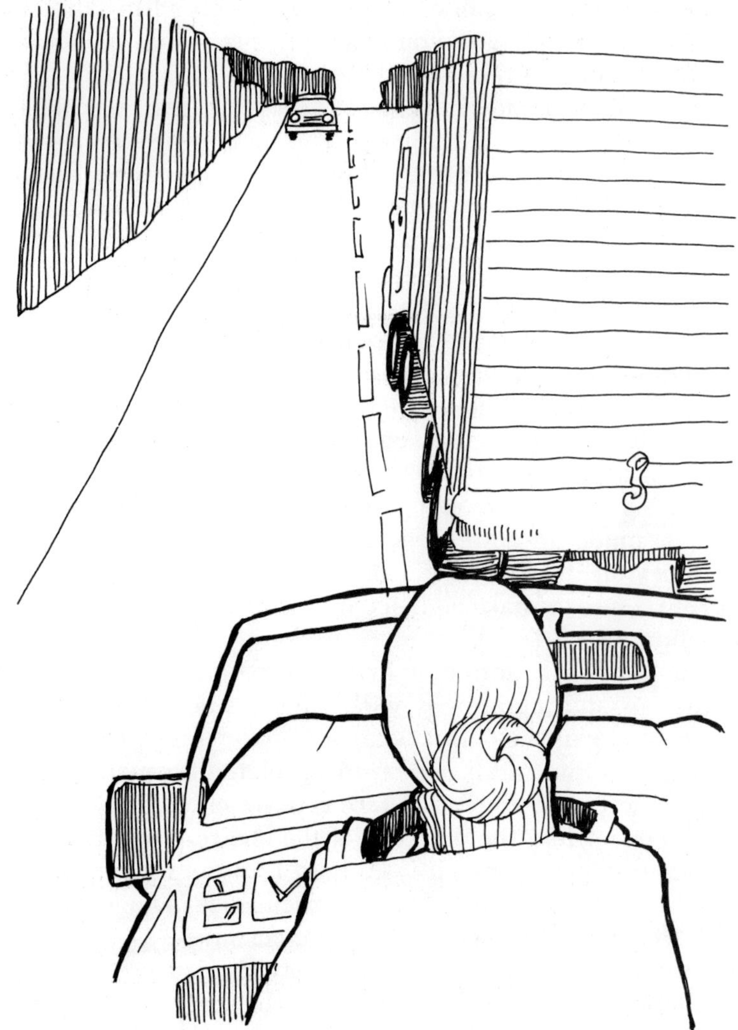

Every decision is made with some uncertainty.

David Viscott, M.D., in his book *Risking,* uses the analogy of passing another automobile on the highway. It is the most dangerous time of driving. The driver must make a committment to take the risk, accelerate, and follow through in his committment. Viscott describes risk as a sequence of five steps:

1. Recognizing your need to risk
2. Deciding to risk
3. Initiating the risk
4. The point of no return
5. Completing the risk

If only we could foresee the future! Every action we would take to improve our situation would be executed with complete confidence. We would select the ideal place to live! We would choose the perfect mate! We would be employed in a job we could not wait to get to every day! Dreams, dreams, sweet dreams.

Everyday conversation reflects our uncertainty. In our own way we try to quantify the range, from absolute certainty to complete uncertainty, about a particular set of alternatives.

Below are some common phrases to which we have assigned degrees of "mathematical certainty."

Phrases	Certainty of Outcome
I'm absolutely sure that ...	100 Percent
I feel quite certain that ...	90 "
I am reasonably certain that ...	80 "
There's a good chance that ...	70 "
There's a better than even chance ...	60 "
There's a 50-50 chance that ...	50 "
There's less than an even chance ...	40 "
There's some chance that ...	30 "
There's a slight chance that ...	20 "
I'm not at all certain that ...	10 "
No way, José.	0 "

The exercise is arbitrary, of course, but there is a point to it. The point is this: Almost without realizing it, we try to convert uncertainties (unquantifiable unknowns) into risks (definable probabilities). The reason is normal human fear of the unknown. Most of us are uncomfortable with uncertainties, but we can live with risk. Although the term risk is often used to mean uncertainty, the two words are not synonomous.

The entrepreneur who is searching for a location to start a new business faces a completely unique situation. He knows that no two pieces of real estate are alike. He knows that in some types of retail businesses the distance of one-half a block, or even which side of the street he chooses, can spell the difference between success and disaster. The decision he is about to make is fraught with uncertainty. He cannot get any wholly satisfactory answer to his uncertainty, and he cannot know the odds against him. He cannot insure against this kind of uncertainty, because the probability of success or failure (for a specific time and location) cannot be quantified.

Once he opens his doors, however, he faces uncertainties against which he can insure. These are risks of loss through fire, theft, vandalism, and personal injury. To his insurer these are not uncertainties. They are statistics that insurance specialists face so often that they are certain of the outcome. The insurance actuary knows that out of every 1,000 businesses of this kind there will be a predictable number of casualty losses. The insurer knows the odds. He will therefore assume the risks for a fee that reflects those odds. Private insurers will not write policies on uncertainties that cannot be quantified; if they did, they would probably become one of the casualties.

This does not alter the fact that we humans will scratch, bite, and claw to have our uncertain futures "covered." To whom, then, do all mortals turn? As we will see in later chapters, we often turn to government in our desperation to protect ourselves from the unique, unknown, and uncertain. As we will also see, modern-day governments rarely refuse the supplications of their citizens. Unlike ourselves, governments have little fear of going down the drain. The outcome is that the size of the insurance tabs borne by governments grow to horrendous and unmanageable proportions.

In his classic, *Risk, Uncertainty, and Profit,* written more than sixty years ago, Frank Knight stated it this way: "If the risk is unmeasureable, but the 'moral factor' or some other consideration makes ordinary insurance inapplicable, some other method of securing the same result will be developed and employed."

In learning to work with the choices around us, we learn to come to grips with uncertainty. We try to transform true uncertainty into probability and then into a quantifiable risk. Once we are reasonably comfortable with the risk, we estimate the costs against the anticipated rewards. Then we make our choice and take the action we think best at the time. That's the way it's supposed to work, anyway.

CC-8 Choices Have Primary and Secondary Consequences

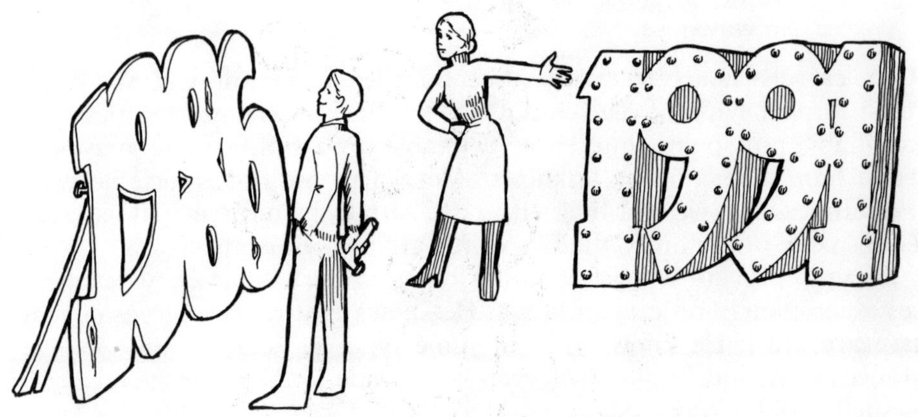

Henry Hazlitt, perhaps best known for his book, *Economics in One Lesson,* contends that "the whole of economics can be reduced to a single lesson, and that lesson can be reduced to a single sentence: 'The art of economics consists in looking not merely at the immediate but at the longer effects on any act or policy; it consists in tracing the consequences of that policy not merely for one group but for all groups'."

Hazlitt gives some examples: The child who eats too much candy has a lot of fun (primary consequence) but develops a belly-ache (secondary consequence). For the heavy drinker, Saturday nights may be a blast (primary), but Sunday morning hangovers and long-term liver damage (secondary consequences) deserve his consideration. The father who permits his family to consume every dollar he earns makes a choice that might be satisfying in the short run; the secondary consequences are a lack of savings for emergencies, education, and retirement.

"In the interest of the individual's long-run well-being, it is necessary for him to make certain short-run sacrifices, or apparent sacrifices. He

24   STRUCTURES

must put certain immediate restraints upon his impulses in order to prevent later regrets. He must accept a certain deprivation today either in order to reap a greater compensation in the future or to prevent an even greater deprivation in the future."

When we choose an action to improve our situation, there may be more than one outcome. In addition to the short-term outcome, usually the more obvious, what are the long-term consequences we should also consider?

The frontier Indiana farmer knew better than to consume his entire corn harvest. Because the long-term consequences could be starvation, he saved enough seed corn to start the planting of his next crop. Similarly, the businessman who drains the last penny of profit from his business may be "consuming his seed corn." A certain amount needs to be plowed back in to assure that his business is as healthy next year (secondary consequence) as this year (primary).

In the sphere of national politics short-term solutions satisfy small pressure groups. The long-term consequences become a burden on the entire society. We will explore this subject in more detail in Chapter 8.

CC-9 We Alone Are Responsible for Our Choices

As Nobel economist Friedrich Hayek wrote in *The Constitution of Liberty:* "Liberty not only means that the individual has both the opportunity and the burden of choice, it also means that he must bear the consequences of his actions and will receive praise or blame for them. Liberty and responsibility are inseparable."

As we make our choices, other persons are frequently involved in our choosing process. Because we respect them or because they have information that appears valuable to us, we turn to other people for their help in making choices: attorneys, salesmen, brokers, accountants, newspaper editorialists, physicians, TV anchormen, consultants, and employers. They may influence our choices either beneficially or adversely.

Assume that you are quite concerned about a forthcoming choice. "I feel uneasy about this situation," you might say. "I am going to choose an action that will improve it. There are things about the consequences that I cannot possibly know or anticipate. I cannot be at all sure that it will turn out exactly the way that I want it to. The choice will be based upon my best personal judgment. I am taking the action because I believe I will be happier with the outcome than with the situation as it is now."

You cannot then add: "Now if this turns out badly, it's not my fault!" An old proverb says: "Success has a thousand parents. Failure is an orphan."

David Viscott in *Risking* makes this point: "You cannot commit to risk unless you are willing to accept responsibility for loss .... You are responsible for what you say, are, feel, and do."

If you don't like your lifestyle, you are responsible.
If you don't like your job, you are responsible.
If you don't like your home, you are responsible.
If you don't like your husband or wife, you are responsible.
If you don't like you, you are responsible.

If you don't like the way you are treated, you are responsible.

How can we rate the value of the advice of others? By using the ten Characteristics of Choice as our guide!

- Does the advisor offer choices that will improve our situation? That is the objective. (CC-1)
- Does the advisor increase the number of choices or reduce them? (CC-2)
- Are the suggestions high-quality alternatives that will improve the quality of the outcome? (CC-3)
- Does the advisor point out the opportunities that we must forgo? (CC-4)
- Does the advisor respect our individual values, or impose his own values as being superior? (CC-5)
- Does the advisor help find additional time for choosing? Or does he rush us? (CC-6)
- Does the advice help us reduce the unknowns and uncertainties and point out the risks? Or does it add to them? (CC-7)
- Are the secondary consequences discussed as well as the short-term? (CC-8)

- Does the advisor help us see the elements needed for a recovery in the event of a mistake? (CC-10)
- Finally, caveat emptor. What effect will the advice have on the advisor's situation? Might his situation be improved even if ours is not?

CC-10 The Weightier the Decision, the More Difficult to Change

A supertanker loaded with Saudi Arabian crude oil heads out of the Persian Gulf at five knots; the tanker is so heavy that it needs ten miles of ocean to negotiate a U-turn. The trucker with the pedal to the metal at seventy miles per hour needs 200 yards of highway to come to a stop. On the other hand, a boy pedaling safely on his bike can stop in three feet of sidewalk.

A wrong decision in a vital situation may take years to correct. A wrong choice on a trivial matter might be corrected in a moment.

Your mom told you that you would make mistakes. And she told you that you would learn from your mistakes. That's the way you grow, she used to say. She probably did not tell you about "turnaround time." Three choices will tie you up for years: (1) how you will earn your living, (2) whom you will marry, and (3) where you will live.

As Peter Drucker has pointed out, several solutions should be sought during the decision-making process. If the most promising alternative turns out to be a poor choice, you have already investigated other courses of action. The plan thought to be second-best may now look the best.

Decisions about real estate are one of the three most important choices we face in life. Our homes, the biggest real estate decision for most of us, can tie up one-third of our annual income for up to thirty years!

The one we decide to marry may fit into one or two of these four classifications: (1) a smart producer, (2) an intelligent consumer, (3) an uninspired producer, or (4) a foolish consumer. Yet, there is a fifty-fifty chance we will learn this only after the vows are said. In addition, there is only a fifty-fifty chance that we will leave that knot tied for the rest of our lives.

Reversing poor choices has one additional complication. We would like to return to the situation as it was, so that a fresh choice can be made.

Surprise! The way it was is no longer. We find out how it now is! We find ourselves dealing not with the old situation but with a new situation similar to the old only in some ways. As Heraclitus stated, "It is not possible to step into the same river twice." The waters in front of us then are now far downstream.

Bob Goldstein likes to tell the story about Moses when he came down from the mountain and met one of the elders of the tribe. "How'd it go?" the elder asked. Moses breathed a sigh of relief and said, "He settled for ten."

The Ten Commandments are religious laws that we disobey at our own risk. The ten Characteristics of Choice are human economics laws. Like it or not, they play an important role in our choosing processes. If we ignore them (as most of us do) we increase the uncertainties and risks of our outcomes. If we use them, we greatly enhance our chances for a better situation.

Here are the ten Characteristics of Choice summarized.

(CC-1) Choices have a common purpose: to improve our situation.
(CC-2) Choices come only in twos or more. A choice of one is force.
(CC-3) To achieve the best outcomes, include the best inputs.
(CC-4) Every choice has a cost.
(CC-5) Choices are subjective value preferences.
(CC-6) Choices are made with limited time and information.
(CC-7) Choices involve unknowns, uncertainties and risks.
(CC-8) Choices have primary and secondary consequences.
(CC-9) We alone are responsible for our choices.
(CC-10) The weightier the decision the harder to change.

Hayek has written: "Knowledge of the world is knowledge of what one must do or not do in certain kinds of circumstances. And in avoiding danger it is as important to know what one must never do as to know what one must do to achieve a particular result."

THE EIGHT PHASES OF THE CHOOSING PROCESS

THE CP's

Choosing Process

The other half of Piece 1, the other surface of our freedom-of-choice disk, is The Choosing Process. This disk is divided into eight wedges.

(CP-1) Awareness
(CP-2) Definition
(CP-3) Analysis
(CP-4) Collection
(CP-5) Decision
(CP-6) Communication
(CP-7) Action
(CP-8) Evaluation

We usually define outcomes as good or bad, right or wrong, an accomplishment or a mistake, a victory or a defeat. Many thoughtful economists, however, suggest there is a better way. In mathematics there is only one right answer to a problem. Every other answer is wrong. Yet, as we discussed (CC-5), most of our choices are subjective value judgments, which means that the outcomes are rarely precise. The "answer" is that the situation has been improved to some degree to our satisfaction or it has not. You are happier with the new situation or you are less happy.

Not So Happy

Consequences and outcomes resulting from human action are better rated in terms of relative satisfaction. In our pursuit of happiness, how far did we get on our latest try? Here are some subjective expressions we use to try to quantify satisfaction. Following each is an estimated percent of satisfaction.

WAYS WE ATTEMPT TO QUANTIFY OUR SATISFACTION
WITH AN OUTCOME

Expression	Amount of Satisfaction
I'm delighted. Couldn't be happier!	100 Percent
I am very, very pleased.	90 "
Suits me. I'm quite contented.	80 "
I'm contented with it.	70 "
I can live with it.	60 "
I'm reasonably satisfied ... I guess	50 "
Just so-so. I have my doubts.	40 "
I am a little unhappy with it.	30 "
I admit I'm disappointed.	20 "
I don't think I can live with this.	10 "
Return to Go.	0 "

Now if we end up with an outcome with which we are "content" (70 percent), have we improved our situation as we saw it at the time? Only if we viewed our situation as being less than 70 percent satisfactory before the outcome!

If we were in a situation that we "didn't think we could live with" (10 percent satisfactory) and improved it to "content with" (70 percent), it would appear that we have made a choice that makes us happier.

But let's suppose we have a "good enough" situation on our hands (60 percent satisfaction). We want to improve upon it. We examine our alternatives. We come up with something that looks better. We make our choice and take our action. But there were—remember?—unknowns. Now we find that we are "a little unhappy" with the outcome (only 30 percent satisfaction). Rather than progressing up our scale of satisfaction, we have retrogressed down it!

"Change," Abraham Lincoln said, "does not always denote progress." Or, in the good-ole-boy lingo of Bert Lance, "If it ain't broke, don't fix it."

It is our unalienable right, the Declaration of Independence tells us, to "pursue happiness." We want to improve our situation, not just change it. Thus we should decide where we are before we decide where we want to go.

The choosing process may better be described in terms of phases than steps. "Steps" suggest a cadence and precision, while "phases" suggest a progression with overlaps. The lines of demarcation may blur. Often we will find that we are in two phases at once.

Because the objective of choice and action is to improve our situation as we see it, (CC-1), we might look at "satisfaction" as a cabinet we are building. To build it, we need both tools and the process for using the tools. The tools, as we have seen, are the Characteristics of Choice. What about the process?

Picture yourself as the carpenter. You have a hammer, saw, rule, pencil, square, and level in your tool box. You reach for the tool designed for the specific need of the moment. You use the rule to measure the board, the square to make sure your cut will be true, the pencil to mark the line, the saw to cut it, the level to make certain the board is properly in place, and the hammer to nail it there. You use one tool after another as needed. It is a process that is repeated again and again until your project is completed. You measure, mark, cut and fit in a cycle that is repeated over and over. The Choosing Process is such a cycle.

In their book *Teach Your Child Decision Making*, psychologists John Clabby and Maurice Elias tell us that even youngsters 3 and 4 years old can benefit from their understanding of the decision-making process!

The objective of this chapter is to establish the Choosing Process as half of Piece 1, the solid pedestal upon which each of us stands. We will build other structures upon this same base. Piece 1 is our "rock," the essential base for the structures of all our free organizations.

The eight phases of the Choosing Process begin with Phase (CP-1), Awareness. Nothing can happen until we are aware. The process continues through intermediate phases. Sometimes all are utilized—sometimes not— until it is completed in Phase (CP-8), Evaluation, where we critique the results of our decision. If for any reason the outcome is not the improvement in satisfaction we had hoped for, we begin the cycle again.

Phase (CP-1) Awareness

We have a "felt uneasiness." Something is not quite as it should be, not quite complete. From our subconscious mind into our consciousness the thought crystallizes. It appears that some sort of action or change is needed. This may be a situation or an unfulfilled need. When we dig into the mind of the entrepreneur in Chapter 4, we will see that this relates to his innate sense of opportunity.

Phase (CP-2) Definition

Find the problem and define it. As Peter Drucker says, "Too much time cannot be spent on this phase." There is a danger that the wrong problem will be solved. Once the problem is defined, determine "the conditions for the solution of the problem. The objectives for the solution must be thoroughly thought out." This may easily go on at the same time as Phase (CP-3). There may be many shifts in our attention back and forth.

Phase (CP-3) Analysis

Analyze the problem. Classify it by considering the various characteristics of choice that can be brought to bear: costs, preferences, unknowns, uncertainties, risks, primary and secondary consequences. Get all the facts and opinions that contribute to a full understanding of the problem. Even then, because of the time and money required to assemble information, a decision may have to be based upon incomplete knowledge (CC-6).

Phase (CP-4) Collection

Collect and create alternative solutions. This is sometimes called "brainstorming"—the input of ideas from numerous sources without yet making judgments on their worth. "It should be an invariable rule," writes Dr. Drucker, "to develop several alternative solutions to every problem. Otherwise there is the danger of falling into the trap of 'either-or'." See (CC-2).

Phase (CP-5) Decision

Decide on the best solution. Consider the Characteristics of Choice that have been discussed in this chapter, particularly the risks and secondary consequences of the various solutions. "There is no risk-less action nor even risk-less non-action'," Drucker wrote. What amount of time, effort, and expense will each solution require? If the alternatives that are chosen turn out to be mistakes, how quickly can each be reversed?

Phase (CP-6) Communication

Communicate the decision. Who is affected and what do they need to know to play their part? People who are likely to be deeply affected should have been involved in Phases (CP-2) and (CP-3), helping to define and analyze the problem. Those who have had a hand in defining it are more likely to understand and accept the changes resulting from the decision.

Phase (CP-7) Action

Take action. Make the change that has been decided upon. This phase is separate from Phase (CP-5), because the optimal time for action may be considerably removed from the time of the decision.

Phase (CP-8) Evaluation

Evaluation, the final phase, is the critique, the feedback. The change has been made and the new action taken. How is the decision working? Has the situation actually improved? Has the objective actually been achieved? If not, return to Go. Passage of time will usually not correct the mistake. The more time that passes the further you are from your original situation. Even when you return, if you must, it will be a different situation from the one you left behind.

Summary: The Freedom to Choose

There were three reasons for beginning *Structures* in the way we have.

First, individual freedom of choice must be Piece Number One in the structure of our personal freedom and the liberty of our society. It is the politico-economic base of all free societies. It is the economic foundation for our market economy. It is the political foundation for our democracy.

Forty years ago, Hayek wrote in the *Road to Serfdom:* "Responsibility, not to a superior, but to one's conscience, the awareness of duty not extracted by compulsion, the necessity to decide which of the things one values are to be sacrificed to others, and to bear the consequences of one's own decision, are the very essence of any morals which deserve the name."

Second, there are practical ways in which most of us can get a lot more mileage out of the choices around us. Pragmatically, choices are helpful in life's everyday struggles. In utilizing choices as our servants, we begin to erase uncertainty and build solidity.

Peter Drucker again:

Of course, searching for and considering alternatives does not provide a man with an imagination he lacks. But most of us have infinitely more imagination that we ever use. A blind man, to be sure, cannot learn to see. But it is amazing how much a person with normal eyesight does not see, and how much he can see through systematic training of the vision.

Third, the individual who understands the character of free choice will be more likely to recognize any external coercion that dilutes the quality of his choices or interrupts his orderly use of a choosing process—ours, or someone else's.

$$(CC's) + (CP's) = Piece\ (1) = Freedom\ to\ Choose$$

We have married the ten characteristics and the eight phases in the process. It is called the CC/CP Grid. Let it help you with your choices. Use it as your checklist and your guide.

CC + CP = Optimal Outcome

Process

1 Awareness
2 Definition
3 Analysis
4 Collection
5 Decision
6 Communication
7 Action
8 Evaluation

Characteristics

1 Purpose:
Improve the
situation

2 Choices come
in two's
or more

3 Best outcome,
best inputs

4 Every choice
has a cost

5 Individual
value
preferences

6 Limited time,
information

7 Unknowns,
uncertainties
& risks

8 Primary &
secondary
consequences

9 You are
responsible

10 Big choices
hard to change

Chapter 2: Symbols, Models, and Structures

> *For the real environment is altogether too big, too complex, and too fleeting for direct acquaintance. We are not equipped to deal with so much subtlety, so much variety, so many permutations and combinations. And although we have to act in that environment, we have to reconstruct it on a simpler model before we can manage it.*
>
> Walter Lippmann

We will resume our exploration of the other pieces in our model in the next chapter.

In this chapter we explore the reasons for models. We examine the ways in which people use symbols and models to communicate with each other. Our wooden model is unique. Its function is to portray the structures of several abstract, related ideas. Once we *see* the structures of these concepts in the drawings in this book—and especially in wood in our models—our minds can recall them more easily.

Most entrepreneurs are not trained teachers. Our models help the businessman understand, retain, recall, and explain our concepts. Although these concepts are discussed in classrooms, they are also important to our families and to our business organizations. Now they can be discussed more easily within our families and businesses.

Americans know about as much about economics today as they knew about sex before Kinsey. Dr. Alfred Kinsey was not nationally known in

1948, but as professor of zoology at the University of Indiana he published *Sexual Behavior in the Human Male*. The results were staggering. It seems incredible now, but at the time the general public viewed his scientific work in about the way they viewed pornography.

On the subject of economics, the typical American is still at grade school level.

Brace yourself: Economic "intercourse" between consenting adults and kids has been going on for centuries. In human nature, to make choices and to take action is just as deeply rooted as sex.

One of our purposes here is to suggest that choice is a suitable subject for dinner table conversation even in nice American homes like yours.

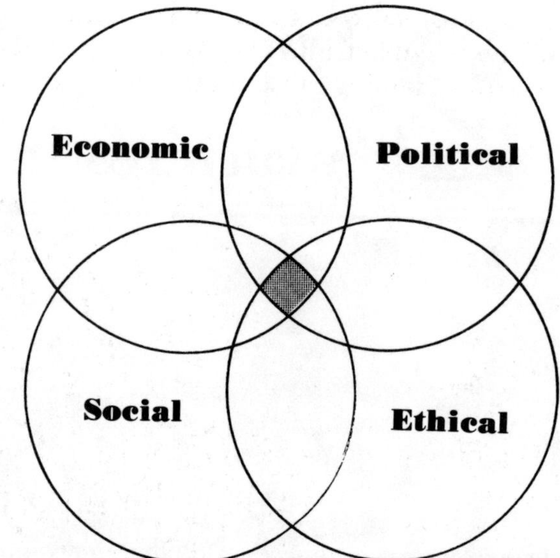

The Human Side of Economics

The aspect of economics that we will explore in this book is broad in scope because it is the *human* side, the area where four of our American heritages overlap: economic, political, sociological, and moral. Being a specialist in none of these fields, I present only the views of a layman generalist, an overview combining all four areas. Do you view the world as an economist? As a politician? As a sociologist? Do you look only at the moral aspect of each event of the day? I doubt it.

We look at the world as generalists. We draw upon our general knowledge of economics, our general understanding of the political system, our general view of the social picture, and our general view of day-to-day morality. We try not to adopt a lopsided view of the daily scene. If pressed, we express this outlook by answering, "I'm middle-of-the-road."

We have introduced and explored the concept that freedom of choice is vital to "changing our situation" (identified in the Declaration of Independence as our "pursuit of happiness"). Individual freedom of choice, represented by a disk made up of meaningful subdivisions, is Piece 1 in our principal structure.

Another "unalienable right" that the Declaration mentions is liberty. In following chapters we will build the structure of liberty upward and outward from the basic freedom-to-choose disk. As we add pieces to our structure and explore the meanings of each, we will encounter economic situations intertwined with the political, the social, and the ethical. The resulting symbols, models, and structures will slice through the boundaries of these old disciplines and may redefine these philosophies in ways that disturb some sensibilities.

SYMBOLS

The dictionary defines the word *symbol* as a visible sign of something invisible ... an act, sight, sound, or object having cultural significance and the capacity to excite a response ... a sign, mark, figure, or indication ... an ideal or otherwise intangible truth.

Below are some strong, familiar abstract symbols and what they stand for.

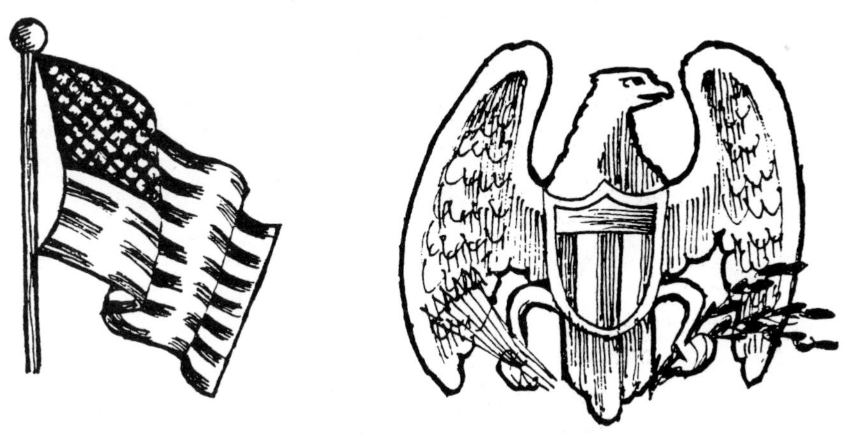

Both the flag and seal stand for the United States of America, a sovereign nation. Both of the following symbols stand for liberty.

The two symbols below stand for the two largest political parties in the United States at the present time.

The next two symbols do double duty. Each is the symbol of a political party but, in addition, is (or was) also the symbol of a sovereign nation.

Each of the eight symbols above represents a bubbling stew of political, economic, social, and ethical philosophies. When tasted, each arouses complicated subjective emotions within us. We attach a subjective value to each. We feel strongly positive about some, revulsion from others.

The three symbols below represent American commercial enterprises. Each trademark is well known throughout many nations in the world today. They are viewed as symbols of America and arouse a wide range of emotion. They are economic only in that they represent free-market products.

Trademarks of good free-market products represent more than motels, soft drinks, or restaurants. After years of association with products such as these, we learn that they represent a *standard*. Past experience tells us the kind of quality we can expect from these three products. Each symbol communicates a complete image. If asked to do so, we could define these images in a few words.

Each of these three commercial symbols suggests indirectly and obliquely certain attractive features of the free-market system. Yet, for all our belief in the free-market system, we have no symbol to represent that system!

We might assume that the American flag and seal represent the free market, but they do so only in an oblique way. Specifically they represent the *government* of the United States, its power and its laws. The free market is not an exclusive function of our government any more than it is of the British or Japanese governments.

The free market is neutral, nonnationalistic. We would not wish to have the British or Japanese flag waved under our noses as representative of the free market. In fact we would bristle at such an aggressive stance. Those countries have no monopoly on the free market, and neither does ours.

The free market is a community of people and organizations transcending all national boundaries. Every nation in the world has within it a number of free markets, and to repeat, even though the philosophy crosses every national boundary in the world, there is no universally recognized international symbol for the free-market concept!

We do have the Adam Smith necktie, worn with pride by many. I doubt, however, that most people would recognize it. *Forbes* magazine recently brought a Swedish symbol to our attention. It is a powerful pro-capitalism symbol. I interpret it as a person holding back the enclosing circle of socialism. Quite graphic. Yet it is a symbol only, not an integral part of a model or structure representing a related group of interdependent concepts.

International Use of Symbols

To the international traveler, symbols are extremely helpful; international highway signs, for example, and other signs in public places.

Consider, as an example, Mr. Toyama, a Japanese man who must travel to Tampa. Where will he stay? A Tokyo friend of Mr. Toyama's stayed at a place called Brown's Motel when he was last in Tampa and recommends it. Mr. Toyama's friend goes into some detail about the hospitable features of Brown's, but it is difficult for Mr. Toyama to visualize Brown's Motel because he has not seen it. Mr. Toyama is still uneasy.

What about one of the Holiday Inns in Tampa? Although he has never seen these specific hotels, the chances are reasonably good that Mr. Toyama can form a good mental picture of a Holiday Inn in Tampa. In his mind's eye, he can identify the large lighted sign that Kemmons Wilson designed.

He knows the quality of room, food, and service to expect. No thanks, says Mr. Toyama, I will stay at a Holiday Inn.

If you suggest to a friend that you meet for lunch at McDonald's, he will instantly have a certain image in mind. But suggest Berne's Steak House, and, unless he has experienced the excellence of that Tampa landmark, he will have no accurate idea of the Berne menu or atmosphere. And how about a soft drink? What will it be, a Coke or a cold glass of Mrs. Watson's Wild Surprise?

Millions of people can instantly form feelings from the symbols of Holiday Inn, Coke, and McDonald's. These corporations protect their identities by zealously protecting their trademarks. Backing up each identity are international operating standards, so that *each is a model of all.* If the Tampa innkeeper runs a shabby Holiday Inn, he risks losing his job. If the McDonald's owner tolerates dirty floors and litter, he will lose his franchise. If the local Coca-Cola bottler thinks he can put out the product in mason jars, he will not be a Coca-Cola bottler for long.

So when Mr. Simpson of Seattle says "Holiday Inn" to Senor Martinez of Madrid, Martinez can picture it immediately. And it is identical to the picture that Mr. Langley of London, Fraulein Hauser of Hamburg, M. Poirot of Paris, and Mr. Toyama of Tokyo also form.

Instantaneous international recognition! What an achievement!

Here are the symbols of two religious philosophies. These philosophies cross the boundaries of every nation in the world. Over milleniums these symbols have been recognized internationally and instantly by billions. The advantage of simplicity!

Could these religions have become as universally recognized and effective without symbols? They certainly would have grown, because they have satisfied the spiritual needs of billions of people, but without symbols I would not have wanted the job of marketing them!

When we look into the methods and strategies of professionals, we almost always find symbols and models. Both the Moscow and the New Delhi mathematicians know that "x" in a formula means "multiplied by." The Argentine pianist can read what Bach composed 300 years ago, because both communicate with music notation.

The Swiss doctor can communicate with the Venezuelan pharmacist by way of a "prescription," a confidential message that he entrusts the patient to transport from his office in Geneva to a drug store in Caracas. The pharmacist does not speak German. The doctor does not speak Spanish. Yet their method of communication is almost foolproof.

Following are some politico-economic labels:

Right	Reactionary	Progressive	Republican
Moderate	Conservative	Liberal	Left
Populist	Dictator	Anarchist	Democrat

This book will use words such as these sparingly if at all. William James would have classified them as "words worn threadbare." Their true meanings, if indeed they ever had one, have long since been lost. They are catch basins of fuzzy philosophical flotsam.

We will abstain from using political party names, even ones 200 years old. Federalist and Whig, for example. Why perpetuate these images? Why drag these ill-defined, changeable labels into a unique, new terminology/symbology whose purpose is to simplify?

We shall introduce economic and political symbols that Toyama, Simpson, Poirot, Martinez, and Hauser can use to communicate with each other. When one uses a phrase such as "individual freedom to choose," or "the entrepreneurial hub," or "centralized governmental power," the others understand the meaning instantly. When any of them sees the symbol or model for the "free market," the thoughts that this symbol conveys are identical in the minds of all.

MODELS

Models transform the abstract into the concrete. They visualize the invisible, make the intangible touchable. Models can provide a working example for emulation and imitation. We can see a model, talk about it, and compare it with other models. *A model may serve as a standard.* As a standard, we can take it off the shelf every so often, examine it, and study its characteristics.

Models aid in understanding many problems. They cut through the semantic fog. They advance logical concepts without the use of tired and ambiguous words. They can allow our fingers to touch intangible philosophical concepts. Models encourage the search for the essential elements of the problem and and help us to understand the relationship of these elements to each other and to the problem as a whole.

Each piece in a model has a function. As we will see in Chapter 4, the Profitable Product, Piece 11, performs the function of holding the entire business enterprise together. By its function and its relationship to the function of each of the other parts, the model imparts a sense of structure.

It is the way in which the wings, the fuselage, and the tail of a model airplane are identified and relate functionally to each other and to the entire airplane. Imagine a twentieth-century man explaining to a tenth-century serf how an airplane flies. How much a model could help! "That is the wing; it provides lift. This is the body, which carries the cargo. The engine here provides thrust. This is the tail; it steers the craft."

What are the characteristics of a good model or symbol? What should it do? It should be designed as an aid to understanding, namely, an educational device. It should be three-dimensional so that it can be held in the hands.

It should be made of a substantial material, such as a hardwood which will take on a patina with time. A good model should be simple to assemble and to take apart, so that even those who are not overly dextrous will have no difficulty in handling it. Neither the fifth-grader, the elderly, the handicapped, nor the blind should find its design to be frustrating.

Each piece should be labeled as to what it stands for and have its own part number. Each part should be designed so that its relationship to all the other parts and to the whole is clear and logical. When assembled, it should look balanced, well-proportioned, and generally pleasing to the eye.

We should be pleased to have the structure sitting on the coffee table in our living room, on the conference room table, or on the credenza behind our desk at the office, almost as though it were a work of art. The structures and their parts should lend themselves easily to computer graphics, especially moving graphics and animation. On the TV screen the structures would be instantly identifiable either in line drawings or in three-dimensional photography or art.

The physical models should be simple in design and light in weight, so that their manufacture and shipping is inexpensive. The design should be new and unique, so that it cannot be confused with any other model or infringe upon the trademark, design, copyright, or patent of any product already in existence in any country.

For hobbyists who would prefer to build the models from scratch or out of other materials, the plans and specifications should be simple to read and the directions for construction easy to follow.

Finally, its graphic representation in print is important, especially when the model is to serve as a symbol. It should lend itself easily to line drawings and should photograph distinctly, even in black and white, so that it will enjoy instantaneous recognition. Good graphics, such as Paul Revere's "Join or Die," are memorable.

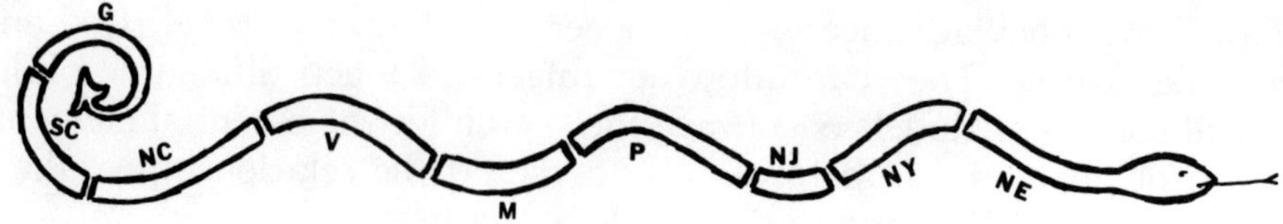

STRUCTURES

Chapters 3 through 6 are devoted to the development and explanation of two model/structures. Each is comprised of specific characteristics. Each represents concepts related to one another. The models are meant to simplify and make visible structural concepts that have heretofore been complex and invisible.

FM Organizations　　　　AM Organizations

PART II FREE-MARKET (FM) STRUCTURE

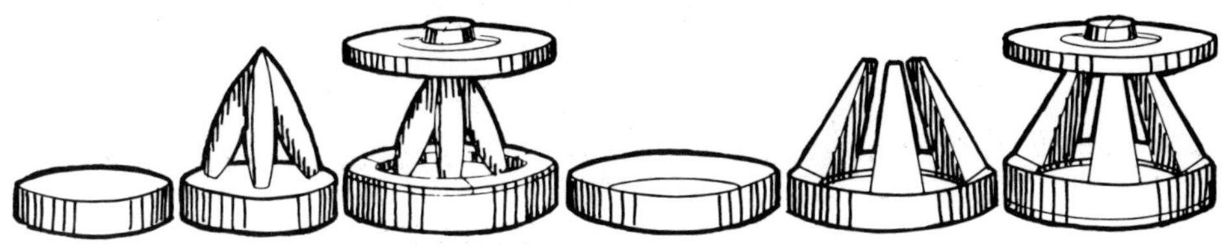

Chapter 3   The Economic Base of the Free Market

Pieces ② **Freedom to Own**
③ **Freedom to Exchange**
④ **Freedom to Fund**

"By removing the organization of economic activity from the control of political authority, the market eliminates the source of coercive power. It enables economic strength to be a check to political power rather than a reinforcement."

Milton Friedman

In this chapter we examine how to put your freedom to choose into action. You do this through owning, exchanging and funding. And for what reason? Why, to improve your situation as you see it, to pursue goals that you believe will make you happier.

Three fundamental economic principles define the free market:

- Freedom to own (Piece 2)
- Freedom to exchange (Piece 3)
- Freedom to fund (Piece 4).

Our first business in this chapter is to introduce the Philomod. If you have your wooden model handy, this is the time to take it out. There are sixteen wooden pieces. For the moment, set aside the three square legs, numbered 12, 13, and 14. They will be introduced in Chapter 6. Philomods are visible, tangible, three-dimensional model/symbols of philosophies.

Each piece has a number and stands for a specific concept. Each structure illustrates the relationships and mutual dependencies of the concepts involved.

Below are exploded and completed views of the first thirteen pieces in the first Philomod.

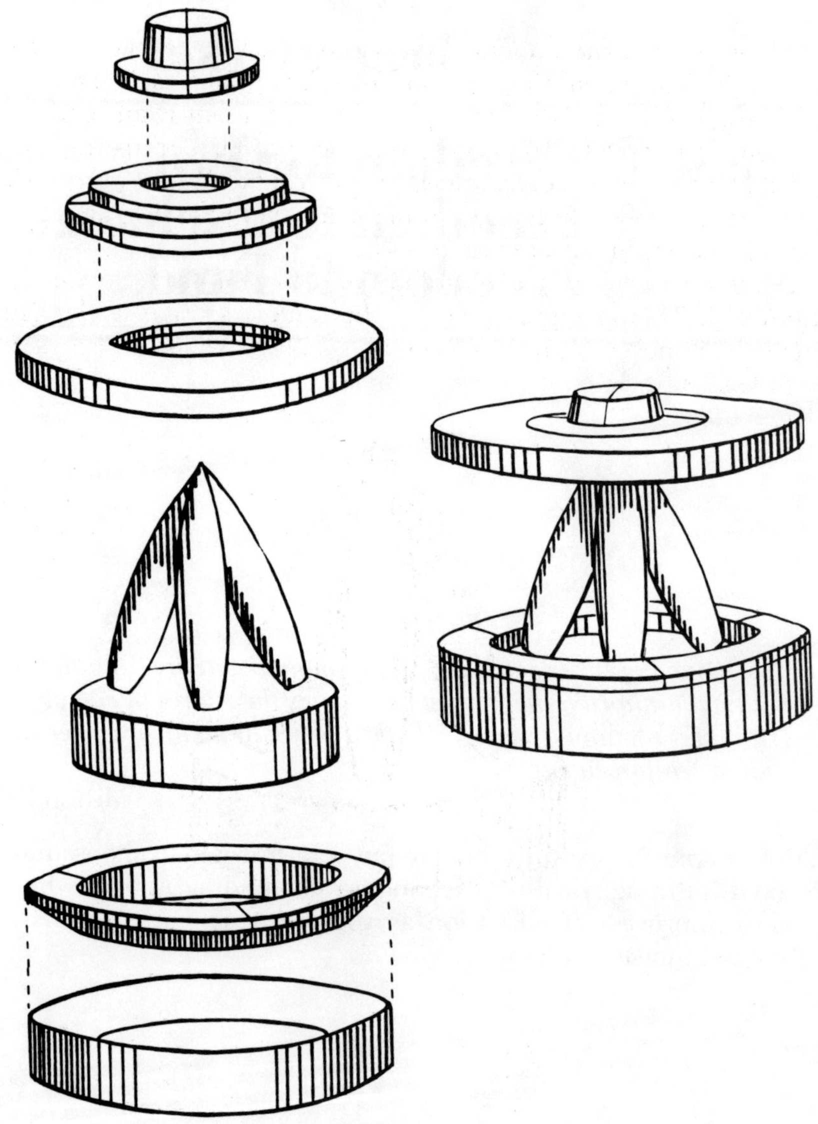

The five pieces at the top that fit together to look like a flying saucer represent the structure of organizations. Most of the people in the world work in organizations. For all practical purposes all organizations have this same five-part structure. We will return to organizations in the next chapter.

If you have our wooden model, go ahead and put the entire structure together now. Note that you will need to put the pieces that comprise the organization together as a unit and then set it on top of the tripod. Otherwise it is difficult to assemble. There is a reason for this, which we explain later.

All we need to know about organizations now is that they can be simple entities, such as gas stations, restaurants, law practices, and farms. A freelance commercial artist, a realtor, or an accountant is an economic organization, even though composed of only one person, because each produces a product or service. A big company is an organization of people. Churches or charities, school systems, fire departments, libraries, and the United States Navy are all organizations of people.

Each organization in every nation in the world rests upon an economic philosophy. This is represented by the middle section of the Philomod, which is composed of three legs on a base. Here we will discuss the three *round* legs on their base.

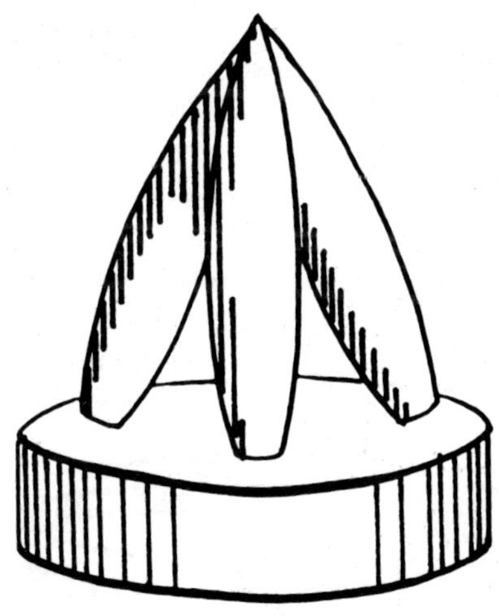

In Chapter 6 we will explain the three *square* legs.

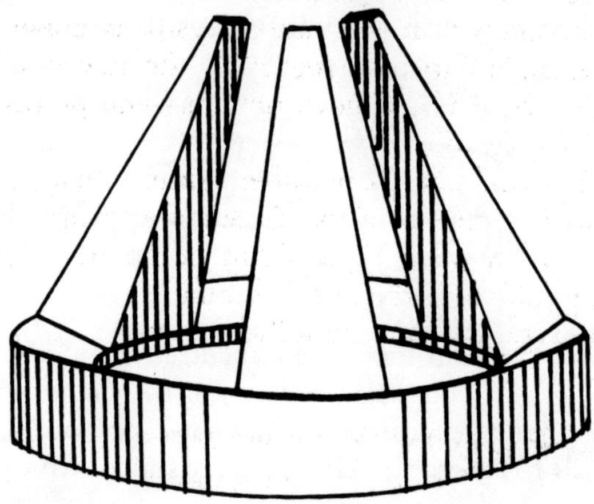

The base for the three round legs is Piece 1. Their lower ends are tapered to fit into holes in Piece 1, which, as we discussed in Chapter 1, represents the freedom to choose. It is the base for all enterprise as well as serving as the personal pedestal for each of us as individuals.

Assembled, the four pieces in this structure are called the Freepod. The Freepod is just one type of economic philosophy upon which organizations are based. There are others. An organization rests either upon the free-market structure that the Freepod symbolizes or upon one of the other economic concepts which we will explore in later chapters. This applies to organizations in the United States, France, Argentina, Sweden, Japan, West Germany, Russia and China. Every nation.

As you may have already guessed, there are many combinations of different types of organizations. These rest upon different kinds of tripods, which represent several different economic concepts.

At the bottom of the Philomod are two rings. These fit around Piece 1, freedom of choice. One of these rings, Piece 5 is solid. The other ring is in three pieces, each number 6.

These two rings, Pieces 5 and 6, represent the structures of *political* philosophies. *Each organization in every nation in the world rests upon a political philosophy.* These pieces will be discussed in Chapter 5.

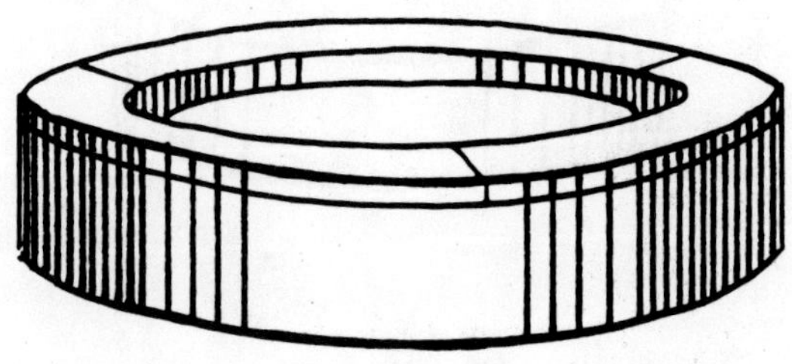

All we need to know about these rings at this point is that they can represent the power of any government. They can represent a county or city government, a state government, or our federal government in Washington with its many branches and offices throughout this country and the world. These rings can also represent the power of the British, Swiss, Italian, Soviet, or Chinese governments—the power of any government anywhere in the world.

There are, then, several possible combinations of organizations, economic tripods (representing the economic concept the organization rests upon), and political rings (representing the political philosophies and policies that may influence the organization.)

To summarize, each Philomod represents:

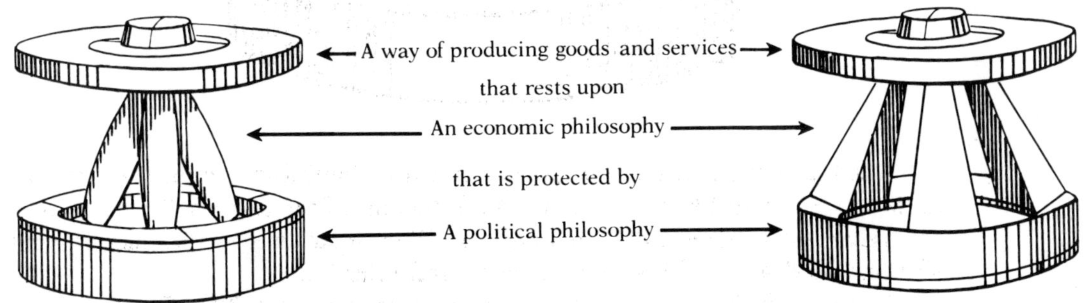

The point to be remembered here is this: Productive organizations never rest solely on an economic philosophy. Nor do any rest only upon a political/governmental philosophy. There is *always both* an economic base-idea as well as a political base-idea that affect each structure. The combination of the two constitutes a distinct politico-economic philosophy.

Our Philomods, then, are politico-economic models, because they include both the political and the economic elements in the real world.

With just five model/symbols, made by rearranging only sixteen pieces, we can reduce the world's major politico-economic concepts to a size that can be held in our hands!

Below is our visual/verbal glossary. These are the six new words and the five new visual concepts that are basic to this book and its accompanying models.

Freepod

The structure of liberty.
The tripod of economic freedom.
The three legs upon their base,
taking their strength from the base.

Freemode
(An FM Organization)

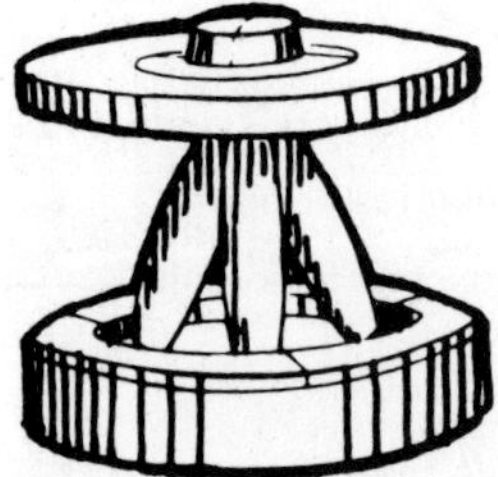

The model of a productive private enterprise based upon economic freedom and protected by a political policy of limited government. This organization is a member of the free-market (FM) community.

Forcepod

The tripod representing the anti-market (AM) economic ideology. Governmental power is the base. The three legs get their strength from this power.

Forcemode
(An AM Organization)

The model of an anti-market (AM) organization based upon the economic philosophy of controlled markets and the political policy of unlimited governmental power. This organization is a member of the anti-market (AM) community.

Hybrimode

The model of a hybrid organization, based in part on economic freedom but also dependent upon the political policy of centralized governmental power.

Philomods   All of the above. Philomods are visible, tangible, three-dimensional models of philosophies. Each piece stands for something of substance. Each piece in each structure represents a specific concept. Each structure illustrates the relationships and mutual dependencies of the concepts involved.

THE FREEDOM TO OWN, PIECE ②

"The close connection between property and freedom is also reflected in the affinity of definition. For if property is the exclusive right of persons over things, freedom is the exclusive right of a person over his actions."

Leopold Kohr

Sally Dawes, age 18, is happy in her first job as a sales clerk in the junior department of a large department store. She sells dresses, slacks, and blouses styled for women her own age. Her surroundings at the store are clean, quiet, and pleasant. Sally feels that she is off on her yellow brick road to happiness.

Sally trades her time and her talents, which are her personal property, for a weekly paycheck. Her take-home pay averages $200. She must plan her spending carefully to buy the goods and services she wants.

She trades her productivity (her property) for money (the property of her employer). With the money she earns she buys things (food, new clothes, cosmetics) and pays for services, such as rent on her apartment.

As a private individual Sally owns many items that she can call "mine," as differentiated from other items in the store and her apartment complex that are "theirs." She has "property rights" to her things. As she cannot take from others what they have earned, neither can others take from her what she has earned. This is simply an extension of the Golden Rule, "Do unto others as you would have them do unto you."

In a free-market economy she is free to own not only property that she consumes, such as food and cosmetics, she is also *free to own property that can be used to produce other goods and services.*

Sally owns a sewing machine on which she frequently makes bandannas on her own time at home. Sally's boss lets her sell her bandannas in the store on consignment (which simply means that the store does not have to pay her for her bandannas until after they are sold). Each one that is sold brings the store a profit and brings Sally a small additional income from her outside independent productivity.

Piece 2 in the Freepod, the Freedom to Own, embodies the concepts of the private ownership of property, including the private ownership of *productive property,* i.e., property used in the production of other property. In Sally's case, her sewing machine and the cloth from which she forms her product are her productive property. This means that a productive enterprise may be based upon the principle of private ownership. Sally's ownership of a sewing machine, plus her ambition and imagination, has led her to her own part-time business, her own productive organization. Sally is an employee of the department store for forty-plus hours a week. On her own time she is an *entrepreneur.*

The organizations that rest atop Piece 2 and the other two legs of the Freepod are called *Freemodes.* They are free-market (FM) organizations. We will use the word *Freemodes* interchangeably with the phrase "free-market organizations."

Freemodes are owned by individual persons or groups of individual persons. They are not owned by the government or any of its agencies.

A related point is that the freedom to own includes the freedom *not* to own, if that is our choice. Piece 2 represents *voluntary* ownership. Sally can own a sewing machine, but she does not have to own one. She can limit her sewing, should she choose to do so, to clothing for her own use and enjoyment. She is a part-time manufacturer because she wants to be. It is an activity that holds value for her. It improves her situation as she sees it in two ways: It is an entrepreneurial sideline she enjoys, and it brings her extra income.

Concepts and Characteristics of Property Ownership

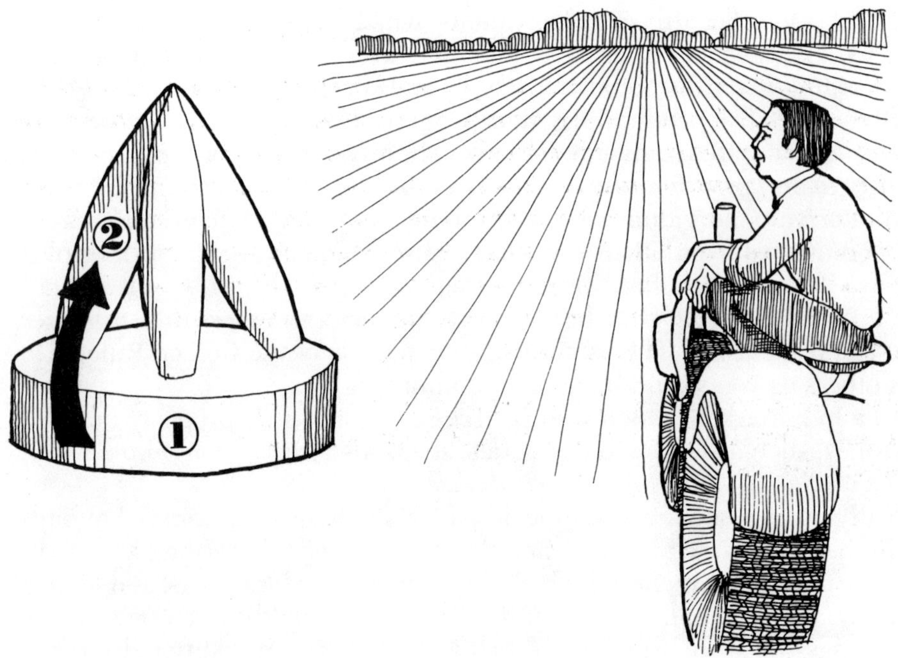

The concept of property rights is not widely understood. I searched the economic literature for four years before I found an explanation that satisfied me. As I had been told by a friend, "Robert LeFevre will explain private property rights, and it will make sense."

LeFevre starts out by explaining that we can only begin to understand the concept when we separate property (the item to be owned) from ownership (the act of owning). The proper relationship can then be explored between man, the owner, and property, the item.

What is property? LeFevre defines it as "anything that is subject to ownership."

Property exists whether it is owned or not.

In a virgin area, where men have not yet penetrated, the land and all the natural appurtenances are property. The advent of man does not change the character of the land, as property. But the relationship of the land to man does change when men acquire this land. I would identify this kind of property before the appearance of an owner as unowned property. *I would similarly identify items in discard, which men have owned and which they now disclaim.*

A second classification of property encompasses property that is correctly owned. *In this relationship an owner (man) has assumed sovereign control over that property which he claims as his own. Assuming that there are no prior or rival claims to the property, and thus decisions respecting the property derive from the authority of the rightful owner, and assuming that the exercise of authority is limited to the property owned, then the ownership is complete and a condition of correct or proper ownership ensues.*

A third classification is property that is incorrectly owned.

There are three characteristics of all owned property. It must be valued by the owner. It must have a boundary that is recognizable to others, so that the sovereignty exercised by the owner can be located with precision. Each property must be subject to the will of the owner in the sense of control already stated. An item that has no value to an owner will not be owned. An item that cannot be bounded, and hence cannot be properly identified, cannot be owned. An item that is not susceptible to the control of the owner will not be owned. Thus, items failing in these characteristics are not properties.

Using LeFevre's three characteristics, let's select twenty items to put to the test. This should give us an idea of what is owned property and what is unowned property.

(a) Has it value to an owner?
(b) Has it definable, describable, measurable boundaries?
(c) Is it susceptible to the control of an owner, exchangeable from one person to another?

	(a)	(b)	(c)	OWNED UNOWNED
The earth's atmosphere	Yes	No	No	U
A liter of nitrogen from the atmosphere	Yes	Yes	Yes	O
Birds in the air	Yes	No	No	U
A duck shot and retrieved	Yes	Yes	Yes	O
The oceans	Yes	Yes	No	U
A liter of seawater	Yes	Yes	Yes	O
Arctic icebergs	Yes	Yes	No	U
An iceberg under tow by tug	Yes	Yes	Yes	O
The fish in the ocean	Yes	No	No	U
A red snapper on the hook	Yes	Yes	Yes	O
Oops! Lost the snapper!	Yes	No	No	U
Seashells on the beach	Yes	No	No	U
A conch shell in hand	Yes	Yes	Yes	O
Beer cans by the highway	No	No	Yes	U
1000 beer cans collected	Yes	Yes	Yes	O
One beer can with rare label	Yes	Yes	Yes	O
A broken chair in city dump	No	Yes	Yes	U
Same chair claimed from dump	Yes	Yes	Yes	O
Your body	Yes	Yes	Yes	O
An hour of your time	Yes	Yes	Yes	O

What Is Freedom to Own?

Accepting these parameters, we can explore five questions that will help to define further our freedom to own:

1. What may we own privately as individuals?
2. How may we rightfully acquire property?
3. Who decides how we can use and dispose of our property?
4. Why differentiate between consumer and producer property?
5. What is Economic Problem Number One, and how do property rights relate to it?

1. What may we own privately as individuals? First, we own ourselves. We own our bodies. No one else can own us. As John Locke wrote in 1690: "Though the earth and all inferior creatures be common to all men, yet every man has a 'property' in his own 'person.' This nobody has any right to but himself."

Second, we own our productivity. Economist Murray Rothbard uses a sculptor and his work as a good example. Who should own the work of art as it emerges from the sculptor's fashioning? The sculptor begins with a piece of stone or a lump of damp clay that he has purchased. From these he fashions the figure of a graceful woman swimmer poised in the starting position for an intercollegiate race. Many of the sculptor's hours and days go into the work—the product. The resultant work of art is an extension of the sculptor himself—the creativity of his mind and the skill of his arms and hands.

Who owns this work? Would anyone be so bold as to say that it no longer is the property of its creator, the sculptor? Rothbard answers. We have three logical alternatives: (1) either the transformer, the creator, has the property right to his creation; or, (2) another man or set of men have the right to appropriate it by force without the sculptor's consent; or, (3) the 'communal' solution—every individual in the world has an equal, quotal share in the ownership of the sculpture ... There are very few who would not concede the monstrous injustice of confiscating the sculptor's property, either by one or more others, or by the world as a whole. For by what right do they do so?

Third, we own our rightfully acquired property. The sculptor purchased the building he uses as his studio (his factory). It is his property, rightfully acquired. Over the years he has bought the various tools he has needed to do his work. They are his property, rightfully acquired. He has also rightfully acquired the clay he transformed into the figure of the poised swimmer.

Privately owned as opposed to what? Here there is a possibility of a misunderstanding. Again, we have become accustomed to fuzzy phrases that confuse rather than clarify. Let us differentiate the phrase "private ownership" from the related concept "public ownership." More precisely we want to differentiate the rights of *individual* ownership from *governmental* ownership.

The possible mixup arises from the ways in which "private" and "public" are sometimes used. Business publications, for example, frequently refer to "publicly-held" or simply "public" corporations and to "privately-held" or simply "private" corporations. They also use the expressions "going public" and "going private."

These terms refer in part to the number of persons who own the stock of the corporation and in part to the state laws and regulations under which corporations are formed and must operate. In Florida, corporations with fewer than twenty shareholders (owners) are considered to be "privately held." They have no legal obligation to report the details of their operations to anyone except the tax collectors at the state and federal levels. On the other hand, there are the "publicly-held" corporations, such as Proctor & Gamble, which has thousands of shareholders or owners. It was necessary that it meet certain legal requirements before it could offer its stock to thousands of investors nationwide.

When we use "public" to describe a structure, it is to describe property that is government owned: city parks, streets, the post office building, the county courthouse, the public schools, and city hall—these as opposed to private homes, farms, timberlands, mines, and other properties and organizations that are property privately owned by individuals or groups of individuals.

Piece 2 in our Philomod or Freemode—the freedom to own—represents the rights of *private* individuals in the ownership of property. The related concept is Piece 12, which represents *governmental* ownership of property. This is expressed as direct ownership by the government, as well as those rights governments reserve that affect our private property rights.

Piece 2 is a part of the tripod (one of the three round legs) upon which the privately-owned organization rests.

The operating organization at the top of any model containing Piece 2 is therefore privately owned.

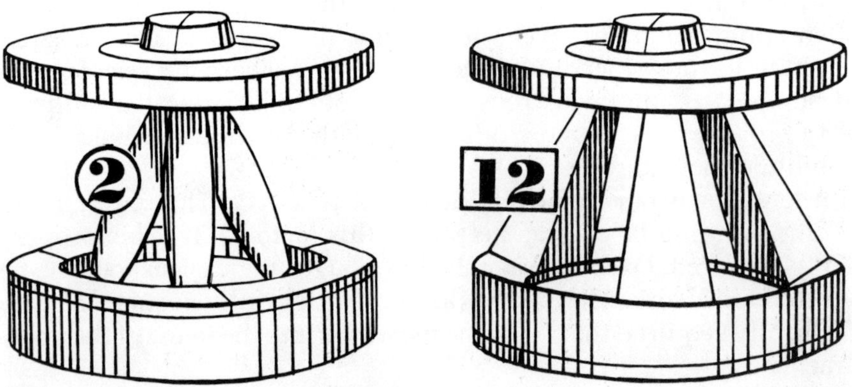

Piece 12, one of the square legs, is the counterpart of Piece 2 in another tripod. Upon it all governmentally-owned organizations rest. These are different structures. We will explain Piece 12 in detail in Chapter 6. For now, please accept this statement: Any organization at the top of a model containing piece 12 is government-owned.

Just for the fun of it, let's make up a list of about 100 owned properties. They have, you will remember, three qualities: (1) they are valued by an owner, (2) they have definable boundaries, and (3) they are subject to the will of the owner.

anvils	antiques	auto wrecking companies
billboards	bonds	bulldozers
cannon	checking accounts	clothing
coal mines	codeine	coins
contracts	copyrights	custard pies
DDT	dogs	drill presses
dynamite	electricity	elephants
energy	farms	firearms
flowers	food	garbage
gin	gold	hammers
hours	ideas	information
ink	jet craft	knowledge
lakes	land	leases
lumber	machine guns	marijuana
money	morphine	musical scores
nails	nuclear power	novels
oil refineries	our body	options
packing houses	parks	Philomods
piranhas	pistols	plasma
plutonium	porn movies	printing presses
quinine	railroads	rifles
salaries	silver futures	steel
stocks	streets	taxicabs
TNT	tractor-trailers	trademarks
underwear	uranium	vegetable gardens
wages	warrants	whiskey
woodlands	X-ray machines	zircons

Please note that properties that may be owned are not always properties that may be owned *privately*. What we may own privately as individuals is dictated by the laws, regulations, codes, morals, and ethics of the society in which we live as well as the time in which we live.

Governments have a penchant for changing the list. Two federal laws of the United States in 1933 are delightful examples. If a man walked down the street in the beginning of that year with a bottle of whiskey in his coat pocket, he would have broken the law. If he had gold coins in his pocket, it would have been perfectly lawful. If, however, at the end of that same year he appeared on the sidewalk with gold in his pocket, he would have been an outlaw. And, if he took a swig from his bottle of booze in public, he would have been within the law. How could this be?

In June of 1933, the United States dropped the gold standard. In December of 1933, prohibition ended.

We shall share more such examples later. Our business at the moment is to move on to the second of our list of five questions that help explain our freedom to own.

2. How may we rightfully acquire property?   Robert Nozick, Professor of Philosophy at Harvard, writes, "Property rights are viewed as rights to determine which of a specified range of admissable options concerning something will be realized."

That word "rights" keeps appearing in definitions related to property. What is meant by "rights"? Economist Leopold Kohr, in his essay, *Property and Freedom,* helps clarify the term. "Property is the full right over a thing. Enlarging it a little I usually render it as the exclusive right of a person over a thing. Property is thus not the thing itself, though by transference we frequently use it in this sense when we speak of a car, or a house, as our property. But legally it is not the car that is our property, but our exclusive right over it."

LeFevre deals with the subject of property "correctly acquired" and with "sovereign rights."

> *A right exists for a man to acquire any property he wills to possess. He may be an original claimant; that is, he may be the first to own an item extracted from the sum total nature has provided.* [The red snapper we caught.] *Additionally he may be a reclaimant; that is, he may become the owner of a property that at one time was owned by another and has been discarded.* [The beer can beside the highway, the chair on the city dump.] *Also he may be a secondary or subordinate claimant, obtaining his right to own a property by the process of exchange with another property owner.* [I trade you 200 of the beer cans I picked up along the highway for your red snapper.] *This explains one meaning of the word 'right.' It is the right to acquire a property. A man's ability to own a property will always be subject to variables, depending upon his captial, his energies, and so on. But his right to acquire property is total. That is, he has a right to seek to own anything, provided in so seeking he keeps in mind that all others with whom he must deal have the same rights he has as a property owner.*

> *A right is expressed in a second way,* LeFevre concludes. *Any man may do precisely as he pleases with what he has totally and honestly acquired ... As an actual owner he is totally sovereign over what he owns and his decisions are final.*

3. Who decides how we can use and dispose of our property?   What is the purpose of property anyway? What is the purpose of goods and services we acquire (whether or not we acquire them correctly)? We want property to use. We want to be consumers of it, or we want to produce further property from it. These are the ways we improve our situation.

It is nonsense to say we are free to choose, Piece 1 and (CP-5) and to take our own actions (CP-7) and that we are fully responsible for our choices (CC-9), if we cannot use our property according to our value preferences (CC-5), in order to improve our situation (CC-1).

When we want to consume it ourselves, we want property to eat, to wear out, to burn, to ride in, to shelter us, or—if we choose—to destroy without a trace. Or we want property to use to produce something else. We, as entrepreneur/producers, want certain properties as producer's goods and services, so that from them we may create more useful goods and services "for the market." That is, for consumption not by ourselves but by others.

A farmer wants land to grow wheat. A miller wants wheat to make flour. A baker wants flour to make doughnuts.

We make choices in the acquisition of property. We choose in a way that we feel will improve our situation. If we did not think a property useful as either a producer good or a consumer good, we would not have acquired it in the first place.

Listen to Kohr once again.

Property, then, means its owner alone has legal command over it. He can give it away. He can throw it away. He can let it rot. He can destroy it. He can bequeath it. He can dispose of it by contract and rent it or sell it. He is free to do with it as he sees fit. In other words, within the limits of his property, he is able to assert his freedom.

And LeFevre again.

The act of ownership is the assumption of sovereign control over property, to the exclusion of the rest of the world. Total control is vested in the rightful owner ... He may be wise or foolish with his own property. He may be profligate or thrifty. Since it is his, he has all rights over it to the exclusion of any possible right of another ... I have used the term sovereignty in relation to ownership to convey the idea that the owner of a property can do no wrong in respect to what he totally owns. He is the sovereign of his property, and his decisions, whether wise or foolish, are not subject to the review of a non-owner.

We make choices to acquire property. We make choices about how we will use our property and about how we will dispose of it. Such choices are either ours, freely made, or they are the choices of some other person. In our Freepod structure, Piece 2 rests directly and securely on Piece 1. Our freedom to own has its base in our freedom to choose. There is a vital flow of strength back and forth between the leg and the disk. The strength of one enhances the strength of the other. Weaknesses in one result in weaknesses in the other.

4. Why differentiate between consumer and producer property?   In a free society, it has been said, we have the right to own not only the shirt on our back but also the machine that makes the shirt.

We are exploring the facets of freedom, which has a structure that operates at the individual level, at the organizational level, and at the national or societal level. We have begun, as you have seen, with the individual. We will build our structures from that personal level up through the organizational and into the societal levels.

As we explore the structure of freedom, we discover a recurrent theme: Power is the enemy of freedom, and one of the ways to preserve freedom is to disperse and limit power. That is basically what our Constitution and Bill of Rights are all about, as we will see in Chapter 5.

If economic power is dispersed among 235 million people—each with the right to be as productive as he chooses with his own property—then this power is not in the hands of the government.

However, if the productive economic power is in the hands of the government along with political power, the potential for totalitarian power is a strong possibility. No one makes this clearer than Nobel economist Milton Friedman in _Capitalism and Freedom._

> _Political freedom means the absence of coercion of a man by his fellow men. The fundamental threat to freedom is power to coerce, be it in the hands of a monarch, a dictator, an oligarchy, or a momentary majority. The preservation of freedom requires the elimination of such concentration of power to the fullest extent and the dispersal and distribution of whatever power cannot be eliminated—a system of checks and balances. By removing the organization of economic activity from the control of political authority, the market eliminates this source of coercive power. It enables economic strength to be a check to political power rather than a reinforcement._

As Nobel economist Hayek wrote forty years ago in *The Road to Serfdom,* "What our generation has forgotten is that the system of private property is the most important quality of freedom, not only for those who own property, but scarcely less for those who do not. It is only because the control of the means of production is divided among many people acting independently that nobody has complete power over us, that we as individuals can decide what to do with ourselves."

If it is important that the individual can buy a car as a consumer, for his and his family's use, it is equally important that he be able to buy it as a producer, to use, for example, as a taxi.

Anti-market (AM) societies do permit privately owned consumer property but little if any privately owned producer property. In the free market (FM) the concept of "consumer sovereignty" is not comprehensive enough. A better phrase would be "individual sovereignty." This covers both the freedom to own as consuming individuals and the freedom to own as producing individuals.

5. What is Economic Problem Number One, and how do property rights relate to it?

The economic problem is *scarcity.*

The economic solution is *productivity.*

Our individual productivity—that which we can produce with our minds and hands—is a personal property. This property serves as a reservoir of potential wealth *not yet produced.*

A farmer, for example, producing for himself, utilizes property in the form of land, equipment, seed, and fertilizer. He transforms these into a different form of property—food. He can consume this new property-form or he can take it to the market and exchange it for another form of property—money.

If you are employed by the farmer, you help him transform his properties—his raw materials—into the new form of property—food. He then pays you for your productivity with his property—money.

Money, as our personal property, then serves as a convenient storehouse of earned wealth that has been produced. We hold it until it is exchanged for other properties. We do not acquire these properties until we choose to, not until they (in our minds) have value. That is, we do not acquire them until we see that they will improve our situation in some way. When we do acquire them, we solve one of our daily problems—personal scarcity.

The economic problem for us as invidivuals is scarcity. The nation's economic problem is the same as ours, only that it is personal scarcity multiplied by 235 million. The world's problem is personal scarcity multiplied by some 5 billion. Strictly speaking, nations are not hungry; individuals are hungry. Nations are not clothed in rags; only individuals are clothed in rags.

The economic solution—individually, organizationally, and nationally—is productivity, which, when totaled, provides the world's productivity.

The properties we as individuals need cannot be taken by force from others. Such action infringes upon others' property rights and *adds nothing to the total of useful properties available.* The problem of scarcity has not been relieved one whit!

By the same reasoning, property we need cannot be printed by government printing presses. *Such action adds nothing to the total property available.* The problem of scarcity has not been relieved in the slightest way. All this does is to increase the supply of money, making each dollar less valuable.

Summary: The Freedom to Own (Piece 2)

The properties we all own are (1) ourselves, (2) our productivity, and (3) our correctly acquired property, as the original claimant to unowned property, or as the secondary claimant through the freedom to exchange (see following section).

Owned property is any item that meets these three qualifications: (1) it is valued by its owner, (2) it has definable boundaries so that it may be identified, and (3) it is subject to the exclusive will of the owner, who has the right to use it in any way he pleases, as long as he does not, in doing so, violate the property rights of others.

Conversely, certain items cannot be owned, which we call, simply, unowned property.

In referring to property, we can divide items into four property classes. The first two have been discussed in this chapter. The third and fourth will be covered in Chapter 6 but are included below.

1. *Unowned property.* Items that are by definition unowned.
2. *Free-market property.* Property correctly acquired in a free market and privately owned with sovereign control over it, as long as property rights of others are not violated. This principle is represented in our structures and Philomods as Piece 2.
3. *Hybrid property.* Property in conflict. Items that have been privately and correctly acquired but are not sovereignly owned because of one or more restrictions on the owner's right to use. Thus, in the FM sense these properties are in contention, subject to the will of a nonowner. This principle may be represented by a hybrid structure named the Hybrimode. This AM/FM conflict may be illustrated in the structures by the presence of both Piece 2 and Piece 12 in the same structure.
4. *Anti-market property.* Government-owned "public" property. Items incorrectly acquired in that the property was valued by an owner, was taken from him against his will, depriving him of his rights of ownership. The principles involved are represented in the structures by Piece 12.

It was necessary to tie ownership concepts down to the deck before we cast off to explore exchange concepts, because we can exchange or trade only what we own. Just as being free to choose is a necessary precondition to our being free to own, being free to own is a necessary precondition to our being free to exchange.

At about age 18 we realize that the most valuable property we own is our own productivity. The fact that we are short on worldly goods when we are young is compensated for by the fact that we are usually long on entrepreneurial expectations. At that time in our lives the concept of economic scarcity is no stranger. It may be our constant companion.

We want to improve our situation (CC-1) to relieve the scarcities. What are we to do?

We have to *exchange* what we have—and which we value (CC-5)—for something the other fellow owns (which we value even more). What we own is our personal productivity, our willingness and our ability to produce. We want to enter into an exchange with another person for money, for it is money—a paycheck—that we value as a way to improve our present situation.

We want to find another person who places a higher value on *our* property (our productivity) than he does on *his* property (his money), which he will pay us in wages. Who is this person?

He is an individual who wishes to improve his situation as he sees it at this time. He has a particular job he wants done. He has a feeling of uneasiness about the situation. His uneasiness will not be relieved until the job is being done to his satisfaction—his definition of a satisfactory outcome. When he first sees you, good looking though you may be, you have no value as a producer for him. If you are the person who can produce, you will then hold value for him. He will go through the choosing process and choose you. He doesn't like his feeling of uneasiness any more than you like your feeling of uneasiness.

When, as a job seeker, we reach an agreement with the other person, who is seeking to get a job done, an *exchange* takes place. Wonderful things begin to happen! Our productivity is our reservoir of potential property. It is all the things that we are capable of doing. Now we are going to have our chance. Our productivity is going to be exchanged for money, which is a reservoir of property *already produced* but not yet acquired.

Our wages remain in reserve form, in our pocket, until we go shopping and find those properties that we value more than the money in our pocket. Then another exchange takes place. We trade our money for the properties in the store.

We talk about "finding a job." The employer talks about "finding someone who can do the job." We talk about "buying" and "selling": We go to the store and "buy" an item we want. The store "sells" it to us. Yet, all these phrases are really another way of describing an exchange of properties that each of us values less for the other fellow's properties, which we value more.

If we don't value the item in the store (the storekeeper's property) more than the money in our pocket (our property), we don't buy. And if the storekeeper does not value our money more than his item, he does not sell. When the exchange does take place, *both* of us are happier. Each of us has exchanged something he values less for something he values more.

Each of us has improved his situation as he sees it at the time. Free exchange is *voluntary* exchange. If we don't think the exchange is a "good deal" we walk away and look for a better one.

Unlike poker, which is a "zero-sum game" (one player's stack of chips grows only as the stack of another player's shrinks), in a free exchange both parties win. In a free-market (FM) economy, when two persons exchange, *both* persons win (CC-1). The young person who gets a job has won a battle to overcome *his* problem of economic scarcity. The employer who gets the job done that he wanted done has triumphed by increasing *his* productivity.

The accompanying diagram illustrates how voluntary exchange works. We are indebted to Bettina Greaves of the Foundation for Economic Education for bringing it to our attention.

Two people, Mr. Langley of London and Señor Martinez of Madrid, see the possibility of an exchange. Langley's situation, as a result of this possible trade, can have one of three outcomes:

1. It would benefit his situation.
2. The situation would be the same; outcome unchanged.
3. It won't benefit his situation.

Martinez's situation can only result in one of the same three outcomes: He will benefit; things will be the same as before; or, he won't benefit.

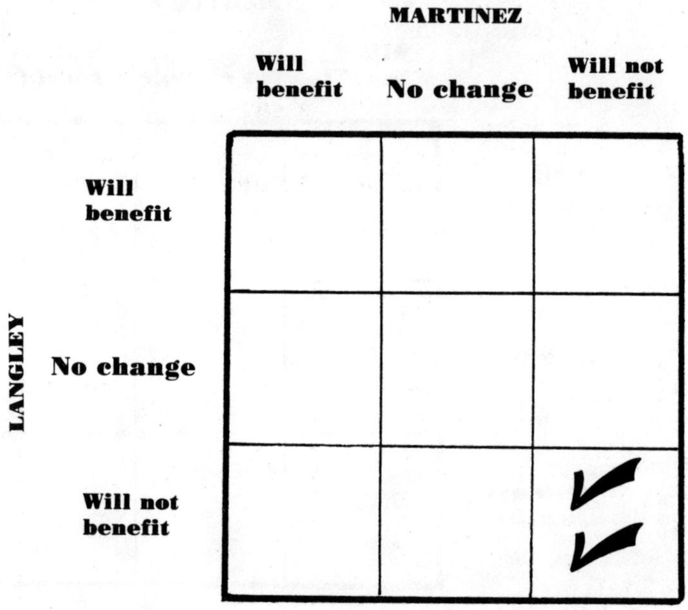

MARTINEZ

	Will benefit	No change	Will not benefit
Will benefit			
No change			
Will not benefit			✓✓

(LANGLEY along the left axis)

If Langley and Martinez decide that neither will benefit from an exchange, nothing happens at all.

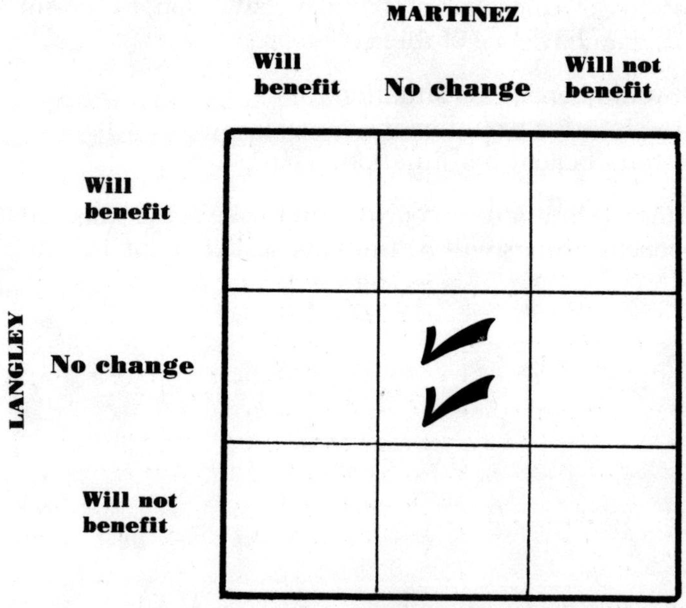

MARTINEZ

	Will benefit	No change	Will not benefit
Will benefit			
No change		✓✓	
Will not benefit			

(LANGLEY along the left axis)

If each ends up with an outcome the same as before, again there is no reason for anything to happen. Let's say that each has a dollar to trade. Why exchange dollars? It would only be a waste of time.

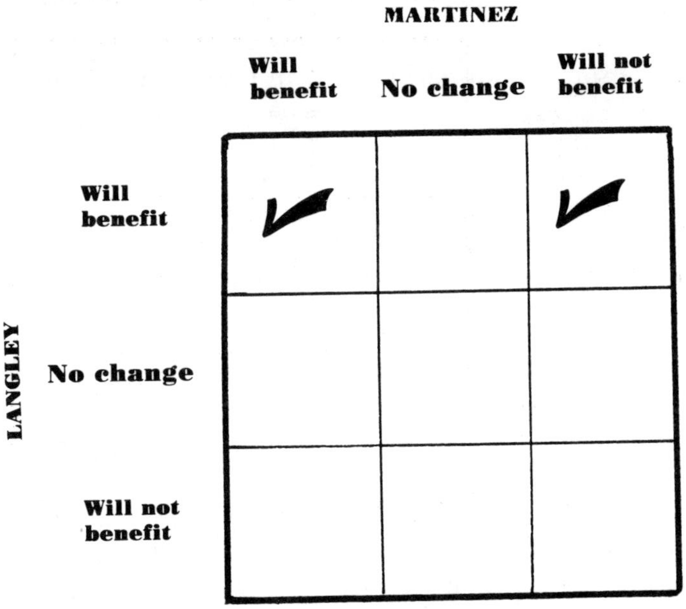

MARTINEZ

LANGLEY	Will benefit	No change	Will not benefit
Will benefit	✔		✔
No change			
Will not benefit			

If Langley benefits, but Martinez does not, Martinez will not trade. Why should he? Where's the motivation? It is not to his advantage to do so. His situation is not improved.

By the same token, if Martinez benefits but Langley does not, Langley will have no reason to enter into an exchange.

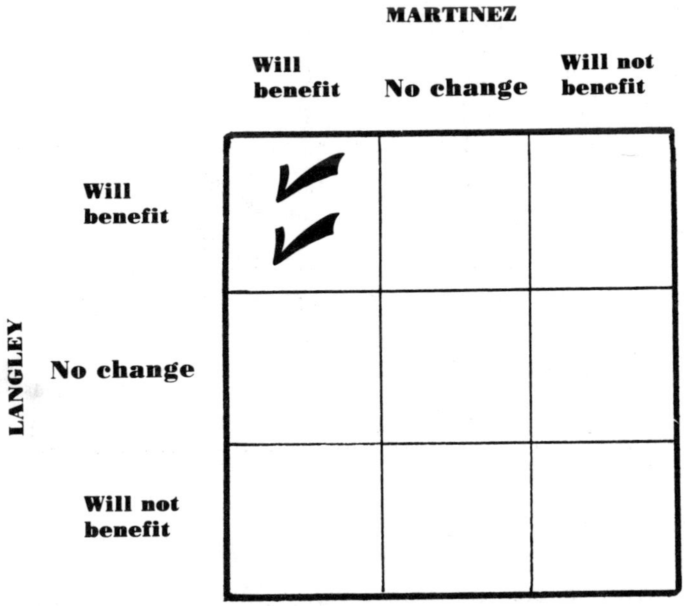

MARTINEZ

LANGLEY	Will benefit	No change	Will not benefit
Will benefit	✔ ✔		
No change			
Will not benefit			

The Economic Base of the Free Market 71

Only if the trade is seen as valuable to both men will they make their exchange. Both say "Yes" voluntarily, because both gain from the transaction.

Whether it is a trade of cucumbers for cabbages between Natasha and Vladimir, who have neighboring gardens in Soviet Siberia, or between two boys in Hannibal, Missouri, who trade a bullfrog for a rusty pocket knife, or between the young person looking for his first job and his first employer, the story is the same. Both participants in the exchange must benefit, or no deal. It must, of course, be a free exchange made voluntarily. Each of the traders has full property rights over what he is exchanging. Neither is being coerced by the other or by a third party who may limit or distort rights of ownership.

And each has other choices. In the environment surrounding the freedom to exchange, there is competition. There is a "competitive market." Both have other choices (CC-2).

COMPETITION: A HEXAGON OF ALTERNATIVES

Let's pause a moment to return to one of the central ideas of *Structures*—the ways in which various organizations touch upon our lives as individuals.

The four-piece structure of the Freepod represents intangible philosophies of economics. But the organization that resides and operates atop this conceptual base is tangible. And the people within it are real and tangible. They smile, cry, shout, whisper, have loves and hates, and can be delightful human beings or first-rate SOB's.

How that organization—whether a company, store, association, church, or charity—helps or hinders our actions as individuals is foremost to our best interest. Does a particlular organization enhance our freedom of choice or does it impair or even destroy it? Is this an organization that I believe in, that I support, and that I want to see grow and prosper?

Our opinions of organizations are very personal. We like them or we don't like them. If we didn't like them twenty years ago we probably still don't. They stuck us with a defective set of tires, or they told us an outright lie. Or perhaps they were close to us at one time: we worked hard and long for them and received no appreciation. And we said, "Nuts to you, Buster." Images and impressions such as these stick with us.

The result is that we usually support a handful of them and we steer clear of many others. In each category of organization, we come to value one—one store, one charity, one tire dealer, one church—above all others (CC-5).

An interesting truth is that we, as individuals, deal only with other individuals. When we initiate an exchange, it is always one individual with another. If we deal with Sears, we deal with one person.

As individuals we exchange with other individuals (1) acting on *their* own behalf, (2) acting for their "unorganized" group, or (3) representing their organizations. In their various roles all these people are competing for our attention.

As for *our* function in the exchange, we enter into a trading environment as individuals (1) acting on our own behalf, (2) representing a group in which we have an interest, or (3) representing our organization.

If we were to illustrate this concept, it would appear as a hexagon with crisscrossed lines. Each line represents an action taking place—or about to take place—between two people.

And does their communication have a reason for being? Yes, each wishes to improve his situation as he sees it at the time (CC-1).

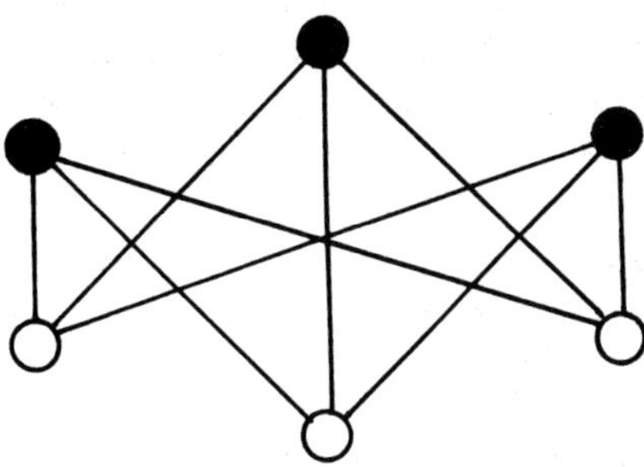

We want to benefit from our freedom to exchange. It is a good idea to employ some Characteristics of Choice from Piece 1.

If we are to accept the responsibility for own choices (CC-9), we must be free to improve our situation as we see it (CC-1), according to our own value preferences (CC-5) without external interference. Faced with scarcities (the economic problem), we must be free to produce and exchange (the economic solution) in order to survive.

Before we exchange, we shop. Shopping is a function of exchanging. Shopping is exploratory action. It is related to (CP-4) in the Choosing Process, which, you will remember, is the collection and creation of alternatives. Shopping is the collection of information. We shop to determine what selections are available. We survey the situation. We let our fingers do the walking. We scan the display and classified ads in our local paper. We go to the reference room of our public library for information on expensive capital goods.

Why do we shop? Because we are assured the best outcome only if we include the best inputs in our choosing process (CC-3). Before we shop, then, there must be more than one choice, because choices come only in twos or more (CC-2). This means that there must be a competitive market. It is essential to the freedom to exchange.

There must be two or more suppliers, or at least an opportunity for two or more. It is best for us when several sources compete for our attention and try to serve our needs, wants, and preferences. Economist Israel Kirzner states it this way: "There must be freedom of market entry and absence of privilege."

Thus we come to appreciate the interdependence of the various freedom-of-choice pieces in the free-market structure. To improve our situation (CC-1), we must be free to exchange, Piece 3. Exchanging is the decisive action. To be free to exchange, we must be free to shop. And, to be free to shop we must be served by competitive markets in which we can shop.

This brings us back to the second big test question: "May I exchange?" This means may I exchange freely, shopping in markets that offer real selections, open to all who wish to enter them, unencumbered by special privileges for a special few.

If the organization in question (and the markets in which it operates) does indeed enhance our freedom to exchange, Piece 3, it serves to reinforce our freedom to choose, Piece 1. If the organization plays a part in blocking free exchange, it is against us.

Piece 3 is a part of the structure of economic freedom. The organization at the top of the Freepod is prepared to exchange freely in a competitive market. There is freedom of entry to all possible competitors. To every individual who interfaces with this market, this means optimal opportunities to shop and to exchange.

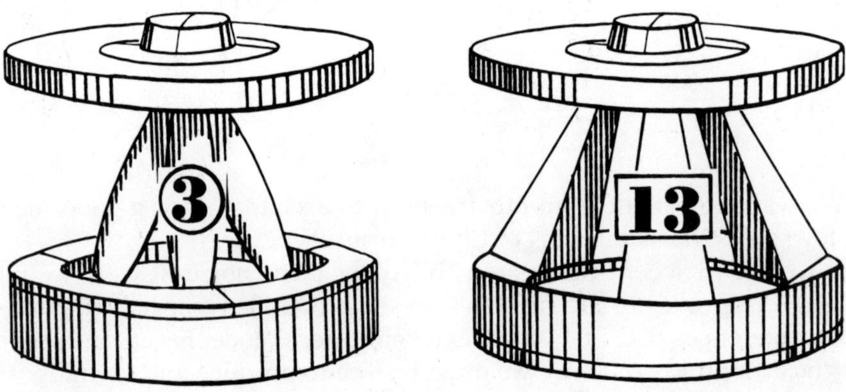

If the organization that rests atop Piece 3 is at the same time supported in our structure by Piece 13, this means that it has gained some sort of monopolistic advantage over its competitors. If it rests *only* on Piece 13 (with Piece 3 completely absent from the structure), *it may have no competitors*. It has been granted a monopolistic privilege. Such privileges, as we shall presently see, are invariably traceable to a political philosophy of unlimited governmental power.

THE FREEDOM TO FUND, PIECE ④

First, we must be free to choose (Piece 1). Second, we must be free to own (Piece 2). Third, we must be free to exchange (Piece 3). Piece 4 in our structure—a round leg identical in shape to Pieces 2 and 3—is our freedom to fund. This allows us to organize our own property and the property of others who wish to participate voluntarily in risk-taking, to fund productive enterprises in the hope of reward.

The first three freedoms carry with them an implicit understanding. They include the freedom *not to choose*, the freedom *not to own*, and the freedom *not to trade*. Those choices are ours and ours alone. Likewise, the freedom to fund always includes the freedom *not to fund*, and we never want to overlook the inclusion of this implied concept. The individual retains his free choice as to which organizations he will support and which he will not.

We may support productive organizations freely and voluntarily in two ways. First, we may support an organization at its inception (when it may be nothing more than a small group of people brought together by an idea they think worthwhile) with our actions and our property. We may invest in it voluntarily—even though there are unknowns, uncertainties and risks (CC-7)—in the belief that there will be an exchange, (Piece 3) resulting in a material or psychic return which we value (CC-5). Second, we may support an organization once it is underway by exchanging freely with it (Piece 3). We help sustain this organization if we prefer the goods and services it produces above the good and services of others. Through Piece 4 we can sustain the organization—not with the assurance of tangible profit—but with the opportunity for profit.

Free organizations are funded at their inception with various kinds of capital (property); and then they are funded on a continuing basis by the profit they earn. As *investors*, we fund the free organizations with our

capital voluntarily, never as a result of coercion. As *consumers*, we help
fund free organizations by purchasing their products voluntarily, never as
a result of coercion.

Reasons for Funding

Why do we fund an organization? We risk in the expectation of reward.
We fund it because we believe it is going to improve our situation in some
way (CC-1). As investors we believe in its future. As consumers we believe
in its present output.

We invest in a company that is going to build 500 homes near our city.
We believe it will be a successful venture, because the homes are needed
in that place at this time. We contribute to the Salvation Army because we
believe in what it is doing as an organization, and we enjoy the psychic
reward in helping. If we buy a Ford, we do so because we believe it is the
best deal available at the time. In doing so, we help sustain the dealer and
the Ford Motor Company as organizations (although we rarely consider
this result consciously). We pledge an amount to a political party because
we believe it is more likely to come up with the kinds of solutions we favor.
We support these organizations by helping to fund them.

In Chapter 6 we will explore related concepts that support anti-market
(AM) organizations within the community of coercion. We will see that we
fund them, not because we *believe* in them, but because we *must*. We must
fund them at their inception. We must provide the funds that sustain them.
We have no choice.

The Purpose of Profit

Profit is a function of voluntary funding, just as are venture capital
and voluntary contributions. All, therefore, are components of Piece 4.
Profit, as Peter Drucker has pointed out, has three purposes: (1) it supplies
operating capital, (2) it measures performance, and (3) it is the reward for
taking risks.

(There is a chance that you may not like the word "profit." Some do
not. Nevertheless, allow yourself to understand the function of profits. They
play a vital role in the free-market system.)

Robert Nozick says, "Often people who do not wish to bear risks feel
entitled to rewards from those who do and win; yet these same people do
not feel obligated to help out by sharing the losses of those who bear risks
and lose."

We have learned that an organization that rests atop the Freepod, an
organization that is a part of the worldwide FM community, is privately
owned, free to exchange, and voluntarily funded. This organization may
be a "profit" organization or a "not-for-profit" organization. The difference
will be apparent to you immediately.

Churches, for example, are certainly members of the free-market community. Yet they are not for profit. Private schools and universities in the
United States are eligible for inclusion in the same classification.

They are not privately owned, strictly speaking, in that individuals do
not own shares of stock in them; and yet they are not bureaus of the
government either. They are run by a board of trustees, a vestry, or similar

group. No one individual or group of individuals, for example, owns Yale or Harvard University. They own *themselves*. We cannot buy shares in these institutions. They are supported by income from private endowments, by voluntary contributions, and by the fees they charge for their services.

While not owned by others, they can and do own property-and do so correctly—in their own names. No individual can be coerced to fund them (although some of their alumni are skilled arm twisters). As organizations they are not expected to "show a profit." They do not survive, however, if their operating expenses continually outpace their incomes. For this reason many private schools and colleges, as well as local church organizations, have indeed gone under.

Because one of the purposes of profit is to measure performance, other yardsticks become more important for non-profit organizations. A church cannot measure how many souls it has saved in the past year, nor how many unhappy people it has made happier. It can, however, measure the number of people in the pews each Sunday—and it does just that. Perhaps you have noticed at your church ushers quietly walking down the aisles after all are settled in their seats. They are "counting the house." If there are fewer people in the congregation each year, the organization is headed for trouble.

A university cannot measure how many of its graduates succeed in life. What is success? Certainly it is not only the amount of a graduate's annual income. It is more likely to be the degree of maturity exhibited as one faces tough problems and trying times. The private university that survives over the years must be believed in by its alumni and friends. They must feel that it produces a good product. Their belief must be strong enough so that their voluntary contributions are generous.

In the absence of profit, trustees and directors of nonprofit institutions must find other objective measurements. They must be sure that their organizations really satisfy the needs, wants, and preferences of the individuals who comprise their "market."

The third purpose of profit is its function as a reward for taking risks. Let's hold this for the next chapter where we will discuss it in detail, when we introduce our hero, the entrepreneur.

Piece 4 is a part of the economic tripod upon which the voluntarily funded organization reposes. The concept which is related to Piece 4 and its antithesis is Piece 14.

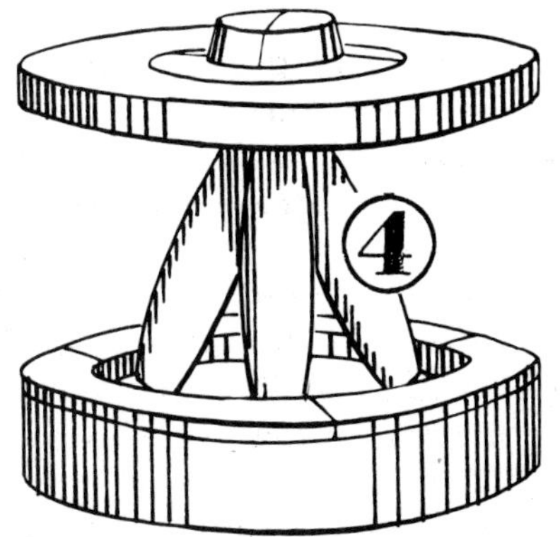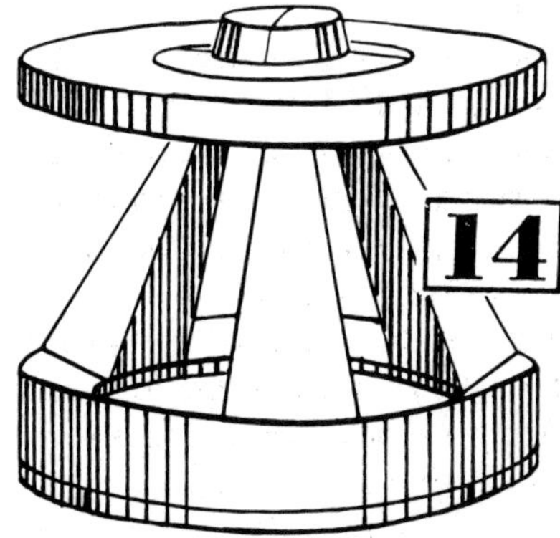

THE THREE-QUESTIONS TEST

One of the purposes of this book is to examine the many ways in which hundreds of organizations influence our lives as individuals. Some organizations help us to exercise our freedom to choose. They reinforce our individuality. They are supportive as we attempt to improve our situation (CC-1) as we undertake to pursue happiness in our own way.

- They increase the choices available (CC-2)
- They cannot force us to exclude the best alternative from consideration (CC-3)
- They tend, through competition (Piece 3) to lower the costs of our choice (CC-4)
- They may try, but they cannot superimpose their own value judgments on us (CC-5)
- They give us time to make a good choice, and they provide us information we need (CC-6)
- They help us lessen risk and uncertainty (CC-7)
- They cannot prevent us from looking at secondary consequences as well as primary ones (CC-8)
- They respect the fact that we alone are responsible for our outcomes (CC-9), but they help us find a way out if we have made a bad decision (CC-10)
- They do not interfere with our choosing process (CP-1 through CP-8), should we choose (Piece 1), to use one.

Other organizations are hindrances to our freedom of choice. They raise objections. They place obstacles in our way. They have many ways in which they can restrict, reduce, or remove our freedom to improve our situation as we see it at the time (see Chapter 7).

The Vulnerability of Our Freedom

We can now count the ways in which our freedom is vulnerable, ways in which we can be coerced.

Our freedom to choose is vulnerable eighteen ways. As we consider the ten characteristics of choice (see Chapter 1), we can understand that not being allowed to consider all ten reduces our ability to improve our situation. As we proceed through the eight phases of the choosing process, any external forces that hamper the process are threats to our pursuit of happiness.

Our freedom is vulnerable to the coercion of our rights of ownership when we cannot acquire property rightfully and freely, when that which we have acquired cannot be traded or utilized in the way that best suits our needs, and when our property is taken from us against our will to fund organizations that are of no interest to us.

We have now completed an explanation of each of the three round legs in the Freepod. You have taken another step toward improving your situation, your self-responsibility, your self-esteem—toward your inalienable right, your personal pursuit of happiness.

One purpose of this examination was to learn to ask three questions as a test to determine the relationship of any organization to ourselves as free individuals:

TEST QUESTION ONE: May I own it?
The free-market answer should usually be YES

TEST QUESTION TWO: May I trade freely?
The free-market answer again should be YES.

TEST QUESTION THREE: Must I fund it, whether I want to or not?
The free-market answer should be NO.

Chapter 4 The Entrepreneurial Structure

Pieces ⑦ **Creativity**
 ⑧ **Management**
 ⑨ **People Resources**
 ⑩ **Property Resources**
 ⑪ **Products and Services**

They have an unremitting desire to create a satisfying new order out of chaos, and the courage to persist to create that order on one's own terms.

Bill Moyers

We now move to the top of the Philomod to the productive operating organization. There are five pieces in this substructure.

- Creativity (Piece 7)
- Management (Piece 8)
- People Resources (Piece 9)
- Property Resources (Piece 10)
- Products and Services (Piece 11)

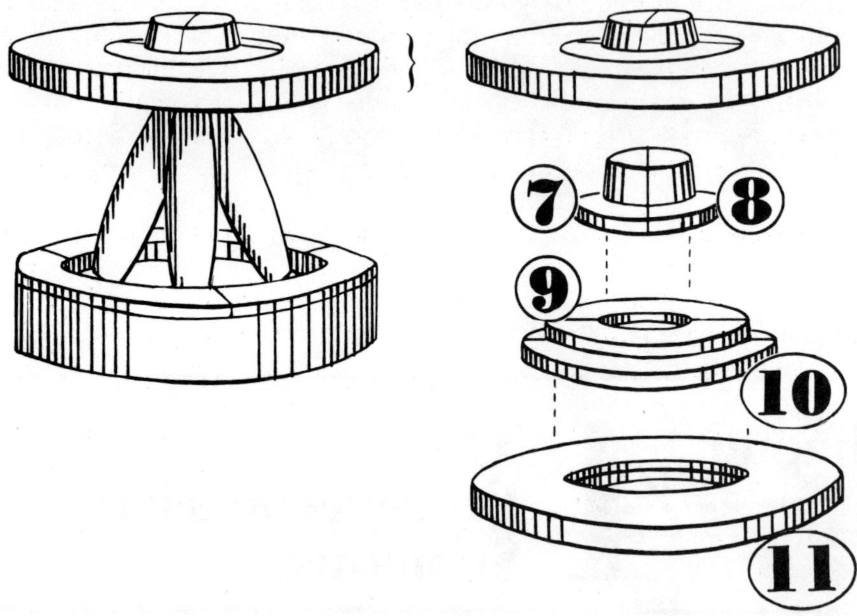

If you have our wooden model handy, please examine it. The hub in the center is comprised of two characteristics: Piece 7 represents creativity or innovation, which is both the original idea, the reason the organization was started, and also the continuing ideas from the organization's research and personnel.

Piece 8 represents management, which guides the organization in turning ideas into marketable goods and services. It is planning, organizing, and controlling. It balances the use of resources available to deliver a product or service that represents good value at a reasonable price.

Pieces 7 and 8 interact with each other. We call these two pieces, when placed together, entrepreneurship or the Entrepreneurial Hub.

The two qualities frequently work harmoniously within one individual. They may also be separate and complementary responsibilities of different individuals within one organization. Or, they may be two different *departments* within an organization: The laboratory or engineering department, for example, representing creativity/innovation, and an executive committee of marketing, production, and financial executives, representing general management.

The entrepreneurial task is to define the market and, as the glove is made to fit the hand, to mold a product or service to fit. In the United States in 1984, a record number of entrepreneurs (an estimated 600,000) launched new business firms. Each felt that he had a new product or service to fit the market.

When we try to place Pieces 7 and 8 by themselves at the top of the Freepod, they do not stay intact. The significance of this is that an idea, namely the creative inspiration, no matter how bright and even when accompanied by good management principles is not enough to hold an organization together. Other components are necessary for any productive organization.

Piece 9 is people resources, which give the organization its unique personality and set it apart from all others. It is the total of the organization's aptitudes, interests, abilities, objectives, motivations, self-disciplines, and appearance. It is the employees who contribute heavily to the creativity and innovation of Piece 7, and who produce the finished product, Piece 11.

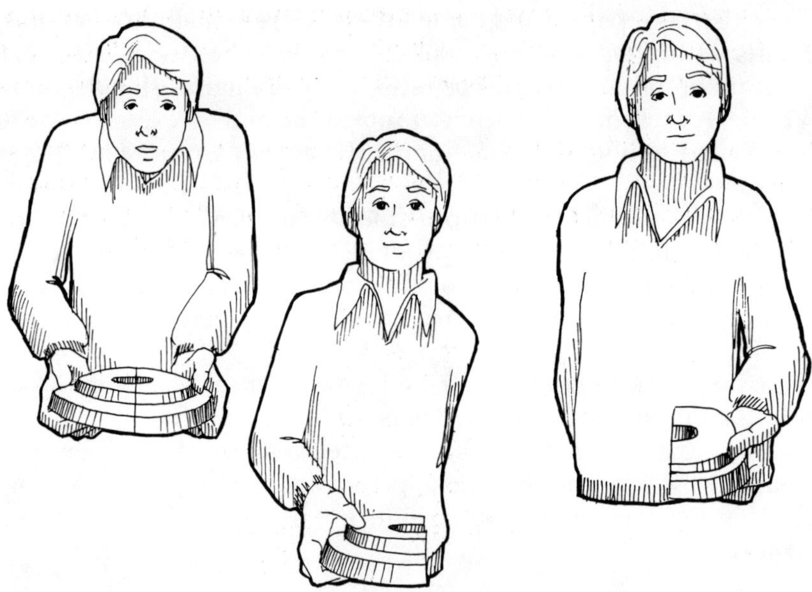

Piece 10 is capital resources and raw materials, the organization's "property" resources as differentiated from "people" resources. The organization cannot "own" its people, though some organizations make the mistake of thinking they can. Organizations can own only that which is represented by Piece 10. It is property that serves as capital, initial funds for salaries and product development in the period before the product is marketed. Piece 10 is land, space, buildings, and equipment, plus the resources and energy which go into the finished goods and services.

Pieces 9 and 10, when fitted together, are called the factors of production, the factor market, or the resources ring. The ring is people resources in concert with property resources.

Note again how our wooden model is constructed. Even with the resources ring in place along with the entrepreneurial hub the structure still will not hold together atop the Freepod. There is still something missing. Missing, of course, is the keystone, the *linchpin*—a profitable good or service.

Piece 11, products and services, is the reason for the organization's being, the end result of the original idea, Piece 7. Piece 11 is a product that matches the needs, wants, or preferences of the market. *Without the successful product the organization falters and collapses.* With it the organization stays together.

The marketable product rests upon the resources ring, which rests upon the entrepreneurial hub, which is balanced atop the Freepod. No piece can be omitted. All are necessary. Each piece, 7 through 11, is completely interdependent upon all the others.

The interdependence extends downward into the structure, relying upon the legs of the Freepod, the rights of ownership, the freedom to exchange, and the freedom to fund. As the free organization draws upon the strengths of its supporting tripod, it reinforces the tripod's strengths through its own existence, its vitality, and its service to its markets.

For this reason, the entrepreneur is the key person in the interdependencies of freedom. More than any other person he represents our various freedoms in action. He has the most to lose if our freedoms are lost. He is the most likely candidate to lead in their defense.

By no means are all organizations commercial. Two of the most long-lived organizations in western society are Oxford University and the Catholic Church. *Organizations, like people, are born, have short or long lives, and die.*

Organizations are born to fulfill a purpose. It may be commercial, artistic, religious, philanthropic, military, or political. Each organization begins as an idea in the mind of one individual. Each is born as a result of a creative idea.

The creative idea may be seen as an opportunity for a new product, a new service, a new symphony, a new piece of sculpture, or a new pair of matching skyscrapers. The idea may be related to a unique religious revelation or a desire to help others less fortunate. It may be a military strategy that will require a new type of submarine, or it may be a political tactic to satisfy a particular bloc of voters.

The creative idea emerges from the mind as a result of a perceived need, want, or preference. This comes first. That an organizational structure may be necessary to carry out the idea may come only as an afterthought. It is not at all unusual for the creative mind to overlook entirely the fact that an organization will be needed to implement the idea. But at some point every innovator realizes: "This idea is going to take some money and materials if I am to go anywhere with it. I may need some expert help from others. And I'll need a place where I can do it. And how can I manage all of this? I've got to get organized!"

Needs beget ideas. Ideas beget organizations. Through organizations things get done.

"Society in this century has become a society of organizations," Peter Drucker writes. "Social tasks, from providing goods and services to education and care of the sick and the elderly, which only a century ago were done by the family, in the home, in the shop or on the farm, are increasingly performed in and through large organizations."

Business organizations are also called *enterprises*. Accordingly, the founder of a business is referred to as an *entrepreneur*, the French word for "enterpriser." Even though governmental bureaus are organizations in every sense of the word, structured from the same five pieces we have just introduced, it is not customary to refer to them as enterprises, and it would be inaccurate to call the founder of a governmental bureau an entrepreneur. He is not, even though he may perform a function quite similar to entrepreneurship. There are several reasons for this, which we will discuss in Chapter 6.

The types of organizations people turn to and the types of new organizations they seek to form have a great deal to do with *the direction in which their society heads*. In a free-market society we expect people to turn *first* to private enterprise for the relief of scarcity, for those goods and services that will answer their needs, wants, and preferences.

THE ENTREPRENEURIAL HUB, PIECES ⑦ AND ⑧

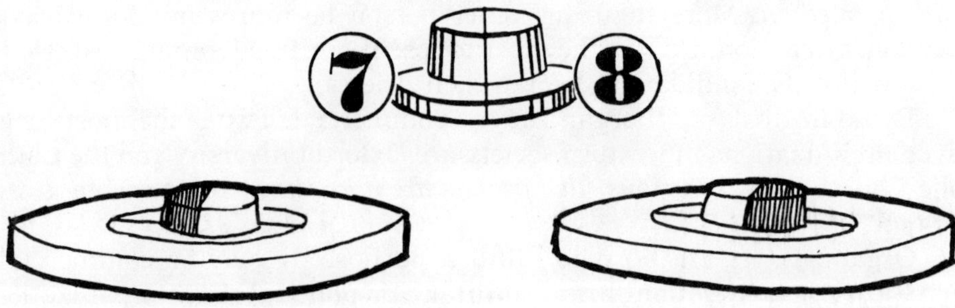

Let's begin at the hub of the wheel, where we will find either an individual entrepreneur or the entrepreneurial function being shared by two or more individuals.

In his 1951 classic, *Capitalism,* David McCord Wright used George Pullman, inventor of the Pullman railroad car, as an example of an entrepreneur with many talents. Pullman had the combined abilities of being the inventor and also the man who could put his ideas across. Wright saw that some men, interested in pure research and wisdom, are psychologically unfit for the struggle needed to put across their ideas. "He either will let his discoveries languish or will willingly turn them over to someone else before they are ever introduced. Accordingly, a special name is needed for that type of man, in any society, who not only thinks up new ideas or adopts the ideas of others but who, in addition, is willing to run the risk and undergo the frequent social onus and difficulties involved in putting across a new social or technological pattern. Such men we call 'enterprisers' or 'entrepreneurs'."

Wright made several other interesting points: Active entrepreneurs and creative artists—"types usually considered to be widely divergent—share a basic attitude. Both conceive of the good life in terms of activity rather than idle contemplation." The entrepreneur, like the artist, *enjoys his work.*

It is supposed that "once an idea has taken shape in the brain of a scientist, or has been discovered in his laboratory, it will automatically become embodied in practical use without requiring anything more than routine effort on the part of a few individuals. Such an idea is entirely mistaken ...."

Wright saw that a large proportion of the human race seems to have an "ingrained dislike for new ideas or ideas which disturb the routine of its existence. Men's minds have a tendency to become set in given molds, and the man who attempts to disturb these preconceptions will encounter little mercy from those whom he is trying to stimulate."

And this: "Entrepreneurs cannot function in a culture which is hostile to change." It is "a requirement of social growth" that we find "ideologies which would permit sufficient freedom of action to new ideas while maintaining adequate order."

Edward de Bono refers to the two types of men as the "originator" and the "implementer" in his excellent book, *New Think.*

Ideas people, he writes, *are not usually powerful organizers; they have so many new ideas that the attraction of the latest one makes it difficult to organize the previous one. Single-mindedness, drive and determination are not characteristics of the ideas man, for he is more interested in having new ideas than in carrying them out.*

Organizers usually fail to distinguish between ideas people, of whom one needs but a few, and implementers, who are the thorough and capable people who do the useful work.

The ideal research team would consist of an ideas man and an implementer ....

How frequently are the originator and the implementer found within one mind? Every day! And, to a degree, in every one of us! In *The Brain Book,* Peter Russell explains that the left and right hemispheres of our brain are areas of specialization. In our *left hemisphere* the functions of *logic, reason, and analysis* are carried out. In the *right hemisphere* are included *creativity and synthesis.*

The fact remains, however, that one of American history's most exciting eras was devoted to our outstanding originator/implementers. Their cerebral hemispheres—their Pieces 7 and 8, if you will—were in fine balance and were fired up. As Daniel Boorstin reminds us, they were what we used to call the "go-getters." Boorstin gives us many examples of nineteenth-century Americans who were originator/implementers.

> *During the nineteenth century, ingenious individual inventors struggled and sacrificed and braved public ridicule. Eli Whitney, Oliver Evans, Elias Howe, Gail Borden, Samuel F. B. Morse, Alexander Graham Bell, George Eastman, John Wesley Hyatt, and scores of others spent their lives, and plagued their families, to make some particular novelty into a marketable commodity. They were inventor-businessmen. Having imagined a sewing machine, they had to fashion it with their own hands, demonstrate it, show how it could be manufactured, and finally persuade someone to do the manufacturing, unless they decided also to do that themselves.*

Robert N. McMurray has written this about the entrepreneur: "He has exquisitely sensitive antennae, which are always tuned to the world about him and to which he is ever responsive ... Companies managed by entrepreneurs have a significantly greater rate of growth than those managed by professional managers. This is probably owing not only to the entrepreneur's greater preoccupation with the daily working of his enterprise, but also to the fact that he has greater freedom of action."

In describing the different stages organizations go through, McMurray entitles only one "the entrepreneurial stage": "At least five stages can be delineated: the beginning entrepreneurial stage (less than 100 people); the transition stage (100 to 200 people); the mature stage (500 to 10,000 people); the bureaucratic stage (over 10,000 people); and the moribund stage (which occurs in all sizes of companies)."

Bridgeford Hunt says that the entrepreneurial type of individual may have difficulty finding a place in today's big corporation. "The very nature of the entrepreneur is in conflict with the basic nature of the corporation. Entrepreneurs are ambitious, creative and energetic people who have the courage to take risks and, if the odds are right, to possibly make a fortune. Basically the modern big corporation is a structured, programmed, conservative organization that goes strictly by the rules."

I have observed that many corporate people learn during their thirties that they may be entrepreneurs rather than corporate "lifers." It is for this reason that I believe age 38 to be so important. For it is from age 40 to age 60 that each of us, if we are to do so, makes the climb to the peak of his own Everest. The corporate person well into his forties is less willing to break away to start his own business, because there is little turnaround time left (CC-10). If he stumbles in his own undertaking after forty, it is more difficult to gain readmittance to the corporate halls.

Jack Yonge, the co-founder/entrepreneur and president of Southeastern Specialties, Inc., likens the MBA-trained corporation executive to a "show dog with a pedigree." Asked what types of dogs entrepreneurs can be compared to, Jack says with pride, "Street dogs!"

Risks, Rewards, and the Few Versus the Many

There is a clear difference between the responsibility shouldered by the entrepreneur as a single individual and the entrepreneurial function as performed by two or more individuals within the large modern corporation. In both cases full responsibility for outcomes (CC-9) is assumed. The difference is the extent of the personal damage caused by a bad outcome.

The Austrian economist Ludwig von Mises told us that there is a simple rule of thumb to distinguish entrepreneurs from nonentrepreneurs. The entrepreneurs, he said, are those on whom the capital losses fall. In 1985 in the United States this changes when a venture capitalist is involved. He is not the originator, but early on, the big risk is his. The entrepreneur is relieved of the financing burden, but he may also not receive as large a reward if his idea is a smash hit. Mises is still correct in over 99 percent of new ventures, however, because the venture capitalist is involved in less than 1 percent.

Just what is the nature of these losses? Take the example of two businessmen, both age 38. Jim Henry is the general manager of a division of a Fortune-500 company. Hal James is a home builder. Both are the hubs of their organizations.

Jim has a new product about ready to market, which he thinks is a winner. His five-year sales projection for the product is $50 million. He readies his marketing program and financial plan for the company's executive committee. He needs $5 million to produce the product, fill the distribution pipeline, and launch his national sales and advertising program. He presents his plans to the committee. It likes them. The committee makes a few suggestions that further strengthen Jim's plan. They OK his $5 million capital committment.

Compared with the personal risks Hal takes, Jim's risks are kid stuff. Hal believes that an area on the Florida Atlantic coast might be a fine opportunity for a PUD (planned unit development—a mixture of homes, recreational facilties, and commercial properties). Three adjacent parcels of land are available, each forty to eighty acres in size. They are, he feels, "in the path of progress." Hal has hired a consulting firm to provide him with population growth projections and housing needs for the area. The firm confirms his sense of the market. Hal pays the consultants $10,000 out of his own pocket.

The probability that a 600-unit residential development will sell out in five years at a $50 million gross appears excellent. Hal selects two of the parcels for purchase. The owners want $3 million. Hal talks them down to $2.7 million and pays them $27,000 out of his own pocket for a six-month option to buy. Hal then commissions an architect/engineering firm to prepare the plans. He also asks for a full-color rendering of the completed project as it would appear from the entrance and from the air. He pays the firm $25,000 "down" out of his own pocket.

Hal takes the consultant's study and his color illustrations to his banker and tells him he needs $8 million for Phase One. After three meetings to hash out the bank's requirements, Hal gets the green light. He must, however, put up his $150,000 home and his $400,000 life insurance policy as collateral. In addition, his personal signature goes on the $8 million note.

Hal then goes to four friends. They form a limited partnership, and in return for a part of future profits, they help Hal buy the land. They pledge him cash from their personal savings. Hal takes one more hard look at his architectural plans, his financial forecasts, and his marketing program. He takes a deep breath and phones his banker to get the papers ready to sign.

Five years pass.

Jim has met the $50 million sales objective he set for his new product. By now his company is paying him a salary of $95,000 a year.

Hal has sold all 600 of his homes and condos and has met *his* $50 million sales objective. He is also enjoying a nice return from the rentals of the stores in his little shopping center in the development. Hal and his friends gross a $4 million profit from his enterprise. Each limited partner clears $250,000. Hal takes home $1 million.

If Jim's new product introduction had bombed and if he had been fired (not very likely) as a result, he would still have a reasonably acceptable corporate track record. He would soon be back in a similar slot in another corporation at a comparable salary. Not too much the worse for wear.

Hal, the entrepreneur, took many times the personal risk of his corporate counterpart. He thereby earned a greater reward. Had Hal's project bombed, he would have been bankrupt. He would have lost his $62,000 out-of-pocket, his home, his life savings, his life insurance, and maybe even his wife. In addition, he would be unemployable in the executive marketplace. "Too much of a wheeler-dealer," the executive-search firms would say, "too little malleability."

The entrepreneurs I have known look back and say, "My God, had I known the risks, I would never have done it!" (I have never heard a corporate manager say this.) Then the "street dog" adds, "But it was fun!"

So the Entrepreneurial Hub (Pieces 7 and 8) serves as the mind of the organization. One hemisphere, the creative mind, *forms*. The other, the management mind, *transforms*.

The creative hemisphere (7) senses what the market wants and forms an idea. The management hemisphere (8) transforms the creative idea into a product and takes it to market. The entire process begins and ends with the market. The creative mind (7) brings forth a property that did not exist before—creates something from nothing. Only in the world of ideas can this be done.

The administrative mind (8), on the other hand, can only obey physical law. It transforms existing raw materials from one arrangement into another—boards into houses, for example.

When the creative and management minds are encased in the same cranium, one does not usually have to "sell" the idea to the other. If the management talent (8) exists that is necessary to take the product to market, the individual in charge (7)(8) simply shifts gears from creative processes (7) to management processes (8) and begins to involve the resources (9)(10) of the organization with the objective of marketing the product (11).

But when these two minds are in different—and sometimes thick—skulls, the administrative mind (8) must first be *convinced*. And therein lies the rub. The two minds do not altogether respect and trust one another. Each harbors a certain amount of prejudice toward the other. The creative mind thinks the management mind is much too preoccupied with facts, figures, production goals, hourly wages, and the bottom line. And the management mind views the creative mind as an impractical luxury, often irritating, always getting off the beaten track, necessitating change, and varying from established policies and procedures.

Myopic madness! Will these two never learn that they cannot live without one another?

How does this relate to the economic problem? The economic problem is scarcity. The economic solution is productivity. The first step in productivity is creativity. The second step is that the creative minority, Piece 7, convince the less creative majority, Piece 8.

THE CREATIVE MIND, PIECE ⑦

Think back for a moment to Piece 1 in our structure. Piece 1 deals with the *logical* way in which free choices are made, situations are resolved, and actions are taken. Piece 7, on the other hand, deals with the *intuitive* way.

Pieces 1 and 8 could be said to represent the *conscious, orderly* mind. Piece 7 is the *subconscious, disorderly* mind.

We are indebted to Edward de Bono for a beautiful analogy:

Lateral thinking is made necessary by the limitations of vertical thinking.

The terms "lateral" and "vertical" were suggested by the following considerations.

It is not possible to dig a hole in a different place by digging the same hole deeper.

Logic is the tool that is used to dig holes deeper and bigger, to make them altogether better holes. But if a hole is in the wrong place, then no amount of improvement is going to put it in the right place. No matter how obvious this may seem to every digger, it is still easier to go on digging in the same hole than to start all over again in a new place. Vertical thinking is digging the same hole deeper; lateral thinking is trying again elsewhere.

It is not possible to look in a different direction by looking harder in the same direction. [A delightful variation on (CC-3) and (CP-4)!]

By far the greatest amount of scientific effort is directed toward the logical enlargement of some accepted hole ... Yet great new ideas and great scientific advances have often come about through people ignoring the hole that is in progress and starting a new one.

Opportunity does not knock. That would be uncharacteristically blatant. Opportunity walks up softly, coming up from behind and standing quietly a few yards from us. We must be able to sense its presence.

The creative idea begins as an elusive wisp in the mind of the individual. We sense a subconscious uneasiness, a moody, cerebral itch. Not rational at all. It's the other side of the brain from rationality. One feels compelled to bring the blurry image of the idea into sharper focus but cannot. Again and again the conscious mind turns its attention to the idea. But over and over the subconscious pushes the conscious out of the way, as if to say, "It's not ready yet. Come back another time. Or better yet, don't call me; I'll call you." It is a time of mental discomfort and frustration.

It is the gestation period of the idea.

Then after weeks or months it happens. From the nethermost repositories of the mind the substantial, formed idea emerges unexpectedly. And accompanying this moment of illumination there is a sense of exhilaration, of relief from a burden. The innovator wants to cry out, "Eureka!" He wants the world to know. The moment is heroic.

But wait.

Ready to be delivered from the mind of the creator, the newborn idea is ever so fragile. The bright idea is frequently portrayed by cartoonists as a lighted light bulb, and indeed it is bright. Also it need not be struck very sharply in order to be shattered. And yet it must now face the first of many shattering, abrasive, and chilling tests. How many ideas perish in this immediate postpartum period? Millions upon millions.

Why so many? The question is pertinent to the focus of this book, because *new ideas—and the way they are handled and mishandled—are central to the essence of enterprise.* When millions of ideas are not only generated but carried forward to market, we have an enterprise system that is working well. But when the outflow is chronically reduced—over years or scores of years—we see the symptoms of a system that is functioning at far below its natural and optimal capacity.

Stimulators of Creativity

What stimulates and enhances creativity? What inhibits and discourages it? Hayek refers to the "process by which the new emerges" as a "voyage into the unknown." If the voyage now challenging us is fruitful, we should discover that the stimulators and inhibitors of creativity, half of the entrepreneurial hub, are the same stimulators and inhibitors of the enterprise system itself.

We should also come to see that certain stimulators and inhibitors appear to exert more of an effect during the gestation of the idea while it is still within the mind. A second group operates more in the postpartum environment after the seed of the idea has been carried to term.

Anyone who has taken a course in firefighting will recognize the following illustration. The first lesson a fire department teaches its fledglings is the "triangle of combustion." Fires are sustained by fuel, heat, and oxygen. To put out the fire, it is only necessary that one of these—any of the three—be removed.

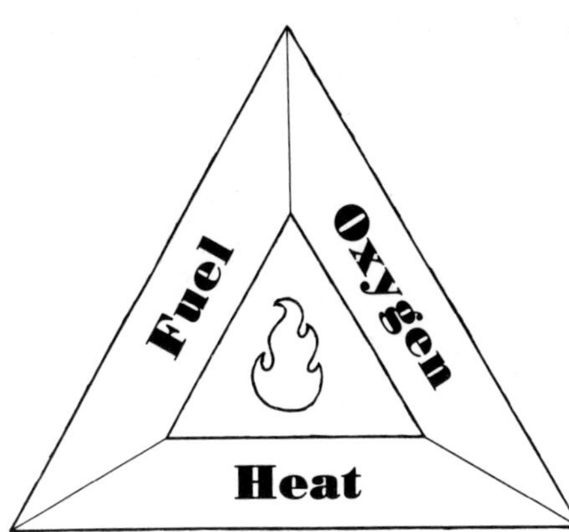

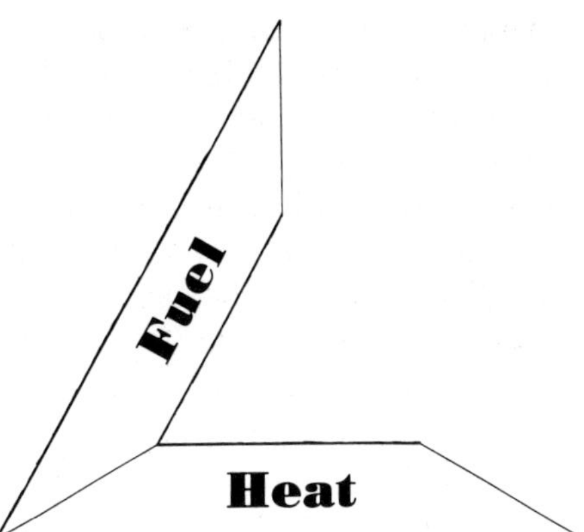

We're going to steal the idea and call it the "Triangle of Creative Combustion." The three elements needed to sustain your creative flame are:

1. input (feed it fuel),
2. motivation (keep it warm), and
3. respite (give it air).

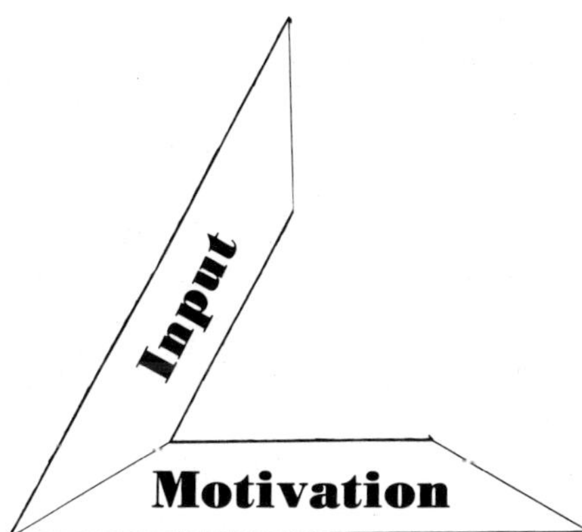

The creative flame burns in all of us to one degree or another. Isn't it probable that the distribution of creative talent around the planet follows the familiar bell-shaped curve?

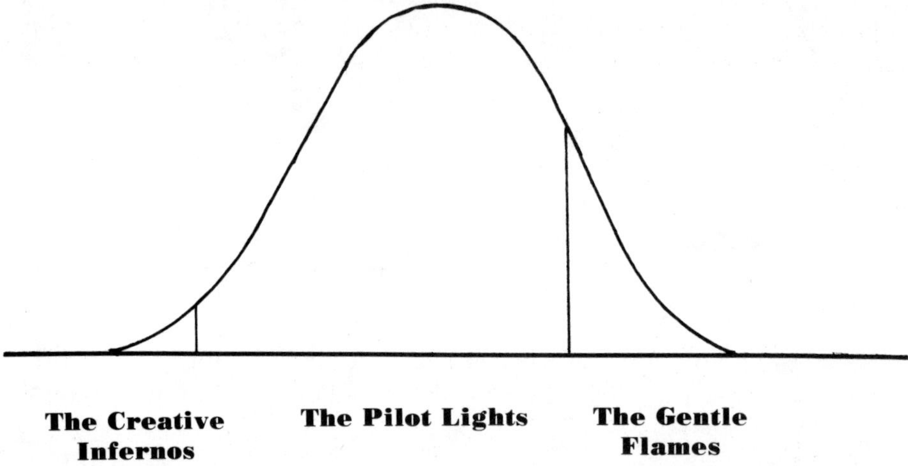

In the tiny area to the left is the highest order of creativity, the intuitive geniuses, the "Raging Infernos." These number, say, one in ten million people, geniuses like Aristotle, Leonardo da Vinci, Charles Darwin, Charles Dickens, Ludwig von Beethoven, Thomas Jefferson, Thomas Edison, and Albert Einstein.

In the larger area to the extreme right of the curve is the next highest order of creativity, the productively creative, the "Gentle Flames." These individuals might number in the hundreds of thousands. They are the top scientists, artists, musicians, engineers, etc., whose creations and ideas affect the world, but of whom history will little note nor long remember.

And then there's that big lump in the middle. All the rest of us, the "Pilot Lights."

The fireman asks, "Where's the fire and what type of fire is it?" Then he goes for the base of it. He wants to put it out just as quickly as he can. If walls, closed doors, or windows stand in the way, he axes them. We want to ask the same question, but we don't want to put it *out*. We want it to burn as *brightly* as possible! And, if there are obstacles in the way, *axe* them!

Because we want to get the most out of our creativity.

For the satisfaction of the individual. For the benefit of the organization. For the new wealth it creates for the planet. Remember? The economic problem is scarcity. The economic solution is productivity.

That there are artistic and scientific creative flames is generally accepted. Less often appreciated is the fact that there are commercial, legal, theological, military, and political creative flames as well. Every vocation and every avocation has its tiny number of Raging Infernos, its substantial number of Gentle Flames, and yes, its masses of Pilot Lights.

According to Dr. Roger J. Williams, in his book, *You Are Extraordinary:* "Our eyes, ears, taste buds and skin senses— in fact, all of our means of gaining impressions from the outside— are highly distinctive for each of us. The wide differences in brain structure contribute to make us all spotted with respect to the ease with which we grasp various thoughts, concepts and ideas. This is why we may speak of someone's having 'a fine legal mind' or of a person's having 'a yen for mathematics' or a student's being a 'language whiz.' Experts agree that every individual tends to have a pattern of mental abilities or potentialities which is distinctive for him or her alone."

Input. What is this process of creativity that Hayek refers to as a "voyage into the unknown?" Eliot D. Hutchinson, former professor of pyschology at the University of Rochester, wrote extensively on the psychology of creative thought. Can the Gentle-Flame original person and the Pilot Lights apply the methods of the Raging Infernos? Hutchinson's studies and his work with Sylvania Electric provide us with some insights and encouragement.

Hutchinson recognized the creative process as intuitive. He categorized four stages of insight:

1. Preparation
2. Frustration
3. Achievement
4. Verification

General preparation, that is, general education, involves a lifetime of input. The mind is fed an incredibly broad mixture of fuel: hard facts, soft impressions, old wives' tales, and dogma. A little that will be pertinent; a lot that will be irrelevant. From birth—even before it—millions of bits of stimuli pour into the brain from the senses of sight, hearing, taste, smell, and touch.

There is, as Russell differentiated in *The Brain Book,* passive stimulation, such as that received from most television programs, which will probably "not be of much benefit in the brain's development." And there is the active stimulation of "directly interacting with the world, with other good minds," which causes us to draw upon our resources.

Russell writes, "A complete education should give equal emphasis to both verbal-analytic thinking (Piece 8) and to aesthetic-synthetic thinking (Piece 7). If only the verbal-analytic side (of the brain) is being educated, the student is effectively being cut off from many ways in which he could directly experience the world around him."

The neurons and fibers of our memory banks retain past episodes, facts, hundreds of thousands of words and their meanings, faces, pictures, skills, instincts, and perhaps memories of a past life. There is a normal "curve of forgetting" where the clarity of information decays with time. But it is possible, through mnenomic techniques, to produce a much higher retention level.

The receptors of the mind, all the while, have also been absorbing unsolved problems, questions, and unanswered challenges. It may be only later that we become aware that our mind took aboard, at some moment in the past, that particular challenge. The "felt uneasiness" has been crouching in a corner of our subconscious, quietly feeding and growing, only occasionally causing discomfort or making its presence known.

All of that is *general* preparation. During the specific preparation for creativity, the original person becomes a student of his chosen subject. The 18-year-old who early learns the nature of his talents through the assistance of a fine teacher, the insight of a loving parent, or the interested guidance of a minister are fortunate. The youngster who learns early that he or she is a Gentle Flame or an "original person" is doubly fortunate. They have found their areas of strength.

We produce according to our abilities. We produce best when we use the best of our abilities. Such producers invariably derive personal satisfaction and enjoy self-esteem. Whether writer, artist, or computer designer, the Gentle Flame—as he or she grows from age eighteen to thirty-eight to fifty-eight— becomes more and more *selective* in the fuels he feeds his mind.

"Invention, strictly speaking," wrote Sir Joshua Reynolds, the eighteenth-century English portraitist, "is little more than a new combination of those images which have been previously gathered and deposited in the memory. Nothing can be made of nothing; he who has laid up no materials can produce no combinations."

The original person, as an individual, grows more extraordinary, grows more unique.

Dr. Frank Barron, a research psychologist at the University of California, Berkley, sees certain common traits in original persons. In *Creativity and Personal Freedom,* he provides five theories that original persons (1) prefer complexity, (2) are more complex psychodynamically and have greater personal scope, (3) are more independent in their judgment, (4) are more self-assertive and dominant, and (5) reject suppression as a mechanism for the control of impulse, implying that they forbid themselves fewer thoughts, that they entertain impulses and ideas that are commonly taboo.

Raging Infernos—the Leonardos and Edisons—apparently become familiar with the patterns of their own creative gestation periods. They realize that the problem/situation upon which they have centered their attention will be difficult to define. There will be false starts. It will be necessary to sort wheat from chaff. Some of the mental process is logical and rational; much of the search is subconscious and intuitional. There is a lot of useless repetition, especially if the problem is difficult. The experienced insightful Inferno takes consolation in knowing that "this too shall pass." He knows that he has given information to his computer—as in choosing-process phases (CP-3) and (CP-4)—and that his computer is whirring and churning, but it does not want to talk to him yet. He has learned that the stage of achievement is preceded by an impatience-with-self stage of frustration.

Frustration—the input phase is filled with it.

Creating is a lonely, nerve-wracking trial. The mind is in labor. The individual's ambition is to deliver a healthy, beautiful child. Tension builds throughout gestation. The rational hemisphere of the brain must work closely with the intuitive hemisphere, something it may not be accustomed to doing. There is no harmony within, only conflict. The original person may encounter a sense of inadequacy and futility. He swings, according to Hutchinson, between the opposite extremes of anger and resignation. In geniuses, Hutchinson says, the outward manifestations may be "extreme irascibility." In his frustration the creative person may attempt to set substitute goals, may try to suppress his own creativity, may turn to excesses. A great deal of energy is required and is expended.

The healthy mind withstands this stressful period. It understands that it is a little out of balance and that as soon as the newborn idea is delivered intact, balance will be restored. It realizes that no one else can give birth to its baby. As Hutchinson says, "In the last analysis the creative act is individual."

Respite.   Now to the second part of our Triangle of Creative Combustion. As the fire must have oxygen, the creative flame must have air. We have selected the word *respite* to label this phenomenom. It is not unlike a religious retreat. Look at respite as an umbrella word that covers time, distance, and periods of neuromuscular refreshment.

Moses got his breath of air—and a lecture from God—by going up the mountain. Jesus removed himself—as did Muhammad six centuries later-to the desert for a month. Those professionals whose livelihood depends upon their continued creativity know that they must likewise have time to think. They structure their lives so that they may spend time away from the daily routine. It opens their conscious minds to become more receptive to ideas that are in subconscious incubation.

"Every man whose business it is to think," wrote Walter Lippmann, "knows that he must for part of the day create about himself a pool of silence."

David Ogilvy, one of Madison Avenue's most unforgettable innovators, put it this way in his *Confessions of An Advertising Man:* "I have developed techniques for keeping open the telephone line to my unconscious, in case that disorderly repository has anything to tell me. I hear a great deal of music. I am on friendly terms with John Barleycorn. I take long hot baths. I garden. I go into retreat among the Amish. I watch birds. I go for long walks in the country... While thus employed in doing nothing, I receive a constant stream of telegrams from my unconscious, and these become the raw material for my advertisements."

Science-fiction author, Robert A. Heinlein, speaks of this essential element through his hero, Lazarus Long, in *Time Enough for Love:* "If you happen to be one of the fretful minority who can do creative work, never force an idea; you'll abort it if you do. Be patient and you'll give birth to it when the time is ripe. Learn to wait."

Thomas Edison took frequent cat naps during periods of scientific experimentation. Hutchinson refers to the technique as an "enforced idleness," as a time of "temporary renunciation of the subject," a time when the creating individual "can listen to the chords of his inner harmony."

de Bono puts it this way: "A new idea does not need to be molded, it can be watched and followed as it grows and temporarily neglected when it does not. If an idea does not form itself into a usable shape there is not much to be gained by forcing it into one .... In general an idea is far more fertile if seduced rather than raped."

Motivation.   What keeps the creative mind pressed to its task? I believe that the "original person" is by nature self-motivated. He strives to get the Big Idea out the door of his mind. He seeks to resolve the matter once and for all. He wants to see his design as a blueprint, to experience the new chemical formula on the laboratory blackboard, to hear his musical notes on the tape recorder, or to see his words on paper. The only way his situation can be improved, as he sees it at the time, is to get his newborn idea out into the world. No one else will experience as he will the joy of labor ended.

The most satisfying reward may be the "delivery" of the idea, but other incentives also motivate. Robert E. Sibson, management consultant, has observed that no single factor motivates everyone. Each individual has his own value preferences (CC-5). Money is usually the number one motivator; people want to improve their situation, (CC-1). Money offers one way to improve a large number of situations but certainly not all. People are motivated by things they do not have or do not think they have—scarcity or a perceived scarcity (the economic problem).

Sibson reaffirms that innovative professionals in industry are motivated by incentives. He investigated the research and development effectiveness in twelve "Fortune 1000" companies in the electronics, pharmaceutical, and chemical industries. Six companies were successful in terms of their creative output and six had poor track records in that area. The study was to determine why. He found the same characteristic present in the successful group and absent in the least innovative group—an incentive compensation plan for the professional people.

Rewards are psychological stimuli. Industry uses them extensively. They may be material; for example, a one-time $5,000 award, for example, for an outstanding achievement. They may be nonmaterial; for example, a personal place in the employee parking lot. Rewards, says Sibson, must be relative. There must be a distinct and direct relationship between what an individual accomplishes and the reward he receives. And rewards must be significant. In other words, the race must be worth the running.

Adversity can motivate. The *Book of Lists* names fifteen authors who wrote best-sellers in their prison cells. Among these were: Cervantes (*Don Quixote*), Hitler (*Mein Kampf*), Nehru (*Glimpses of World History*), O. Henry (short stories, such as "The Gentle Grafter"), Sir Walter Raleigh (*History of the World*), and Oscar Wilde (*The Ballad of Reading Gaol*).

People can be spurred to creativity by the adversity of hard times. James L. Hayes, President of the American Management Association, noted in *Manager's Forum:* "In the recent downturn (1974), even employees who felt secure in their jobs felt the tension of the time and responded with new ideas and experiments as never before. In non-union groups the change was noticeable."

The list of factors that stimulates people is endless because of our differing preferences (CC-5).

Inhibitors of Creativity

While the idea is still *within* the mind, what are the factors that inhibit and discourage creativity? Here is a partial list.

- A low level of creative talent; the strengths of the individual are simply elsewhere
- Lack of input or the wrong input (CC-3)
- Fear of failure or ridicule (CC-4 and/or CC-7)
- Restriction upon rewards (CC-2)
- The wrong kind of rewards (CC-5)
- Orientation to security rather than opportunity (CC-5)
- Regimentation; a framework of arbitrary rules (CC-2)
- Too little time to think, to retreat from day-to-day routine (CC-6)
- A heritage or atmosphere that lacks respect for intuitive thought

Result of Creativity—the Idea

"Then in a twinkling all is changed." So Hutchinson describes his third stage in intuitive thinking. The intuitive seed has been passed up from the subconscious, has taken shape in the preconscious, and has finally been delivered to the conscious mind. It has been fed the proper fuel. It has been given air. It has been kept warm.

The entire nervous system has been engaged in the gestation process. All accumulated tension disappears at the moment of creation. After days or months of being stumped and frustrated, the creator experiences a feeling of fulfillment. The creative mind, elated by its new idea, wants to race through the streets sharing its moment of joy. It forgets that people who race joyfully through streets are looked upon as freaks.

Before the originator, Piece 7, approaches the implementers, Piece 8— whose support he must now have—he should verify his idea (Hutchinson's fourth and last stage in the creative process.)

The painter steps back from his canvas to see if he has captured what he set out to do. Sound familiar? It is akin to the evaluation phase (CP-8). The scientist sets his new hypothesis aside for awhile before running more tests. It gives the logical hemisphere in his brain time to evaluate what the intuitive half has created. Then he may run some more tests. The writer sets aside the chapter or the poem, written in the heat of creation, to cool. When he goes back to his work, he finds misused words and fuzzy phrases that had not been apparent before.

What each innovator wants to achieve is called "objectification." Each seeks to be his own critic, knowing that he is the first of many. Each is aware that the creation of intuition will have to face the scrutiny of logic (Pieces 8 and 1).

Accompanying the text are confrontations as old as civilization itself. Each is the creative minority of one (Piece 7) about to meet the less-creative majority of many (Piece 8).

The country and western songwriter, age 18, with a catchy tune and lyrics, making the rounds in Nashville, seeking someone who will publish his song ...

The pharmaceutical chemist, age 58, with a promising new compound for migraine, waiting outside the conference room where the corporate research and development committee is about to call him in ...

The home builder, age 38, with an idea for a new cluster-housing development, taking the seat across from his banker ...

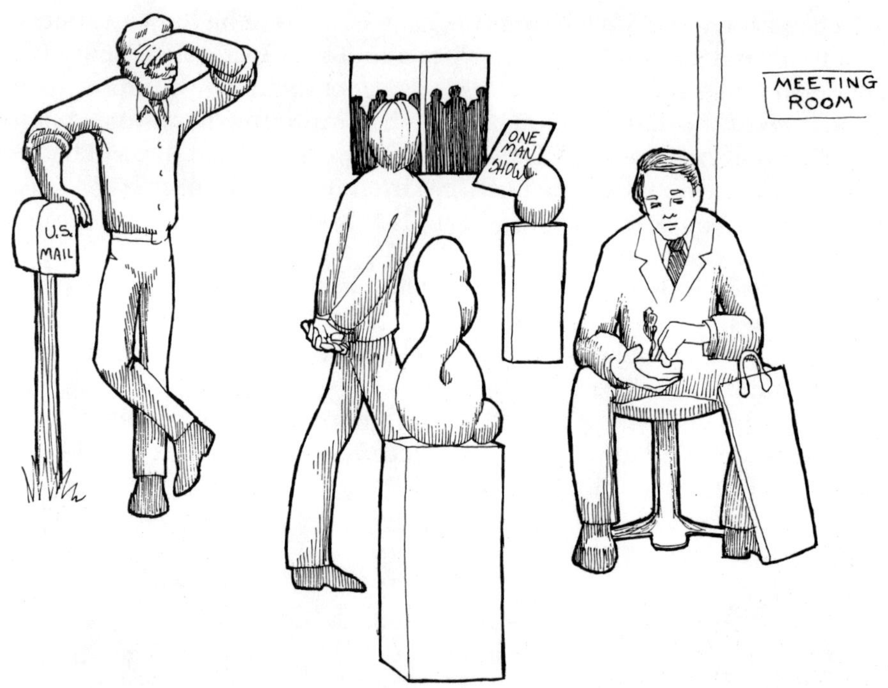

The novelist, age 58, with an exciting story outline, waiting for the mailman to bring him word from his publisher in New York ...

The sculptor, age 38, pacing back and forth within the San Francisco gallery, waiting for the public to be admitted to his first one-man show ...

The advertising account executive, age 38, with his theme for the new campaign for Tide detergent, dousing his cigarette as he is called into the marketing committee meeting at Proctor & Gamble in Cincinnati ...

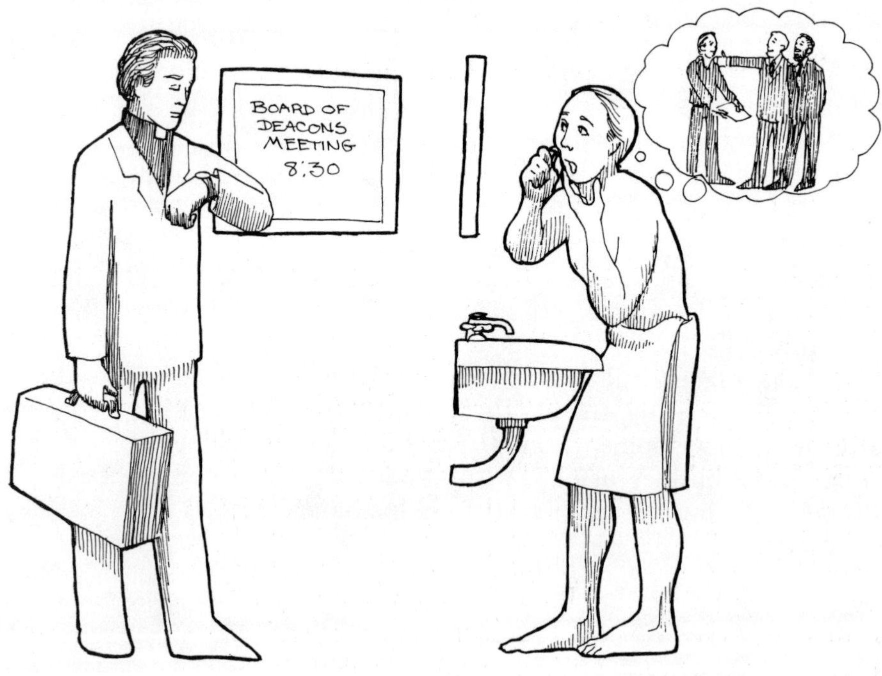

The minister, age 58, in Paducah, Kentucky, waiting for his board of deacons to convene so that he can present his thoughts on going ahead with the new Sunday school addition ...

The production-line machinist, age 38, nervous as he shaves at home in the morning, because this is the day he is to present his ideas on a better milling method to his foreman and to the production manager ...

Galileo, age 69, in June of 1633, ready to face the Roman church's Court of Inquisition, to defend his theory that it is the sun, not the earth, that is the center of the universe ...

Christopher Columbus, age 41, in April of 1492, with his idea about sailing west to India, waiting with hat in hand to be admitted to the courtroom of Isabella of Spain ...

Thomas Jefferson, age 33, having written the rough draft of the Declaration of Independence, waiting to see how it is received by the other members of the Committee of Five and the full body of founders ...

In all these situations the common element is an innovator with an idea fully formed in his mind, bursting with excitement. He wants others to know and wants his idea to be utilized. He wants to improve his situation.

ENTERPRISE'S OPPORTUNE MOMENT, PIECE ⑦ TO PIECE ⑧

[Darwin] *would not take on the establishment. He would complete the job even if it took a lifetime. He would arrange for its publication after death. Then let the hurricane roar.*

from *The Origin* by Irving Stone

Any worthwhile invention must be startling, unexpected and must come to a world that is not prepared for it.

Dr. Edwin Land, founder of Polaroid

In 1945, when Admiral William Leahy was first informed about the completion of the atom bomb, he stated: "That is the biggest fool thing we have ever done. The bomb will never go off, and I speak as an expert on explosives."

The *intuitive* discovery will now be subjected to the close scrutiny of the *reasoning* process. The Raging Inferno or the Gentle Flame is about to be judged by Pilot Lights. As a condominium developer described his appearance before the zoning board: "The cool bubbling mountain brook ran smack dab into the smelly green swamp."

One lone individual with his outrageous new idea is about to be outnumbered, outranked, and outgunned. He is on the defensive because he is out of his field. He will be expected to defend with logic that which came to him intuitively. *He* knows he's got something, but will *they?*

James Brian Quinn paints this picture:

"Most corporations fail to tolerate the creative fanatic who has been the driving force behind most major innovations. Innovations, being far removed from the mainstream of the business, show little promise in the early stages of development. Moreover, the champion is obnoxious, impatient, egotistic, and perhaps a bit irrational in organizational terms. As a consequence, he is not hired. If hired, he is not promoted or rewarded. He is regarded as 'not a serious person,' 'embarrassing,' or 'disruptive'."

Little wonder that for many scientists, artists, innovators, and inventors, enterprise's opportune moment is an invitation to ulcers, tachycardia, migraine, and incontinence! As David McCord Wright stated, they are psychologically incapable of putting the Big Idea across.

David Ogilvy minces no words:

"In the modern world of business, it is useless to be a creative original thinker unless you can also sell what you create. Management cannot be expected to recognize a good idea unless it is presented to them by a good salesman."

The more unique and unusual the creation the more resistance will the creator encounter and the greater will be the risk of rejection. When Charles Darwin presented his theory of evolution to the Royal Academy, his publications were "engulfed in silence." Darwin was shattered.

Aristotle put it this way: "To be sure, we are not hard on a man who goes off the straight path in the direction of too much or too little, if he goes off only a little way. We reserve our censure for the man who swerves widely from the course, because then we are bound to notice it."

Will enterprise recognize one of its finest moments and grasp the unusual? If it does, *the world in that instant will be a little changed.*

Wherein lies the key?

Perhaps the key is understanding the dual character of the entrepreneurial function. The originator and the implementers must at this moment be of one mind, not two. They must act like one entrepreneur would act. Their combined task is to bridge—to originate *and* implement, to form *and* transform. The originator's responsibility is to impart, it is the implementer's equal responsibility to recognize and to grasp. Otherwise, the creation or innovation will be left in limbo.

The quarterback and the down-field receiver cannot ignore each other. Without understanding each other's interdependency they cannot complete the pass. If management ignores the original person, he could become dissatisfied, frustrated, and unhappy. If he is a 38-year-old electronics engineer, he may even pick up his ball and start his own game in Silicon Valley.

The organization does not benefit. Enterprise—in that organization, anyway—aborts. No new wealth for society has been created. That particular problem of economic scarcity remains.

It has often been said that big companies did not get big by being stupid. But some are very slow. Many of today's well-known products took years between origination and realization. From David Wallechinsky's *Book of Lists*, here are twenty-five products and the interval between their conception and their realization:

	Conception	Realization	Interval (Years)
1. Antibiotics	1910	1940	30
2. Automatic transmission	1930	1946	16
3. Ballpoint pen	1936	1945	7
4. Filter cigarettes	1953	1955	2
5. Fluorescent lighting	1901	1934	33
6. Frozen foods	1908	1923	15
7. Heart pacemaker	1928	1960	32
8. Helicopter	1904	1941	37
9. Instant coffee	1934	1956	22
10. Long-playing records	1945	1948	3
11. Minute rice	1931	1949	18
12. Nuclear energy	1919	1965	46
13. Nylon	1927	1939	12
14. Photography	1782	1838	56
15. Radar	1904	1939	35
16. Radio	1890	1914	24
17. Roll-on deodorant	1948	1955	7
18. Silicone	1904	1942	38
19. Stainless steel	1904	1920	16
20. Telegraph	1820	1838	18
21. Television	1884	1947	63
22. Transistor	1940	1956	16
23. Videotape recorder	1950	1956	6
24. Xerox copying	1935	1950	15
25. Zipper	1883	1913	30

Source: Stephen Rosen, The New York Times, June 18, 1976

MANAGEMENT, PIECE ⑧

Whenever you look at a piece of work and you think the fellow was crazy, then you want to pay some attention to that. One of you is likely to be, and you had better find which one it is. It makes an awful lot of difference.

Charles F. Kettering

When the creative mind, Piece 7, passes the ball, the management mind, Piece 8, should be prepared to catch it. Whether the idea is good or not, management must take hold of the idea before it can examine and evaluate it. The ball must be solidly in the hands of the receiver if points are to be posted on the scoreboard.

In the beginning, when the entrepreneur/founder first forms his Freepod-based organization, its task is clear: to produce his Big Idea. Pieces 7 and 8 are in the same brain and body. Motivation need only prod neurons—just centimeters away— within the same brain. When Piece 7 talks, 8 listens.

Then time passes. The founder's little organization grows.

Those centimeters that separated Pieces 7 and 8 now stretch out to meters—even kilometers! Responsibilities have been divided and shared among the managers, Piece 8, and throughout the organization, Piece 9. Foulups are common. Solutions are sought. Ideas start circulating, pouring in from everyone and everywhere. Few are big ideas. Most will be supportive ideas that help carry the big ideas forward. Their quality will range from terrible to terrific. Management must grasp, sort, and select, weighing the risks against the rewards.

In the innovative organization Piece 8 is pelted with creative and innovative ideas. The players recognize that solutions come in twos or more (CC-2), and the best outcomes are achieved only when the best inputs are included (CC-3). If the game is to proceed smoothly to provide many good choices, Piece 8 must have the skill, experience, judgment, and guts to select and act upon the most promising ideas.

How Does Management Take to New Ideas?

Peter Drucker rates innovation so highly that the final chapter of his classic, *Management,* is devoted to the "innovative organization." He has also written that there are really only two functions in business: "Innovation and marketing. All others are costs."

What are the conditions that make an organization welcome creativity and innovation?

Peters and Waterman, in their book on well-run corporations, *In Search of Excellence,* say this: "Creativity is thinking up new things. Innovation is doing new things .... A powerful new idea can kick around unused in a company for years, not because its merits are not recognized, but because nobody has assumed the responsibility for converting it from words into action. Ideas are useless unless used. The proof of their value is only in their implementation. Until then, they are in limbo."

When I started out as a young pharmaceutical salesman, I often visited hospital obstetrics departments and newborn nurseries. What happy places they are! In the center of an organization that deals with sickness and death, here is this happy, upbeat island devoted to new little lives. The nurses take delight in each newborn arrival. They welcome, love, and cuddle each child.

Comparing management's attitude to new ideas with obstetric nurses' attitudes is exaggerated, of course. The point is the necessity for nurturing the new. Are newborn ideas welcomed throughout Pieces 8 and 9? Are there receptive attitudes toward change? The new ways always challenge the old established ways. The comfort of familiar policies and procedures may have to yield to the temporary discomforts and dislocations of new ways.

According to Drucker, an awareness of the importance of innovation should pervade the entire organization for it to succeed, or—in our structure—an innovative awareness must run throughout Pieces 8 and 9. Another way of viewing the same thing: Improving the situation (CC-1), the first charcteristic of choice, begins with *awareness* (CP-1), the first phase of the choosing process.

If management develops a hard defensive shell—understandable but inexcusable—part of the reason is that it understands the characteristics of choice. In new products and services the risk factor deserves respect.

Over half of the 600,000 new businesses that were founded last year will fail in the first three years. In ten years 90 percent of the new product introductions will have failed. So managements become careful. They prefer "to dig the same hole deeper," stick to familiar territory. Digging new holes is necessary but risky.

Yet choices—like the digging of new holes—have a common purpose (CC-1), to improve the situation, which means moving forward through the phases of the choosing process.

The objective, remember, is Piece 11, a successful, profitable product. This happy outcome is achieved through people: management people (Piece 8) interacting with and motivating the "people resources" of the organization (Piece 9); and utilizing a fine-tuned mix of "property resources" (Piece 10).

Peters and Waterman discovered in excellent corporations what they call the "championing system." Three different movers work to get new ideas into use: (1) the product champion, who is apt to be a loner, egotistical and cranky, but believes in a specific product; (2) the successful executive, who knows what it takes to protect a new idea from the organization's tendency toward negation; and (3) the godfather, who is typically an aging leader who provides the role model for championing.

THE COORDINATION OF "PEOPLE" PIECES, PIECES ⑦ ⑧ AND ⑨

> *Treat people as adults. Treat them as partners; treat them with dignity; treat them with respect. Treat* them—*not capital spending and automation—as the primary source of productivity gains.*
>
> Peters and Waterman

Let's take another look at our wooden model. Note that Pieces 7, 8, and 9 are touching.

Creativity, Piece 7, and Management, Piece 8, have one entire flat surface touching each other. Piece 8, Management is touching Piece 9, Human Resources, the organization's people. Is the director of marketing in touch with his salesmen? They are touching his market every day; he had better be. IBM and P&G became great by keeping in touch with their markets through their salespeople. The organization's people, Piece 9, touch Piece 7, Creativity. Neither management people nor R & D people have a monopoly on creativity and innovation. Management has the main responsibility, but creativity touches and flows from all personnel.

Among the other facets of Piece 2, you will remember, we listed examples of the properties people can own. One of these is ideas. People "own" the ideas that their intuitive processes create. People make subjective value judgments (CC-5). Their own ideas are valuable to them. The quality of their ideas may range from awful to excellent, but behind every idea there is a *proud creator*.

Management's Responsibility to Identify, Reward, and Protect

The good manager identifies the person who originated the good idea. The originator owns the idea. If it is valuable and usable, he wants it to be known that it was his baby. If someone else swipes it and gets credit for it, the originator will be disappointed, angry, and perhaps bitter.

As discussed, good managers try to reward innovation according to the innovator's value preferences. The good manager protects against idea theft. Big ideas are covered by patents and copyrights, which provide years of protection against theft. Smaller ideas *also* deserve rewards—congratulations, special recognitions, awards, bonuses.

In this chapter, we listed elements that inhibit creative thought while it is still *within* the mind. A companion list of inhibitors affects ideas once they are *outside* the mind. Anthony Downs's fine work, *Inside Bureaucracy*, describes these inhibitors:

- Research in an unlawful area (addictive chemicals; nuclear, genetic, laser technology)
- Envy or personal bias from less talented peers
- Intolerance (departing from the usual seen as immoral)
- Need for superiors' approval
- Time lag necessary to gain acceptance by a heirarchy
- Or, conversely, time pressures exerted by a heirarchy
- Fear of censure ("Don't rock the boat")
- Theft (originator not protected)
- Need for majority decisions in committee
- Lack of innovator persuasiveness (inability to "sell" the idea)
- Inability to find a backer (lack of a "champion" or capital)

Human resources are every organization's greatest asset. As Sibson has pointed out, human resources differ from property resources in another important way. Unlike property resources, Piece 10 (buildings, furniture, fixtures, and equipment) which wear out, as time passes human resources learn and become more valuable to the organization.

Hank Aaron was paid lots of bucks because he produced home runs. Julie Andrews gets paid lots of bucks because she performs her lines well in front of the camera and produces lines at the box office. We produce according to our abilities. We produce best when we use the best of our abilities. We are paid not according to how hard we work but according to how well we produce.

THE RESOURCES RING, PIECES ⑨ AND ⑩

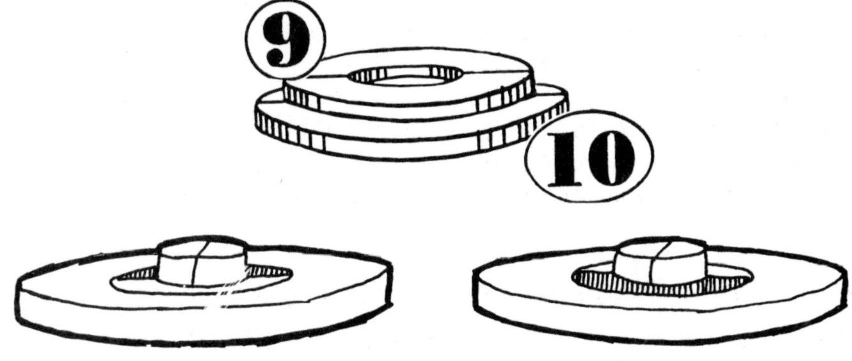

The Resources Ring represents what is called in Economics 101 the "four M's." Men, money, machinery, materials. We have discussed "men," Piece 9. Piece 10 covers the remainder.

Capital

Money, more commonly called "financial resources," "funding," or "capital," is limited in quantity like all other resources. The organization must have money to fund its operation. Where do entrepreneurs find money? What are venture capitalists looking for in the entrepreneur?

Venture Magazine is a gold mine of information about entrepreneurs. In a recent issue it reported the results of a survey of its readers. There were 399 responses on how entrepreneurs raised their money and the average amount raised.

WHERE ENTREPRENEURS FOUND MONEY

Method	Amount Raised, Millions
Public Offering	$7.2
Equipment Lease	7.0
Public or Private Sale of Debt	3.9
Family and Friends	3.7
Private Placement	3.6
Loan or Credit Line	1.4
Personal Savings	1.0

Arthur Lipper III provides some general observations on the character of the entrepreneurs in whom he invests. The entrepreneur

- Has been generally lucky in his childhood, where he lived, and in his associations with people
- Has good timing, meaning he is not too early or too late in entering the market
- Is an achiever
- Is frequently a first-born or an only child
- Is an early riser
- Has a high energy level
- Is usually married

After the enterprise is successfully underway, the financial burden can be shifted away from the shoulder of venture capital toward the other shoulder of funding called profits.

I have been close to venture capitalists and to venture capital associations. I have heard many emerging entrepreneurs bemoan the lack of venture capital. In my opinion there is an ocean of capital out there. It is looking for—sometimes desperate for—good new ideas and a reasonable return on the investment. Peter Drucker recently said, "Money is coming out of the woodwork. Anybody with a track record today of having started two successful new ventures can get all the money needed in maybe two telephone calls."

Let's say I have $100. With my freedom to fund, Piece 4, I can do what I want with my $100. It is property that I acquired rightfully.

I could destroy it. Let's say it is in the form of five $20 bills. I could light a match to each bill one by one. But there is a near 100 percent chance that I won't do that. It just doesn't provide much satisfaction. So I have a decision to make. I want to place my $100 where it will be most likely to improve my situation as I see it at this time (CC-1).

I have several choices (CC-2). I can spend my $100, buying something for myself or someone I love. Lots of choices there. I must think about this. In order to get the greatest satisfaction from my $100, I should review many possibilities. To get the best outcome, I must be sure that I have included the very best alternative in my list of selections (CC-3). My preference (CC-5) is to invest my $100 with a financial institution.

Now investments are filled with unknowns, uncertainties, and risks (CC-7). And my time is limited, because my $100 of capital is not earning any rent. In addition I don't have a lot of information about investing (CC-6).

I can choose 6 percent interest on my investment by putting my $100 in a federal savings & loan passbook account. It will be quite safe there, insured by the FSLIC. Very little risk, but not a great rent paid on my $100 either.

Until recently I could get a 10 percent return on my $100 invested in a money market fund. The fund I prefer invests exclusively in U.S. Treasury Bills. I don't think our federal government is going to go broke in the next few months, so the risk here could also be slight.

Now I have a benchmark. I can get a 10 percent return on my investment without doing anything and without any real worry. I will use that benchmark to evaluate any other investment. If I can get ten percent without effort and without worrying about the safety of my investment, I know that riskier investments must bring me substantially more than 10 percent.

I have a friend who is an entrepreneur. He is smart, honest, and works hard. I have great confidence in him. If my friend wants me to invest in his new business idea, he must start with a number quite a bit higher than a projected 10 percent return in order to get my attention. The reason is the risk.

I also have the opportunity to buy a piece of land. It is in the path of progress. The city is growing rapidly in that direction. In a few years, according to the real estate broker who wants to sell it to me, "it will be worth a lot of money." It had better be. My benchmark is 10 percent. Considering the risk, and considering the difficulty in selling land during bad times, I believe that the piece of land should appreciate at 20 percent a year, or I am not going to get too excited about it. Only two to four years out of every twenty does land increase in value at a rate above twenty percent. Many years it will not appreciate at all. No, I think I will not buy the land. My sense of timing tells me it is not the right time.

Capital must be free to flow. The minds that control capital want a rate of return on their investment that reflects the riskiness of the venture. "Without-risk" returns 10 percent. Risky business comes higher. How much higher? The professionals who invest with entrepreneurs know that nine out of ten companies formed in 1985 will not be in business in 1995. The bell of bankruptcy tolls for 90 percent of all start-ups.

Arthur Lipper, in his excellent guide, *Investing in Private Companies*, believes the compound annual rate of return should be between 25 percent and 115 percent. Here are acceptable ranges of profit targets for the venture capitalist:

PROFIT TARGETS	COMPOUNDED ANNUAL RATES OF RETURN
Triple their money in three years	44%
Triple their money in five years	25%
Four times their money in four years	41%
Five times their money in three years	71%
Five times their money in five years	38%
Seven times their money in three years	91%
Seven times their money in five years	48%
Ten times their money in three years	115%
Ten times their money in five years	58%

The economic problem is scarcity. The economic solution is productivity. Because capital is scarce, this process preserves a scarce resource. When we consumers, Piece 1, like a product and buy it repeatedly in the marketplace, Piece 3, the producer's rate of return increases. Conversely, if we consumers are less satisfied with the output of an enterprise, his rates of return will go down. Capital will be withdrawn from that company. The use of scarce resources for that purpose will decline and will thereby be preserved. The consumer's choice— your choice—Piece 1, determines which enterprises shall live, which shall die.

Other Resources

Besides capital, Piece 10 contains other properties, such as materials, machinery, and land. Recall that creativity, Piece 7, *forms*, and management, Piece 8 *transforms*. The organization's people, Piece 9, carry out the transformation using tools and machinery, also Piece 10.

Natural resources are the wealth supplied us by nature. Natural resources fall into two classifications: Those that are replenishable, such as timber, grains, cotton, cattle, and the fishes in the sea. And, those that are depletable, such as coal, oil, copper, chromite, and iron.

These then are physical resources that are used up. Machinery and buildings are worn out. We are learning that land, rivers, and lakes may also become "worn out."

Raw materials, Piece 10, are put into the productive process. What is produced is output, Piece 11 at the top of our structure.

The same material can be *input* to one productive organization and *output* to another. Phosphate is a natural resource put out by the phosphate miner. That phosphate plus seed, fertile soil, sun, and rain are inputs to the farmer. His output is wheat, corn, or soybeans. Wheat is input to the miller. His output is flour. Flour is input to the baker. His output is hamburger buns. The buns are input to your McDonald's down on the corner. The output is a Big Mac hot to go.

Raw materials, like other economic goods, are scarce. It is our position that they are best conserved by the free market. The anti-market invariably misallocates and frequently squanders them. We will discuss the reasons for this in Chapter 6.

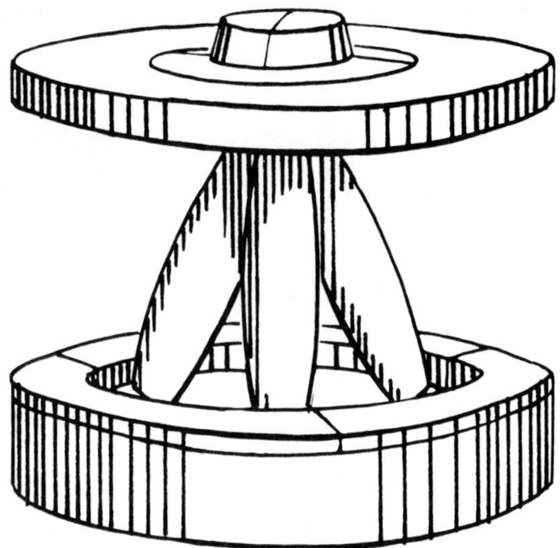

THE PROFITABLE PRODUCT OR SERVICE, THE LINCHPIN, PIECE ⑪

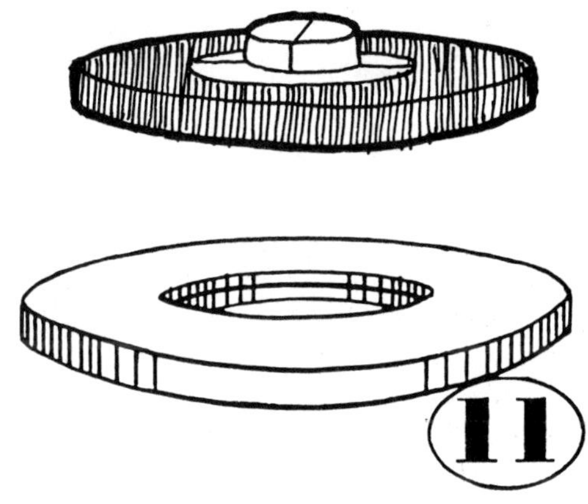

The finished, profitable good or service, Piece 11, is based upon an initial idea that was created to satisfy a consumer need, want, or preference. This disk represents a profitable product or service only because it has satisfied the preferences of its market.

Literally and figuratively, this piece holds our free-market organization together. *The principles of the free-market, the Freepod, are so structured that they bring to a rapid end those FM organizations that do not provide us consumers with the product we prefer.*

Without a profitable product or service the free-market (FM) organization *self-destructs*. Our wooden model clearly dramatizes this significant principle. When Piece 11 is not in place performing its linchpin function, this signifies that we the consumer, Piece 1, have chosen not to fund the organization through Piece 4.

Of equal significance is the fact that only this *one* organization is destroyed when it does not have a successful Piece 11. Only the resources of this *one* organization were wasted. The loss of scarce and precious resources was stemmed at that point and went no further.

Lose your linchpin, and your productive machine falls apart!

Such are the concepts of enterprise atop the free-market structure. Next we turn our attention to the structure of limited government, that type of government specifically designed to protect FM structures.

Chapter 5 — The Political Base of the Free Market

Pieces ⑤ **Centralized Governmental Power**
⑥ **Limitation and Dispersion of Governmental Power**
① **Freedom to Choose**

Government is instituted to protect property of every sort .... This being the end of government, that alone is a just government which impartially secures to every man, whatever is his own.

James Madison

Government is not reason, it is not eloquence— it is force! Like fire it is a dangerous servant and a fearful master; never for a moment should it be left to irresponsible action.

George Washington

The business of Chapter 4 was to describe in general terms the creation and administration of an enterprise. The subject of this chapter is the founding of another organization to protect enterprise and economic freedom through a policy of limited government. That organization is the United States of America.

When the 38-year-old corporate person breaks away from the parent company to found his own enterprise, he is concerned, of course, but he also has a sense of relief. There are many mixed feelings. Yet he is filled with hope.

When the thirteen colonies broke away from Great Britain in 1776, the founders felt relief, deep concern, and hope, and the well-founded fear that they might all be hanged. (As the American Revolution ground through eight years, the British captured five of the signers of the Declaration and tortured them. Nine of the signers died from wounds or the harsh exposure of the Revolution. The homes of twelve others were burned.)

In breaking away from the mother corporation, the aspiring entrepreneur goes through three phases:

1. He reaches a point of exasperation where he resolves, "Enough! I think they're running this organization improperly. I'm leaving!"
2. He faces the necessity of preparing his general business plan for his new endeavor.
3. He lists specifics. He says to himself, "These are the things I want to do. Those are things the corporation did that I don't want to do."

In breaking away from mother England the founders of the United States also went through three phases:

1. The Declaration of Independence was the point of exasperation. In effect it said, "Enough! They are running this organization improperly. We're breaking away!"
2. Eleven years later, the founders prepared the Constitution, which was an improved general plan they felt they needed in order to manage the new nation.
3. The founders wrote the Bill of Rights, which said, "These are the particulars that we want. And, these are the things 'they' did that we don't want."

Dozens of good men had a hand in the founding of this nation. John Adams, John Hancock, James Madison, Benjamin Franklin, John Jay, and Alexander Hamilton played key roles. Though each played an important role at one time or another, there were two whose lights shone brighter than all others. Two Virginians best represent the founder's hub.

One of the nation's finest creative minds (Piece 7) was Thomas Jefferson. At the time he wrote our Declaration of Independence in 1776, he was 33. Complementing Jefferson's scholarly personality was the organizational and administrative genius, George Washington. Age 43 in June of 1775, when he was unanimously appointed commander-in-chief of the Continental Army, Washington ideally represented the new nation's Piece 8.

The 6-foot-3, loose-jointed, sandy-haired Jefferson was a scholar of political history and philosophy. He was a gifted writer. As an idea guy, a creative inferno, he ranks right up there with Leonardo da Vinci, Thomas Edison, Einstein, and Beethoven. Not only did he author the Declaration, he had a hand in the development of Virginia's constitution— after which the federal constitution was partially patterned— and contributed to our Bill of Rights, which became law in 1791. He was particularly proud that the Virginia constitution contained his specifications for religious freedom. He took equal pride in the fact that he founded the University of Virginia. Jefferson was a lawyer, architect, inventor, plantation owner, and he would satisfy our definition of an entrepreneur.

Washington, a muscular 6-foot-2, dark hair and dark complexion, was a military wizard. With no formal military training, he learned everything he knew about military tactics in the field. Starting with a bunch of undisciplined shopkeepers, farmers, and woodsmen with little more than their squirrel rifles, Washington organized them and led them to victory at Yorktown. He chaired the Constitutional Convention of 1787. Beginning in 1789 he served for eight years as the first president of the United States. He was a born leader, an executive. The stamp of his natural administrative skills remains on the office of the president to this day. His Farewell Address of 1796 is still read in the Congress on his birthday each year. Washington was a surveyor, a plantation owner, and he believed in real estate as an investment. At the time of his death he owned tens of thousands of acres of land in Virginia and what is now West Virginia.

Jefferson and Washington fathered our nation's first two opposing political parties. Each also had a "lieutenant." Jefferson's lifelong lieutenant was James Madison, who was, as we know, president after Jefferson. George Washington had a philosophical lieutenant in his secretary of the Treasury, Alexander Hamilton.

Jefferson represented not only creative genius, Piece 7, complementing Washington's administrative genius, Piece 8, he symbolized decentralization of power to the people, whereas Hamilton—to a much greater degree than his chief, Washington—stood for a strong centralization of power within the new federal government.

Two historic comments in the words of Jefferson and Hamilton themselves will help differentiate these philosophies. Writing from Monticello on January 16, 1811, after his retirement from the presidency, Jefferson recalled: "Another incident took place on the same occasion which will further delineate Hamilton's political principles. The room being hung around with a collection of the portraits of remarkable men, among them were those of Bacon, Newton, and Locke. Hamilton asked me who they were. I told him they were my trinity of the three greatest men the world had ever produced, naming them. He paused for some time: 'The greatest man,' said he, 'that ever lived was Julius Caesar'."

Henry Adams, in his history of the Jefferson and Madison administrations, provides additional insight into the Hamiltonian viewpoint: "Hamilton, at a New York dinner, replied to some democratic sentiment by striking his hand sharply on the table and saying, 'Your people, sir—your people is a great beast!'"

Our point is this: At their hubs, all organizations must have both Pieces 7 and 8 to succeed. Rarely is that hub a place of peace and quiet. At the structural hub of the new United States of America, symbolic of these two complementing pieces, were Jefferson the philosopher/purist and Washington the administrator/pragmatist. They disagreed, bitterly at times: Jefferson with his belief that power should be controlled by the people, Washington with his belief that power should be retained by the central government. Yet the organization they founded grew and prospered.

Let's turn again to our Philomod, specifically to its base, where we find three vital pieces—1, 5, and 6. Piece 1 we discussed in detail in Chapter 1.

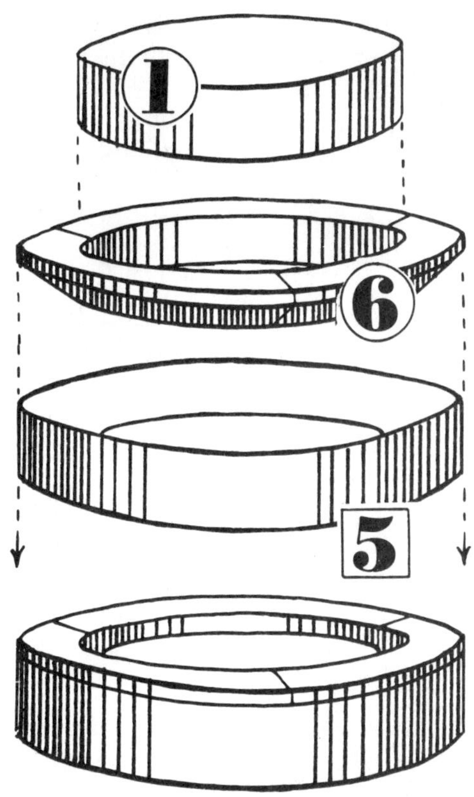

BALANCE OF POWER

To this point in our book all pieces in our substructures have been identified by numbers in circles. These pieces represent elements of the free market (FM). Now we will introduce four pieces identified by numbers in *squares*. The first of these is Piece 5. Pieces 12, 13, and 14 will be the subject of the next chapter. When combined, the four represent the basic components of the anti-market (AM).

Pieces 5 and 6 are rings that protect Piece 1. They represent government.

The Purpose of Government is to Protect...   Freedom of Choice

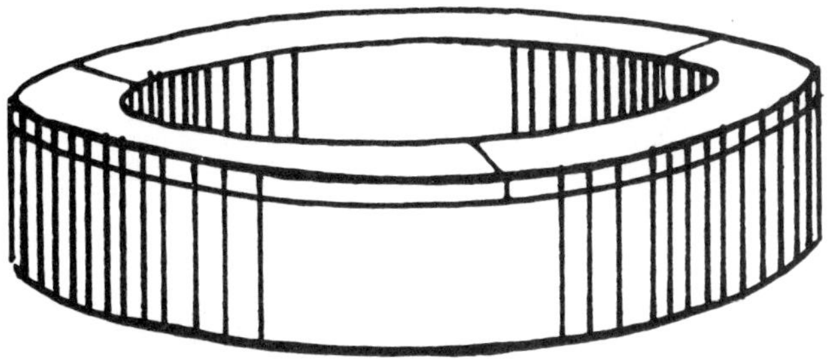

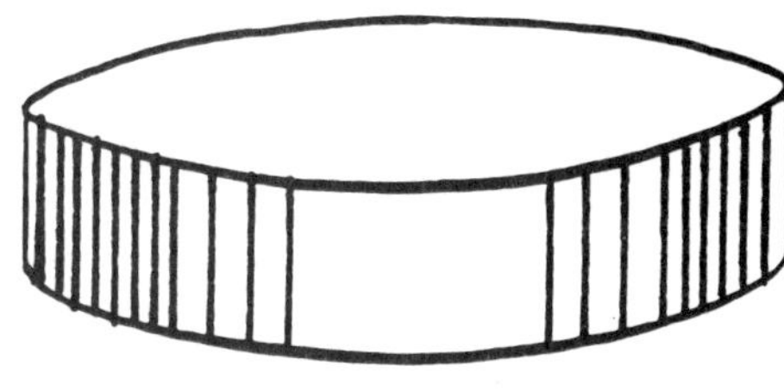

Piece 5 is centralized governmental power, such as the Marines, Air Force, Army and Navy, and the Department of State. Their purpose? To protect our freedoms from aggression.

"But hold on there," said the Founding Fathers, as they were writing the Constitution, "what will protect us from centralized power itself?" Thus they gave birth to those unique ideas which are the basis for Piece 6.

In several different ways, governmental power is decentralized and limited by the Constitution. Piece 6, for that reason, is actually composed of three different pieces representing dispersion of power into three functional branches: the executive, the legislative, and the judicial. Then there is decentralization by strata and geography—federal government, state government, and the people.

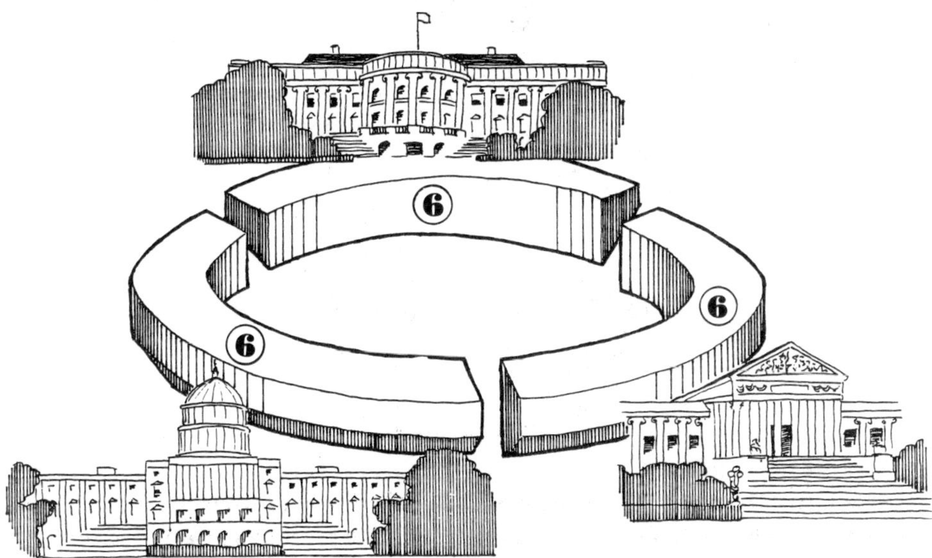

To limit governmental power, the Founding Fathers created a system of checks and balances: The House must originate all money bills, subject to the review of the Senate and the veto of the President. The Senate must approve the President's appointments to the Cabinet, and so on.

Limitation and Dispersion of Governmental Power (Piece 6)

The freedom to choose is best protected by *a delicate balance of force and dispersion of force.* Freedom of choice is best protected from external aggression by organizations such as the armed forces with the legal right to use force. These rely upon the centralization of governmental power (Piece 5).

The freedom to choose is best protected from internal aggression by articles in the Constitution and Bill of Rights whose purpose is to limit and disperse governmental power (Piece 6).

Simply stated in our Structures "shorthand," the purpose of Piece 5 is to protect Piece 1. But what is to protect 1 from 5? That is the role of Piece 6—to check and restrain Piece 5!

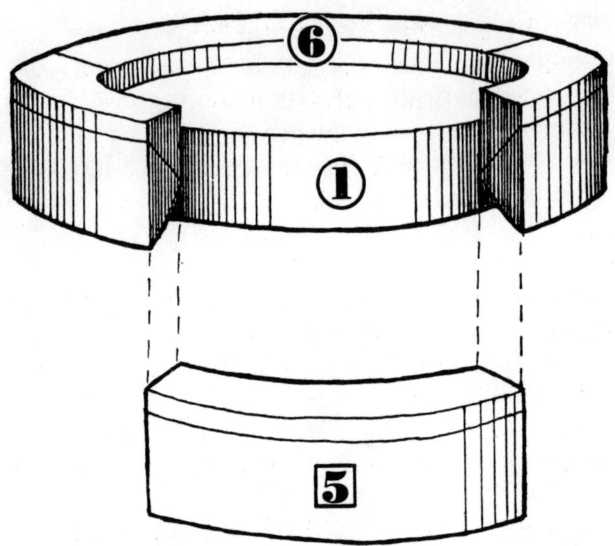

If we were to saw through Piece 5, the cross section would appear triangular. From the vertical outside wall, the surfaces of this piece are tapered inward. There is a reason for this design. Piece 5 must provide a footing for the three square legs in the Philomod. When Piece 6 is on top of Piece 5, the square legs (next chapter) cannot get a foothold. As we will see, Piece 6 *is not always on top*.

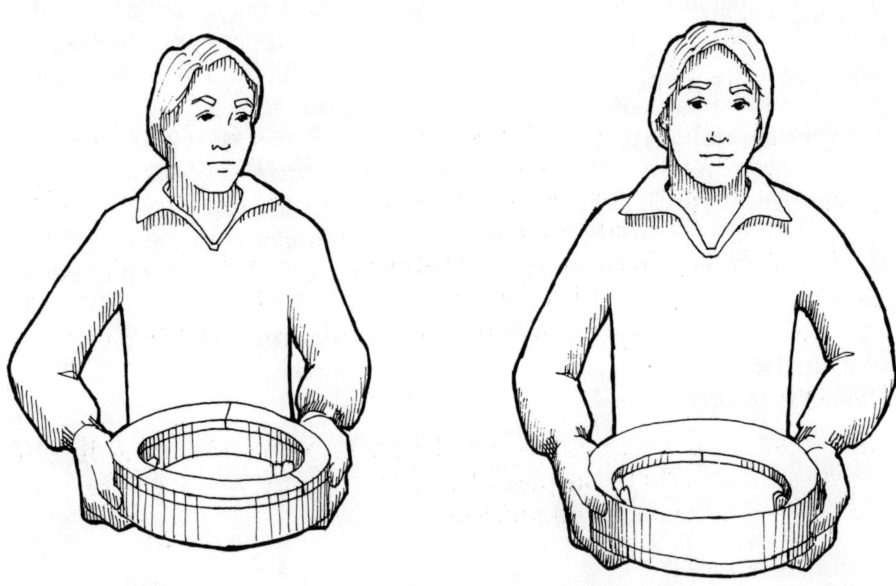

Centralization of Governmental Power (Piece 5)

In order to preserve law and order and to protect against external aggression, government must have the exclusive legal right to use force. Government must have a monopoly on the legal use of force. The explicit mark of the free society is that it is based—economically as well as politically—upon individual freedom of choice. Fundamental to the free society is that it use force only in a defensive manner, never in an aggressive, offensive manner.

Limitation and dispersion of political power was further ensured by the Tenth Amendment in the Bill of Rights and was a particular favorite of Jefferson's. He quoted it frequently, before, during, and after his term as president.

Writing from Philadelphia on January 26, 1799, just before his first term, Jefferson stated the philosophy of his party in a letter to Elbridge Gerry:

"I am for preserving to the states the powers not yielded by them to the Union, & to the legislature of the Union its constitutional share in the division of power; and I am not for transferring all the power of the states to the general government, & all those of that government to the Executive Branch. I am for a government rigorously frugal & simple, applying all the possible savings of the public revenue to the discharge of the national debt; and not for a multiplication of officers & salaries merely to make partisans, & for increasing, by every device, the public debt, on the principle of its being a public blessing."

We will return to Jefferson's feelings about the national debt later in this chapter.

The Original Cabinet

The Founding Fathers of the United States thought the scope of governmental power should be quite narrow. The best evidence we have of this is the original number of cabinet positions in George Washington's 1789 cabinet. There were five cabinet officers: the Secretaries of State, Treasury, and War, an Attorney General, and a Postmaster General. Their five functions were: to get along with other nations, to pay the government's expenses, to defend the shores, to settle citizen disputes, and to move the mail.

That was it.

Since 1789, nine more cabinet positions have been added. They have a common denominator. The purpose of each is to exert political control over an area of economic goods and services.

- 1849: Interior
- 1862: Agriculture
- 1903: Commerce and Labor, divided ten years later into:
- 1913: Commerce
- 1913: Labor
- 1953: Education and Health and Human Services, divided 26 years later into:
- 1979: Education

- 1979: Health and Human Services
- 1965: Housing and Urban Development
- 1966: Transportation
- 1977: Energy

Jefferson, even Washington, would have viewed these new bureaus as an improper role for government in a free society.

Historian Esmond Wright puts the size of the 1789 United States government in delightful perspective. Washington, as President, had fewer federal employees than he had on his staff at Mount Vernon!

In the last quarter of the twentieth century, the size of government is one of our greatest sources of uneasiness. The cabinet positions added since 1849 illustrate areas of governmental control over economic function. They are examples of a long-term shift in the balance of power from the economy to the government. Economists Friedman and Hayek tell us that economic power is best decentralized among the people and their enterprises, rather than reinforcing the power of the government.

We either have freedom *of* choice or freedom *from* choice. Either we are in control of our situation, or someone else is in control of our situation. Either we pursue happiness according to our own individual value preferences, or we are coerced to live according to someone else's value preferences. If we alone are to be responsible for our choices, then no one else should assume that he is responsible for our lives.

Thomas Jefferson understood the principle as well as any man. He phrased it this way when he wrote the Declaration of Independence: that we are "endowed by our Creator with certain unalienable Rights, that among these are Life, Liberty, and the Pursuit of Happiness."

Who judges as to which of two pursuits makes us happier? Only we ourselves. In this chapter one of the objectives is to try to see liberty and the pursuit of happiness in the same way the founding fathers did.

Pursuing happiness and being assured it are entirely different ideas. In pursuit we make choices. In pursuing what appears to us as the happier situation we cannot be certain that we will catch what we pursue or that—once caught—it will indeed be the happier one. The pursuit is overshadowed by unknowns, uncertainties, and risks (CC-7). Only after phase (CP-8), when we evaluate our new situation, can we judge whether we are happier. We may have made a mistake. We may find that we moved ourselves from a happier situation to one less so. But the important thing is that we did it our way. No one else's.

In his *Philosophy of the American Revolution*, Morton White writes: "If the essence of government was identified with the purpose proposed for it by God, then one philosopher who saw God's intention in one way might define government so that it was obliged to aid and abet man in the pursuit of happiness, whereas another might think it obliged only to protect man's right to pursue happiness—a critical difference in political philosophy."

It is significant that Jefferson used the word *pursuit*. He used it in his rough draft of the Declaration. Jefferson, the articulate man, was free to choose the words *assure* or *guarantee*, but he was wise enough to perceive that such an assurance would be impossible to fulfill. And while the Committee of Five— Jefferson, Benjamin Franklin, John Adams, Roger Sherman, and Robert Livingston—made other changes, they did not change that word, nor did the full body of the founding fathers when the fifty-eight members approved the final document.

Strains upon the commercial freedoms of the colonists led to the American Revolution. If the founding fathers did not have a similar mind-set when they arrived in Philadelphia in the summer of 1776, they were more of one mind when they departed there.

THREE PHASES OF ESCAPING FROM TYRANNY

Escaping from tyranny, they believed, would involve three phases: (1) The break—the Declaration; (2) the general plan—the Constitution; and (3) the specifics desired—the Bill of Rights.

Phase 1: The Break

At the time of the Declaration the founding fathers had a general perception of what they were against (tyranny) and also a good idea of what they were for (liberty). Several radicals, such as John Adams of Massachussetts and Richard Henry Lee of Virginia, pushed for independence. The conservatives from New York and Pennsylvania wished to proceed more deliberately. There were steady hands, such as Franklin's, in the middle. They did not think in terms that divided political policy from economic practice. While their grievances with Great Britain covered both, their enumerations of grievances were politico-economic mixtures.

Their feeling of uneasiness was strong. The situation had become one of tyranny. They knew they wanted an improved situation. Most had come to realize that they first had to fight a war—which had already started at Lexington and Concord—and win it, to gain their liberty. They knew they faced unknowns, uncertainties, and grave personal risks.

They agreed to break from Britain. They acknowledged and fought their war. And under General Washington they won it.

The Articles of Confederation were still the central law of the land. Approved in November, 1777, the Articles endorsed a central government that was relatively weak in relation to the governments of the individual states.

Phase 2: The New Plan

The Constitution was written ten years after the Articles and eleven years after the Declaration, in Philadelphia, during the summer of 1787. James Madison, Jefferson's "lieutenant," is called the "father of the Constitution," although its parts were hammered out by several committees. (Jefferson, our minister to France at the time, was in Paris.) George Washington, by then the hero-general, was chairman of the convention. The meetings were closed to the public. Complete secrecy was agreed upon. No reporters were allowed. There were no leaks. No press releases until the job was done.

The fifty-five men who framed our Constitution were well-rounded men. They shared a sense of identification with the sages of classic Athens and Rome. And when they spoke of "liberty" and "tyranny," each had an image in mind that the others fully understood. Their individual value preferences (CC-5) had grown toward a unanimity, a consensus.

John Locke, one of Jefferson's trinity of heroes, was an English philosopher. Locke's writings of a hundred years before, in 1690, had a profound effect upon these framers: "Freedom of men under government is to have a standing rule to live by, common to every one of that society, and made by the legislative power erected in it; a liberty to follow my own will in all things where that rule prescribes not, and not to be subject to the inconstant, uncertain, arbitrary will of another man."

Clinton Rossiter has condensed the key ideas of the colonial era. Our forefathers believed strongly in "natural rights." They believed, he writes: "The greatest of these rights are: the right to life, which carries with it the power of self-preservation; the right to liberty, to act as one pleases without external restraint; the right to property, to use and dispose of the fruits of honest industry; the right to happiness, or at least to pursue it on equal terms with other men; and the right to free conscience, to reach out for God without the permission or even help of other men."

According to Rossiter, there was a "consensus of constitutional thought." The key ideas were that government should be:

- plain, simple and intelligible; reasonably educated men should be able to comprehend its structure and functioning
- limited in purpose, reach, methods, and duration
- kept as near to the people as possible through frequent elections and provisions for rotation-in-office
- constitutional, that is, composed of laws rather than men, in which "power is reduced to the lowest level consistent with effective operation of the political machinery."

Phase 3: The Specifics Desired

The original ten amendments of the Bill of Rights were ratified in December, 1791. These are some of the political rights of the individual. These are the major facets of Piece 6 of our Philomod, which forms a protective ring around the individual's freedom to choose. The numeral "6" in our structure is therefore illustrated within a circle, allying it with the free market (FM).

Combining the Bill of Rights and checks and balances, the founding fathers wrote about twenty restrictions into the federal law to strengthen individual choice, Piece 1, and to defang and declaw centralized power by specifying certain limitations and dispersions of power, Piece 6. The Bill of Rights assured these protections:

- Prohibition of a state religious establishment; freedom of speech, press, and right to petition
- Right to keep and bear arms
- Conditions for quartering soldiers in homes
- Right of search and seizure regulated
- Provisions concerning prosecution, trial and punishment; private property shall not be taken for public use without just compensation

- Right to a speedy trial
- Right of trial by jury
- Excessive bail or cruel punishment prohibited
- Enumeration of certain rights in the Constitution not to be construed to deny or disparage others retained by the people
- Powers not delegated to the United States, or prohibited to the states, are reserved to the states or to the people.

The three basic documents were now the law of the land. They were political documents, but their purpose was the protection of both our political and our economic freedoms.

Had our new nation escaped those things it found onerous in the mother nation? Only partially. When we explore the reasons, we will better understand the uneasiness of modern-day America.

HOW GREAT BRITAIN CENTRALIZED POLITICAL POWER AND CONTROLLED THE AMERICAN ECONOMY

The problem lay in London, headquarters of the mother organization. In the 1760s the American colonies had become too vast, too diverse, too distant, and too dynamic to be well managed from London, 3,000 miles away. The very fastest communication time between London and New York was almost a month by sea.

London in the 1760s didn't see the writing on the wall. The colonies were ready to do business on their own.

The Treaty of Paris in 1763 ended the Seven Years' War between England and France. France ceded to England all of her territories east of the Mississippi River, except New Orleans. As a result of the long war, England was heavily in debt. As a result of London's attention being occupied by the war, the American colonies had been generally free to grow and prosper. With the objective of increasing tax revenues from the colonies, the British now began reasserting their control.

The colonial economy had for years been under London's thumb. Parliament and the king eventually controlled American commerce in four ways:

1. For 100 years, the colonies could ship sugar, cotton, tobacco, wool, rice, furs, and other commodities *only directly to England.*
2. They were permitted to trade with other nations, but *only through British agents.*
3. Later all imports into the colonies—from all other nations—had to be shipped *by way of England.*
4. Still later, most colonial manufactured items were *restricted to distribution within the colonies,* so that the colonies would not compete with British manufacturers in all other parts of the world.

Following 1763 came several onerous acts, all meant to centralize power in Parliament and the Crown and to pull revenue out of the colonies by way of taxes, importation stamps, and the like. Each action on London's part led to rioting and reaction in the colonies. Each new colonial action brought new restrictive reactions from London:

- 1763: customs officers were relocated from London to America; naval officers became deputy customs agents
- 1764: the Sugar Act disrupted trade in molasses and rum between the colonies and the French islands; the Currency Act made paper money illegal
- 1765: the Stamp Act imposed heavy duties on pamphlets, newspapers, legal documents, cards, and dice; reaction: non-importation associations in the colonies to boycott British goods
- 1765, 1766: the Quartering Acts provided housing for British troops in the taverns and warehouses in the Colonies (later quartering in homes was crammed down the throat of the colonists)
- 1767: the Townsend duties on imported products
- 1768: customs officers tried to seize John Hancock's ship with a load of wine; reaction: a Boston mob drove the customs officers to take refuge in Castle William in Boston Harbor
- 1770 reaction: Bostonians snowballed British troops; five colonists were killed in what became known as the Boston Massacre
- 1773 reaction: the Boston Tea Party was staged
- 1774 British reaction: the Coercive Acts, the British closed the port of Boston until the dumped tea was paid for

The escalating economic controls all discouraged or prohibited free American commerce. Try as it might, centralized political power in Parliament and the King could no longer hold back the economy of a young country now ready to break loose.

New England was bursting with granite, timber, fishing and ship building. By 1800 there would be 7,000 British and American ships on the high seas, half of which were built in New England shipyards. New York and Pennsylvania had manufacturing and banking industries. The mid-Atlantic colonies supplied the wheat and corn. The South was bursting with cotton, indigo, and tobacco.

Our brief summary cannot do justice to the color and texture of the times. Suffice to say, America was ready to do business with the world, and to kiss the mother organization goodbye.

JEFFERSON AND THE NATIONAL DEBT

Before we return from Colonial America, we should gain one more pertinent insight into the attitudes of the founding fathers by examining Jefferson's ideas on debt. We find them in a letter from Jefferson in Paris, to Madison in America.

Thirteen years had passed since Jefferson had written the Declaration. He was stationed in Paris as our ambassador to France. It was September 6, 1789. Jefferson himself would not be President Jefferson for another ten years. His good friend Madison would not be president for another eighteen years. Madison, on this fall day in 1789, was probably riding north to New York, as a Representative from Virginia, bound for the opening of the first session of Congress (under the new Constitution).

Debt was foremost on Jefferson's mind. His letter to his friend developed his beliefs on that subject. He addressed "the question whether one generation of men has a right to bind another."

"I set out this ground which I suppose to be self evident, that the earth belongs ... to the living; that the dead have neither powers nor rights over it ...."

Jefferson believed that no man should be permitted to "bind" the next or succeeding generations. No one should obligate his property beyond his lifetime, for debts contracted during his lifetime. Were he able to do this during his life, he could obligate his children for several generations. The result would be that the property would then "belong to the dead, and not the living"—the reverse of his principle.

"I say the earth belongs to each of these generations during its course, fully, and in their own right. The second generation receives it clear of the debts and incumbrances of the first, the third of the second, and so on."

Jefferson believed that a person should be permitted to "bind" his property only for the remaining years of his own life—one generation only. Men lived in Jefferson's time to about 55 years of age. A man of 21 would be allowed therefore to encumber his property for only 34 years, a man of 45 for only 10 years, and so on. One generation, in colonial America, was considered to be nineteen years.

On September 25—not enough time for Jefferson's letter to cross the ocean—Congress submitted for the approval of the states the first amendments to the Constitution, usually called the Bill of Rights. Let's continue Jefferson's letter from Paris:

"But with respect to future debts, would it not be wise and just for that nation to declare in the constitution they are forming that neither the legislature, nor the the nation itself can validly contract more debt, than they may pay within their own age, or within the term of nineteen years?"

Jefferson, stuck at his post three thousand miles away in Paris, knew his friend Madison possessed one of the sharpest legal minds of the day. He had virtually authored the Constitution. Jefferson had one more amendment in mind, and he wanted his friend to go to bat.

"This principle that the earth belongs to the living not to the dead is of very extensive application and consequence in every country... Your station in the councils of our country gives you an opportunity of producing it to public consideration, of forcing it into discussion ... It would furnish matter for a fine preamble to our first law for appropriating the public revenue ..."

On September 29, 1789, the first Congress adjourned. The "opportune moment" arrived and passed.

Jefferson's historic letter was still in the diplomatic mail pouch aboard a ship sailing for New York.

There is little doubt that these two men at that particular time could have had the moon, had they wanted it. What a pity they were not together in New York. Their talents, focused on an amendment to curb the national debt and backed up by their excellent public images, would have assured passage. Jefferson, as Piece 7 in the new organization, felt that tug of uneasiness: Congress was overlooking a debt ceiling limited to our ability to pay "within the time of our own lives."

PART III ANTI-MARKET (AM) STRUCTURE

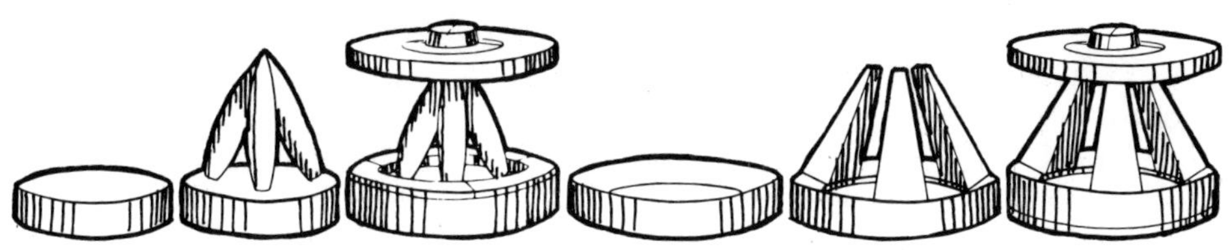

The preservation and expansion of freedom are today threatened from two directions. The one threat is obvious and clear. It is the external threat coming from the evil men in the Kremlin who promise to bury us. The other threat is far more subtle. It is the internal threat coming from men of good intentions and good will who wish to reform us ... The two threats unfortunately reinforce one another.

Milton Friedman

The next two chapters explore the antithesis of the free market—the antipode or anti-market. By looking at related-but-opposite concepts we can improve our understanding of our own.

If Jefferson were alive today, he would be bitterly disappointed that we Americans are so frightfully uninformed of the concepts of the free market. I say "frightfully" with reason. In a republic, as he preached, widespread misinformation among the majority represents a danger to the whole. It *is* frightening. The anti-market mentality is excitable and unpredictable. It can range from benign to belligerent, from passive to activist, from the bullheadedness of the blue-collar to the sophisticated, ivory-tower intellectual.

AM/FM STRUCTURES

In Parts One and Two of *Structures* I have relied heavily upon my political-economic mentors. I have advocated the virtues of the free market and its hero, the entrepreneur. In Part Three we will explore how those same mentors perceive the vices of the international anti-market community.

Hayek's view, for example, is that the anti-market is not "over there" on some foreign continent but right here in American organizations and people.

Every nation is an AM/FM mixture. Each holds within its borders a community of free-market organizations (Freemodes) and a community of anti-market organizations (Forcemodes). This is quite normal both for the past and the future. Both the anti-market and the free market—like them or loathe them—have their durable qualities.

In military matters, anti-market organizations excel. In producing goods and services, the free-market organizations excel. As with Piece 7, creativity, and Piece 8, management, the two may not be particularly enamored of each other, but they still must rely on each other. Each is incomplete without the complementary facilities, services, and protections offered by the other.

In addition, it is neither accurate nor enlightening to label nations as "free" or "totalitarian." The matter is akin to quantifying "happiness," with which we dealt in Chapter 1. We make choices that result in our being happier or less happy; it is the *direction* that is more meaningful. We try to improve our situation from one with which we are only 20 percent satisfied to one with which we are, let's say, 70 percent satisfied.

Within any nation it is, first, the *current ratio* of Freemodes to Forcemodes that tells the tale of the status quo. At this moment in time, how strong is the community of free-market organizations in comparison with the community of anti-market organizations?

Of interest next is the historical *trend*. Is the nation's community of free-market organizations growing or shrinking?

And third, what is the *rate* of change? Is the rate of growth of one of the two communities accelerating or slowing?

By measuring the current ratio, the trend, and the rate, we obtain a nation's moving AM/FM profile. A society or nation moves toward liberty or toward tyranny. "Liberty" and "tyranny"—Jefferson, Washington, Franklin, and John Adams liked those two words. In their eighteenth-century conversations they used those two words every day. They wrote those two words into our revered national documents. (I have observed that twentieth-century Americans rarely use these two words in conversation. Be aware of this.)

As the AM/FM conflict unfolds, we shall see scores of differences and misunderstandings. These become antagonisms and hostilities that can cause deep splits in the psyche of society. We are going to put the finger on these schizophrenias.

We shall see that the AM/FM profile of the United States—one of the bastions of the entrepreneur—has moved in the direction of the anti-market for three generations. That puts the free market as our grandparents knew it beyond the scope of our memory. The free market was like hundreds of full bolts of natural bright woolens, cottons, and linens. Now we have only the remnants of those natural-grown FM fabrics and the synthetics and polyesters of the AM generation.

Our free-market organizations have been thoroughly and constantly constrained and vilified. And yet our entrepreneurial organizations still vibrate with vitality. Those of Japan, Switzerland, Singapore, and Hong Kong are even more vibrant.

It is the strength, direction, and momentum of the anti-market movement—a pronounced shift in our current AM/FM ratio that is the cause for this late-twentieth-century "felt uneasiness."

What follows is an exposition of three related concepts (the trinity of tyranny, if you will) that are universal. Not only have they existed in every epoch, they grow naturally within every society and, as we shall see, from very natural human feelings. The three work synergistically, that is, in combination they achieve effects that each alone could not. Like a mixture of alcohol, tranquilizers, and antihistimines, they are a deadly dose. They can be the death of liberty. They have been precisely that for several nations.

Before we examine the structure of the anti-market, let's summarize with a glossary of our Philomod substructures. Following are all the related concepts divided into groups.

PHILOMOD SUBSTRUCTURES:
Related Mutually-Dependent Concepts

The Free-Market (FM) Principles Group

① Freedom to Choose

② Freedom to Own (Private Ownership of Property)

③ Freedom to Exchange (Competitive Markets)

④ Freedom to Fund (Voluntary Funding)

The Anti-Market (AM) Ideologies Group

⑤ Centralized Governmental Power

⑫ Public Ownership of Productive Property

⑬ Controlled Markets (Restricted Exchange)

⑭ Mandatory Funding (Taxation and Inflation)

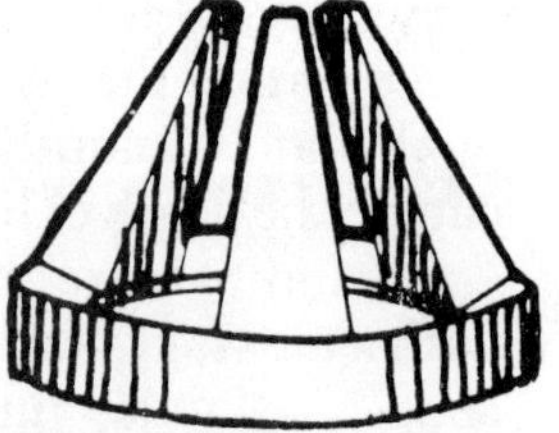

The Operating Organization Group

⑦ Creativity and Innovation

⑧ Management

⑨ People Resources

⑩ Property Resources

⑪ The Product or Service

The Entrepreneurial Function Sub-Group

⑦ Creativity and Innovation

⑧ Management

The Productive Resources Sub-Group

⑨ People Resources

⑩ Property Resources

The Constitutional Balance of Governmental Power

⑤ Centralized Governmental Power

⑥ Limitation & Dispersion of Government Power

① Powers Reserved to the Individual

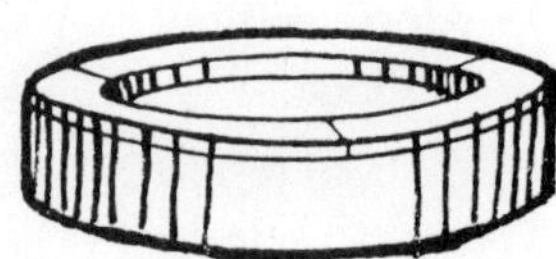

Chapter 6 — The Structure of Coercion

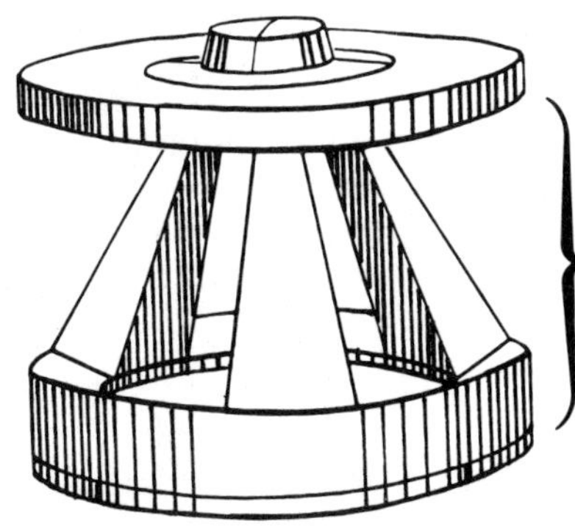 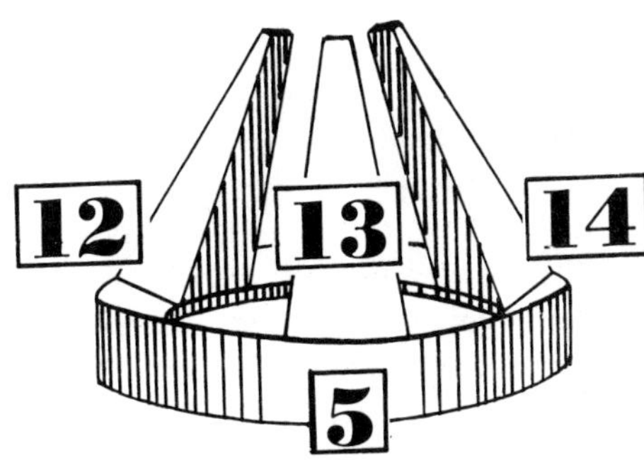

Coerce: To restrain or dominate by nullifying individual will.
Webster's Dictionary

Coercion is King; coercion, the ultimately destructive force, is rampant throughout the world today. It is not merely that coercion has become commonplace. Worse yet, it has become acceptable.
George C. Roche

The business of this chapter is to introduce the antagonist, the anti-market organization, or "Forcemode," based upon the AM *economic* ideology of *controlled markets* and protected by a *political* policy of *centralized governmental power*. These are the uses of power that limit your freedom to choose as well as your economic individualism.

Pieces 12, 13, and 14 are the last three pieces to be introduced into our study of structures. Here is a Philomod of a different philosophic persuasion.

If you have our wooden model, please construct a revised model that looks like this. Assemble the saucer-shaped organization. Hold it in one hand by its top, the entrepreneurial hub. With your other hand place the three square legs upright on Piece 5. Support them as you guide their top ends into the channel on the underside of the organization. You should include Pieces 6 beneath Piece 5 and also Piece 1, but note that neither Piece 1 nor 6 is necessary to the stability of this structure!

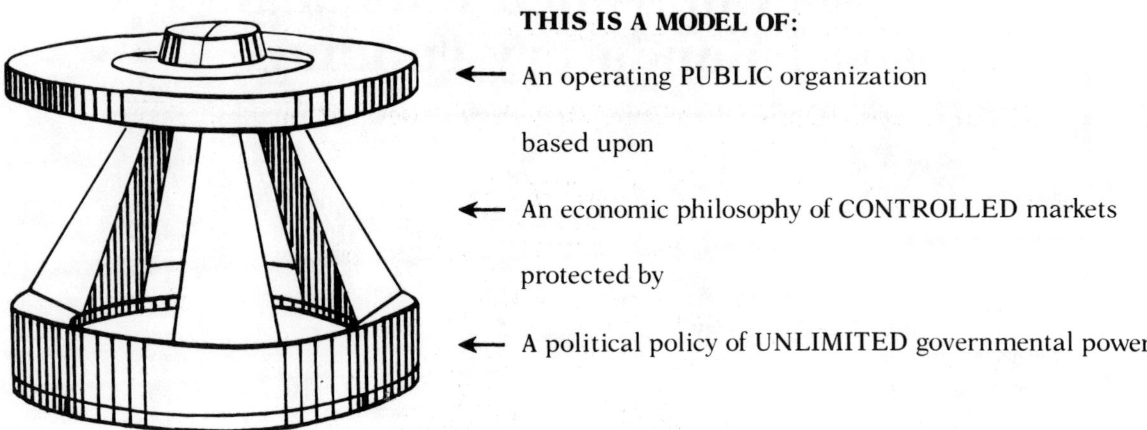

THIS IS A MODEL OF:

← An operating PUBLIC organization

based upon

← An economic philosophy of CONTROLLED markets

protected by

← A political policy of UNLIMITED governmental power

As with our model of the free-market organization, we have the operating organization at the top. There is the hub at the center, the same two pieces. Around it is the resources ring. And then, of course, the reason why any organization exists, the outer rim, the products and/or services that an organization provides.

At the bottom of this Philomod, we have the same two rings, unbroken Piece 5 and Piece 6 in its three parts, representing the limitation upon and dispersion of that power. Yet in the anti-market Forcemode, centralized governmental power now rests atop limitation and dispersion! Centralization has gained an advantage! Limitation/dispersion appears to have its shoulders pinned to the mat!

Utilizing centralized power as its base, the three square legs represent:

- Public Ownership of Productive Property (Piece 12)
- Controlled Exchange (Piece 13)
- Mandatory Funding (Piece 14)

There were *eleven* pieces in the Philomod of the free-market organization, but only *ten* pieces in this Philomod. Which piece is missing? Perhaps none; it's very difficult to tell from the illustration. We cannot see whether Piece 1, freedom of choice, is present or not.

Two conclusions appear obvious.

As long as Limitation and Dispersion of Governmental Power, Piece 6, had the upper hand, it would have been impossible for these three strange new legs to secure a foothold here. As the wooden model demonstrates, the new legs would have slipped off the horizontal upper surface of Piece 6. But Centralized Government Power, Piece 5, is beveled to provide a footing for the square legs.

The other conclusion is that Freedom of Choice, Piece 1, is not a necessary part of this structure. The structure is not dependent upon it. The structure is perfectly stable without it! The three square legs rest securely on Piece 5.

The structure of an anti-market organization can take freedom of choice or leave it. Whether choice is present or absent makes no difference in the stability and continuation of any organization atop this structure.

PUBLIC OWNERSHIP OF PRODUCTIVE PROPERTY, PIECE 12

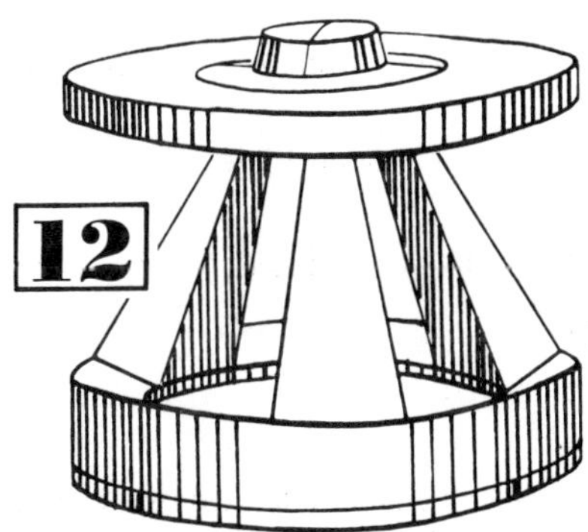

It is because we have departed from the ideal so much further than most people realize, and because, unless this development is soon checked, it will by its own momentum transform society from a free into a totalitarian one, that we must reconsider the general principles guiding our political actions.

Friedrich Hayek

The Soviet Union is wall-to-wall anti-market. The government owns all power-generating facilites, all the steel and aluminum companies, all the automobile manufacturing facilities, all the recreational facilities, all the banks, all the transportation systems, and all the educational facilities.

The Soviet government also owns all the printing presses, all the paper mills, all the printing ink manufactures, and even all duplicating equipment. "Subversive" authors can never expect their manuscripts to be published as books. Their manuscripts remain forever manuscripts, retyped laboriously by loving hands, over and over again, and then passed quietly from one trusted person to another.

The Soviet Union finds many advantages in owning all the printing presses. Want to conceal a city of 50,000, because it is manufacturing something secret for space? Hide a gulag? That's easy—don't print the name or location on any maps! American intelligence has uncovered several unidentified Soviet cities of 30,000 to 50,000 people. How do the Soviets identify such cities for internal communications purposes? A post office box number!

Soviet radio and TV airways are owned by the government. Circuses, ballets, symphony orchestras, hotels, and department stores are government owned properties. The anti-market extends into the farthest territories of the Soviet Union as well as to its satellites, Poland, East Germany, Cuba, and others.

The same may be said about almost all similar properties of production in Red China. These are totalitarian anti-markets because the production of most goods and services is not allowed in private hands.

What is the current ratio of anti-market organizations to free-market organizations in the Soviet Union and in Red China? We have no way to know. A large portion of all production in the Soviet Union is wasted, left rotting in the fields or too poor in quality to be allowed to leave the factory. The amount of waste is perhaps a little less in Red China. The CIA has estimates but will not reveal them. I have been unable to find trustworthy statistics on the Communist nations or their satellites.

Let us assume an eight-to-two ratio of expenditures controlled by the state to expenditures by the private sector— anti-market 80 percent; free market 20 percent.

How the AM/FM Ratio Is Determined

From those nations, let's turn to the AM/FM ratio in the West. A nation's AM percentage is found by dividing its central government expenditure (CGE) by it gross national product (GNP). To arrive at the FM percentage, the AM percent is merely subtracted from 100. In other words,

$$AM\% = \frac{CGE}{GNP}$$

$$FM\% = 100\% - AM\%$$

Central government expenditure is used as the primary measure of anti-market. State and local governmental expenditures make up the remainder of the anti-market. These additional numbers are readily available for the United States, but reliable numbers are not easily obtained for the other nine nations on our chart.

TEN NATIONS
AM/FM RATIO
1972

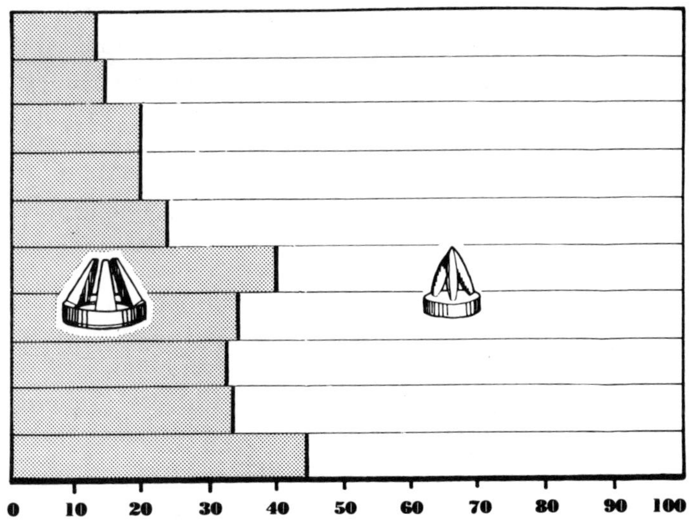

Source: World Military Expenditures and Arms Transfers 1972-1982, U.S. Arms Control & Disarmament Agency, Department of State, April, 1984

To illustrate the wide variation, we have chosen ten western industrialized nations and, of course, Japan. Japan had the smallest anti-market in 1972, only 13 percent. Thus the ratio in 1972 for Japan was AM 13/FM 87. Switzerland was a close second at that time at AM 14/FM 86. The United States and Canada tied for third position in 1972 at AM 20/FM 80. The Netherlands was at the other end of the spectrum in our sample of ten. In 1972 the anti-market stood at a 44 percent share: AM 44/FM 56.

In 1972, then, the scope of the anti-market ranged from about 13% to about 44%, which would give us an average of roughly AM 28/ FM 72. Japan, Switzerland, the United States, and Canada appear to have been the four most dedicated free-market nations.

Basic to the concept of the anti-market, then, is the public ownership or control over organizations producing economic goods and services. Examples are a federal power utility (Tennesee Valley Authority), municipally-owned power utility (Jacksonville Electric Authority), a steel company (British Steel), an automobile manufacturer (Renault), government-owned transportation (British Railways, Air Canada), or the New York subway system. Others include government-owned schools and state universities, government-owned recreational facilities (state and national parks and campgrounds), and health care (federal and state hospitals). Who is the largest producer of movies in the United States? The federal government. Who is the largest printer in the United States? The federal government.

How do governments come to own productive properties?

1. They acquire them as the original claimant.
2. They purchase them as the secondary claimant with funds obtained through (a) borrowing (the sale of bonds), (b) taxation, or (c) inflation of the currency.
3. They take title through legislation.
4. They take them through military action.

Entrepreneurs learn to finance their productive organizations through several methods, including the sale of stock (selling part ownership) and—less frequently—through issuing bonds (borrowing). To understand state ownership, we need to know the difference between stocks and bonds.

Acquisition of publicly-owned property is frequently financed through the sale of public bonds. Bonds may be sold, for example, to build a school, a civic auditorium, an expressway system, or a bridge. The individual or organization who buys such bonds is making a voluntary investment choice. The purchaser is free to invest, knowing that there is a fixed percentage rate of return. He may be further interested if the bonds are backed up by the governmental body's power to tax. The point is that there is no force or coercion. It is a free choice. The bonds are the subjective value preference (CC-5) of the investor.

Other organizations are competing (Piece 3) in the bond market for the buyer's attention and his capital. The bond market is immense, many times larger that the market for corporate stocks, which receives much more media attention. Not only are there hundreds of other "public" bonds available, there are transportation bonds, utility bonds, and corporate bonds, all of which are sold to help fund (Piece 4) private corporations.

With none of these bond purchases does the buyer acquire ownership in the organization. If he wished to own a piece of the railroad, the corporation, or electric utility, he would buy stock in it (Piece 2). To own or not to own, his free choice— whatever he feels will most likely improve his situation (CC-1).

Therefore, when he buys public bonds, he does not own part of the organization, the school, auditorium, or the bridge. Ownership of these properties is denied him. The ownership is governmental. The control of the organization is through a special agency or authority that has been chartered through governmental legislation. It is not Piece 2, but Piece 12.

Because he cannot *buy* ownership, he cannot *sell* ownership.

If, as "one of the people" he assumes that he "owns" the picnic tables in the state park, let him try to sell one of them. If, as a citizen, he thinks he "owns" the paintings on the walls of the White House, let him try to sell one of them. If he believes that "public property is really your property," let him explain to the sheriff why he is carting one of the mohogany desks out of the court house to sell it.

The fact that the individual cannot sell these properties is solid evidence that they are not his.

We cannot buy stock in governmental organizations. We can only buy the bonds they sell. Only the bonds are our property (Piece 2). We own only a promise to pay.

Now we begin to see the difference between Freemodes and Forcemodes.

Most shares of stock can be sold (if someone wants to buy them). Most shares of stock include "voting rights." We the owner may "vote our shares" or assign our vote by proxy to another. In this manner, shareholders who are the owners have some control over the company's management. If we disapprove of the way management is running "our" company, we can take action to improve our situation.

"See here," you scold the CEO at the stockholder's meeting, "we the owners are dissatisfied with your profit and your growth. We expected better performance from you. We're selling out and will invest in another company more to our liking. If you do not mend your ways, you may be out on the street looking for another job!"

If the risk is too great, the profit too small, or the growth too slow, we pursue happiness in greener fields. If we perceive more "value" elsewhere, we sell our shares, take our money, and depart.

We don't own governmental organizations because we can't kiss them "goodbye" for a "good buy." Controls over governmentally-owned organizations are much less direct, are exerted much more slowly and very inefficiently. Politicians forget, ignore, or never heard of the secondary consequences of ill-advised legislation—borne out only after many years. They who voted it in are long out of office. Fire them? How?

The secondary consequences of federally funded mistakes may become apparent only twenty, thirty, or fifty years later. Get rid of the Federal Trade Commission, the Federal Housing Authority, or the Department of Energy? Just withhold your financial support. Write across your next income-tax return, "I no longer wish to 'own' the FHA. Deducting $1,000. OK?" Sure.

Think the Social Security system, the giant among Forcemodes, is a 50-year-old mistake because it keeps going broke? Don't support it. Withhold from your withholding. Sure.

The Department of Energy has offered no service of value to you? You as its funds supplier would like its 17,000 employees off your back? Sorry, you are without power. Your individual will has been nullified. By definition, you have been coerced.

Why the fuss? Is public ownership of productive property all that significant?

In Chapter 3, Milton Friedman stated the significant principle: Economic power should be separate from political power. In Piece 2, ownership of property is diffused and dispersed by individual ownership. Even the largest corporations are owned by thousands of shareholders. But in Piece 12 we see ownership concentrated and empowered by political power. That "public" being the federal, state, and local governments. When both the *economic power* and the *political power* are in the hands of the government, that can become *total power*.

In 1972, according to our chart, economic power in North America was broadly decentralized. Eighty percent was in the hands of 220 million independent-minded Americans and 20 million Canadians and in about 15 million privately-owned productive business organizations or Freemodes. Only 20 percent of the economic power was controlled by central government expenditures in the two countries.

Apparently power was dispersed in similar manner in Japan and Switzerland. When we look at the AM/FM ratios in Sweden and the Netherlands, we cannot help but be concerned by the threatening appearance of combined economic and political power in their anti-markets. When the question is: "May I own?" and the answer is "No," some organization within our society is moving us in the wrong direction.

In the never-ending AM/FM conflict—the threat of the Forcemodes over the Freemodes—the sovereign rights of the individual over his property are a basic defense. Not just consumer's rights or producer's rights, but sovereign rights over property, extended as far as they can possibly be extended over the usage of property, without, of course, ever going so far as to violate the property rights of another.

Hybrid Ownership Rights

In Chapter 3 we discussed how property could be placed into the following classifications: (1) unowned property, (2) free-market property, (3) hybrid property, and (4) anti-market property.

What are the characteristics of hybrid property? The owner of hybrid property cannot be certain of his property rights. For example, a man finds a beautiful shell on the beach or purchases one through voluntary free-market exchange with another person. He becomes then the secondary claimant to the shell. As the owner of the shell, he now has the freedom to do with it exactly as he chooses. He may even destroy the shell. The FM requires only that he not use his property in any way that violates the property rights of other individuals.

Now let's move to a bit more complex example.

In front of a county courthouse, a mass of people extends from the sidewalk in through the big front doors, up through the hallways, and into the meeting room of the County Commissioners. A developer stands before the commission. He has purchased a fifty-acre estate in a nice suburb. The crowd of people is from that neighborhood.

The purpose of his purchase was to transform the estate into condominium homes. The 50-year-old original home will serve as the clubhouse. He needs a zoning variance; condominium ownership in this county is a little different from the single-family home ownership. His neighbors are up in arms. "It will destroy the personality of the neighborhood environment." The commissioners are terrified. They picture their losses at the next election. They deny his petition. Try telling the developer that his very best alternative (CC-3) has not been denied him. His best alternative has been yanked away. Tell him that he is free to improve his situation as he sees it (CC-1).

The wills of nonowners have triumphed over the property rights of the rightful owner. Were the rights of the neighbors endangered? Not really. The value of their homes would not have been adversely affected. They just don't like condominiums. The developer's will as the rightful owner has been "nullified through restraint." This by definition is coercion.

A farmer, an entrepreneur, owns 800 acres adjacent to an interstate highway. He is having a tough time making ends meet. The land is his but has been mortgaged. He has almost a half mile of frontage on the interstate.

Six 40-foot billboards would bring in $600 a month from advertisers. That $7,200 a year would be the difference between keeping the family farm and losing it. He tells the outdoor advertising company to go ahead, put up the signs.

The State Department of Transportation sees the billboards. It plants seedling trees in the state right-of-way. In three years the signs on the farmer's property can no longer be seen by passing motorists. The advertising company cancels its contract with the farmer. He is forced into bankruptcy. Tell the farmer all about Pieces 1 and 2. Tell him all about (CC-9), that he alone is responsible for the outcomes of his decisions. His will as the rightful owner has been coerced by a nonowner, the state. Were motorists' private property rights endangered? In no way, though the State assumed they were.

On the other hand, if the farmer adjacent to the interstate had a peat bog on fire causing smoke that blinded the passing traffic, his property would be endangering others' safety and property.

Controversial examples. Precisely. Hybrid property.

When the rights of individual ownership, Piece 2, are muddy, the freedom to exchange, Piece 3, will be spattered. Free-market foundations are weakened. Anti-market ideologies are strengthened. This is the greater tragedy. This is where we all become transgressors.

Either we are in charge of ourselves and our rightfully acquired property, or someone else is in charge. There is no middle way. Unfortunately, what we think of as property rights in an FM economy are frequently only hybrid rights.

Recall the test question from Chapter 3: May I own? When the answer is "No" or "Yes, but," you are being coerced by the force of the anti-market.

CONTROLLED MARKETS; RESTRICTED EXCHANGE, PIECE 13

When you prevent me from doing anything I want to do, that is persecution, but when I prevent you from doing anything you want to do, that is law, order and morals.

George Bernard Shaw

When we explored the freedom to exchange (Piece 3) in Chapter 3, we saw that in the free, competitive market the individual is king. He is free to shop and free to exchange, with nothing more to concern him than his own value preferences. He buys only what and when he wishes. He sells only when he thinks it is to his advantage. He trades the property that has less value in his eyes for another's property that he sees as having greater value. He does this to improve his situation.

What then are the related concepts in the anti-market? How does governmental power alter the workings of the market? Does it alter the effectiveness of the productive organization at the top of the structure? If so, in what ways? Does it diminish or enhance your sovereignty as an individual?

The economic problem is scarcity; the economic solution is productivity. Anti-market organizations can be productive, thereby helping to alleviate the problem of scarcity.

The Tennessee Valley Authority, for example, does produce electricity that it sells to businesses and homes. British Steel does produce I-beams, sheet steel, and pipe. Renault does produce automobiles for producers and consumers. Amtrak does produce rail service so that you may vacation in Florida. And so on. Some of these organizations have the privileges of a monopoly, others do not. The TVA has a monopoly within its area. In its geographical areas Amtrak has a monopoly on rail passenger service. British Steel must compete with other basic steel fabricators. Renault faces competition from GM, Ford, Nissan, Mercedes, and others.

Our contention is that free-market organizations would perform these tasks in a more accountable manner and certainly at less cost.

Anti-market organizations or Forcemodes interfere in our free-market choosing processes in three ways.

1. They control market prices.
2. They control market products.
3. They limit market entry.

Anti-Market Interference through Price

When the anti-market interferes with the free market through price, the interference causes either shortages or surpluses. If the anti-market sets a price too high, the free market produces too much. If the AM sets prices too low, the FM will produce too little.

The Department of Labor, an anti-market organization, administers minimum wage laws. The current minimum wage is $3.65 per hour. The price is too high for many small entrepreneurs to pay for unskilled labor even though they may badly need it. As a consequence they do not hire. The result is a surplus of labor. The unskilled 18-year-old wants to enter the work force for the first time and gain some marketable experience. If he were able to start at, say, $1 or $2 an hour, he could gain this experience. Once experienced, he could work his way upward through $3, $4, $5 and more. Anti-market policy produces mass and permanent unemployment by setting too high a wage threshold.

Another anti-market organization, the Department of Agriculture, sets an artificially high farm price on peanuts. Because of the prospects for more profit by growing peanuts, many farmer/entrepreneurs choose to plant peanuts instead of some other crop. Why not? It improves the farmer's situation as he sees it at the time. As a result, there is a surplus of peanuts.

The excess must be stored in peanut warehouses. Too high a price by the AM has resulted in another surplus produced by the FM. Economic resources have been wasted.

On the other hand, in a period of price controls, as during the Nixon administration, the Agriculture Department set a low price on what free-market cattlemen could charge for beef. Because of the fixed low price by the anti-market— "to protect the consumer"— cattle rancher/entrepreneurs began to incur losses. They could not afford to feed their beef cattle. Naturally, they chose to raise less beef, an improvement in their situation as they saw it, resulting in severe meat shortages. Supermarket meat counters had long lines of people looking for meat they could not find. The anti-market had set too low a price and the result was shortages.

In April, 1986 the Department of Agriculture began its program to reduce the output of milk. It paid dairy farmers for slaughtering their cows. Outcome: a sudden and dramatic increase in the supply of beef. Secondary effect: cattle farmers lost $25 million per week because of lower demand for their beef.

The Federal Reserve and the Congress have almost complete control over monetary and fiscal policy. Through the expansion of credit they mislead the businessman and throw the marketplace into confusion. Economist Hans Sennholz writes, "The credit expansion misleads businessmen into costly errors of expansion and modernization for which their is no consumer demand. The fiscal deficits that are to stimulate economic recovery and full employment bolster some industries while depressing others. If the housing industry becomes the receipient of federal largess it will prosper and expand so long as the federal support is forthcoming. But when a few years later the injection of government funds is halted because other industries suffer from stagnation and are now are clamoring for their share of the federal favors, the housing industry must fall into depression and unemployment."

Secondary consequences (CC-8) have been at work. Anti-market organizations are notorious for their ignorance, disregard, and oversight of secondary consequences. Their actions might "solve" one problem, but the secondary consequence turns out to be an even knottier problem, either an embarrassing surplus or a painful shortage.

The anti-market disrupts the free market millions of ways each day when it interferes with prices. Who pays? You, as the consumer and the producer invariably suffer the outcome.

Anti-Market Interference through Product Control

One of the heavyweights in the anti-market is the Food and Drug Administration (FDA). Pharmaceutical products that have been safely prescribed by European doctors for years are withheld from American patients. Pharmaceutical manufacturers know all about (CC-7); the unknowns and uncertainties in marketing new drugs are enormous. Pharmaceutical manufacturers do not want to risk multimillion-dollar liabilities by marketing drugs that are dangerous to you.

Aprenolol, used in Sweden since 1967 to prevent death after heart attacks, is not yet available to American patients. Ulcer sufferers have been denied carbenoxolone and similar drugs for years. For depression, viloxazine is a safe effective treatment, available to British patients but not to Americans. The FDA has delayed hundreds of such fine products for years. Thousands have suffered because of this Forcemode's delays.

Coming soon are mandatory airbags in your automobile at an extra expense of $600 a car. How did you get so lucky! Already there are mandatory seat belts, mandatory helmets for motorcyclists, mandatory emission controls with expensive catalytic converters, and a mandatory fifty-five miles per hour speed limit wasting hours of valuable travel time. Ask your family if they would rather have $600 in cash or an air bag. Let the choice be theirs, not that of the Forcemode, the United States Department of Transportation.

Zoning codes are an anti-market device for prohibiting us from using our personal property as productive property. When we reach 58, many of us become "empty nesters." This means the kids have grown and left the nest, and parents have two empty bedrooms on their hands. The 58-year-olds could sell the house, but a very favorable mortgage makes that sound like a poor deal. Why not "take in roomers?" That's what great grandma used to do. Invite in some nice people (many singles are looking for rooms),

The Free-Market (FM) Principles Group

① Freedom to Choose
② Freedom to Own
③ Freedom to Exchange
④ Freedom to Fund

adopt some simple living rules to preserve the peace and tranquility of the neighborhood, and earn extra money each week. If you live in many single-family, homeowner neighborhoods, forget it. The Forcemodes say you cannot be a Freemode.

(CC-3), your freedom to include the very best alternative in your list of options, has been denied you. You cannot include it in your choosing process. You are aware that your situation could be improved (CP-1), but you are not permitted to improve your situation as you see it at the time (CC-1). The economic problem of scarcity (in this case, comfortable living quarters) cannot be solved through your individual productivity. You have been so thoroughly coerced that the obvious and simple solution to your problem does not even enter your mind!

At the base of Piece 13 is Piece 5, centralized governmental power. These are some of the ways in which we feel this power. Restrictions upon our freedom to trade result in thousands of products and services that cost you more than they should and thousands of economic opportunities lost.

Anti-Market Limitations on Market Entry.

Would you like to own your own taxicab in New York City? Just fork over $25,000 for a "medallion." That will be your first cost to enter that market as a producer of that service. This is an example of an occupational license limitation on entering that market as an entrepreneur. In Boston, not only must you obtain a license to operate a taxi through the Hackney Carriage Unit of the Boston Police Department, you must obey a dress code which prohibits cab drivers from wearing shorts and tank tops and requires that they shave.

Occupational licensing, an anti-market device, usually begins, strangely enough, in free-market trade organizations. A group of entrepreneurs, such

The Anti-Market (AM) Ideologies Group

5	Centralized Governmental Power
12	Public Ownership of Property
13	Controlled Markets
14	Mandatory Funding

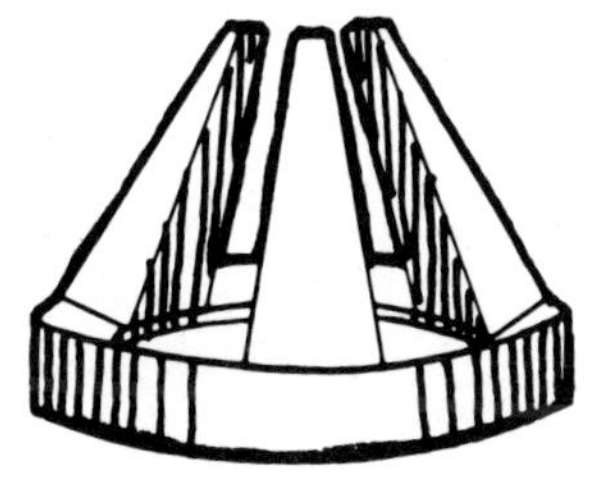

as plumbers, electricians, barbers, and beauticians, decide that everyone is getting into their act. They team up and march to their state legislature. "We must have laws requiring examinations," they plead. "Everyone wants to be in our trade. It's dangerous to the safety of the consumer if these people are not properly trained!" As a result we have state licensing boards. And, as a result there are fewer electricians and the supply is short.

Of course, many professions should require licenses for safety purposes. Brain surgeons should be licensed. But open the anti-market door for one entrepreneurial group and they all flock in. Where should the line be drawn? Strict licensing means lower supply of that specialty and higher prices. Higher prices mean more people do their own electrical wiring. Now that can really be unsafe!

How about setting up your own lottery? Sorry, against the law. That is a monopoly that seventeen states have now set aside for themselves. The free-market gambling casinos in Las Vegas and Atlantic City can make millions in profits by paying out $94 in winnings for every $100 the house takes in. On a 6 percent gross profit they thrive. But the state lotteries? They pay out only $50 of every $100 they (as the house) take in! Worse yet, they lie to you. If you win "a million dollars," they pay $50,000 a year for 20 years. If they paid you a million dollars up front, you could invest it, enjoy $80,000 to $100,000 a year in interest earnings for twenty years and still have your million. But they invest it and earn the interest. At 10 percent interest, they need to have only $468,000 to pay you $50,000 a year, and they still have the money at the end! Anti-market skullduggery.

You are 38, a mailman, and you are very tired of hearing the people on your route talk about your lousy service. Why not set up a delivery service for mail? Not for first-class mail you don't. That market is not free; it is closed by law. It is a monopoly of the United States Postal Service.

You get the picture.

When Forcemodes control market prices, control your marketable products, and restrict your market entry, you can understand the meaning of Piece 13.

The test question is: May I compete? When the answer is "No," you are feeling the coercion of the anti-market.

MANDATORY FUNDING; TAXATION AND INFLATION, PIECE 14

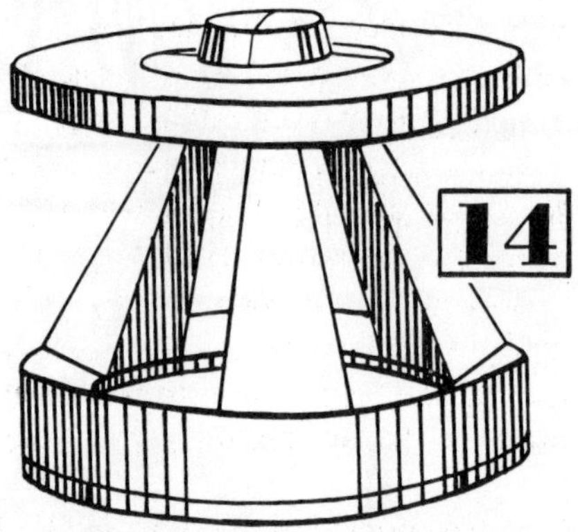

But how is this legal plunder to be identified? Quite simply. See if the law takes from some persons what belongs to them and gives it to other persons to whom it does not belong. See if the law benefits one citizen at the expense of another by doing what the citizen himself cannot do without committing a crime.

Frederic Bastiat

There's an odd twist to taxation. It is this: free-market economies are dependent upon taxation. "In the socialist economy," Mises explains, "the government swallows the whole orbit of the individual's actions and becomes totalitarian. It no longer depends on its financial support from means extracted from its citizens."

The third square leg of the Forcepod, the anti-market tripod, is involuntary or forced funding. Piece 14 is the related concept—the antithesis—of Piece 4, the freedom of the individual to fund or not to fund, whichever he chooses.

The difference between the Freemode and the Forcemode is the 'difference in the way the organization is paid," Peter Drucker tells us.

The anti-market organization cannot create wealth. It can only take it from free market organizations. Thus it forcefully diverts capital resources, natural resources, and human resources for its own purposes from the free market. Rather than providing consumers with what *we want*, the AM organization provides consumers with what *it thinks they should have*.

As individuals, we fund the private productive enterprise if we like what we see. We do this, you will remember, in two ways: (1) we invest in the private enterprise by buying its stocks or bonds, thereby providing it with captial funds, and risking in expectation of reward, and (2) we buy its goods or services, thereby contributing to its profitability. If we like the free organization, its policies, and its products, we support it voluntarily. If we do not like what we see, we withold our support entirely, or even "punish" it by purchasing instead from a competitor.

Not so in the case of Piece 14.

Anti-market organizations are funded wholly or in part by taxation. Government, as viewed by the writers of the Constitution, is supposed to be relatively simple. The reason is that we can best understand simplicity. If we the people can understand it, we can control it. Jefferson had this great faith in us. If we cannot understand the issues, the anti-market has a splendid opportunity to coerce or "fleece" us.

Over the past 200 years, as the number of governmental organizations has increased (the number, not the need) the need for funds to run them has also increased. Because in FM economies governmental organizations cannot create wealth, they are obliged to take part of the wealth earned by their citizens. This wealth, generated in and by the free market, is taken from the citizenry in several ways. Most—but not all—of these ways are made "legal" by tax laws. The various legislatures—federal, state, and local—spend a great deal of their time searching for new sources of taxes and writing new tax laws, to be backed up, if necessary, by the use of armed force.

Let's assume that your personal income is $1,000 a month, an easy amount to work with, and that you are single. Off the top there are two federal taxes you must pay. Your income tax and your social security. These total about $240. In most states the next tax to be taken from your paycheck is your state income tax, about 6 percent or $60. Thus $300 of your $1,000 is withheld by your employer. He matches your social security contribution, say $60, and sends $360 to the federal division of the anti-market to fund its many anti-market activities.

You have $700 left. Next is state sales tax, about 5 percent. That will be $35 on whatever you buy with your $700. The obliging Freemode/store pays this to the state division of the anti-market to run its various Forcemodes. The value of your take-home purchasing power is now at $665 a month.

This is getting depressing, isn't it? As a consumer of goods and services you pay the taxes that productive FM organizations must pay to remain in business. (These costs are built in to the price of what you buy, so you end up paying.) These are workman's compensation, unemployment taxes, property taxes, the employer's share of his employees' social security, and others; these total about 10 percent of all goods and services. The net effect is that your take-home is now $600.

Are the federal and state forcemodes finished with their plunder? They are already taking $40 out of every $100 you earn. Looking at it another way, you work January, February, March, and April— four months— solely for the support of the anti-market before you get a dime.

Now comes the biggie. The hidden tax. Because the government cannot live within its income, it inflates the currency. It prints money to distribute free to people who cannot or will not produce goods and services.

Governments are strangely selective in what they learn and how quickly. Some things, like free-market concepts, they never learn. But other things, such as how to inflate the currency, they all learn—and very quickly.

Inflation in the United States has run as high as 14 percent recently. While we have seen a lower rate in the mid 1980s, there remain underlying reasons for higher rates again. In Israel, Argentina, Brazil, and elsewhere in recent years inflation has run as high as 200 and 2,000 percent per year!

At this point, let us return to some illustrations.

The chart shows that at 10 percent inflation, your $600 shrinks 10 percent a year.

At the start, you keep 100 percent of your $600. But in one year, you will keep only 90 percent of the value of your take-home. Year Two: 81 percent. Year Three: 73 percent. Year Four: 66 percent. Year Five: 59 percent.

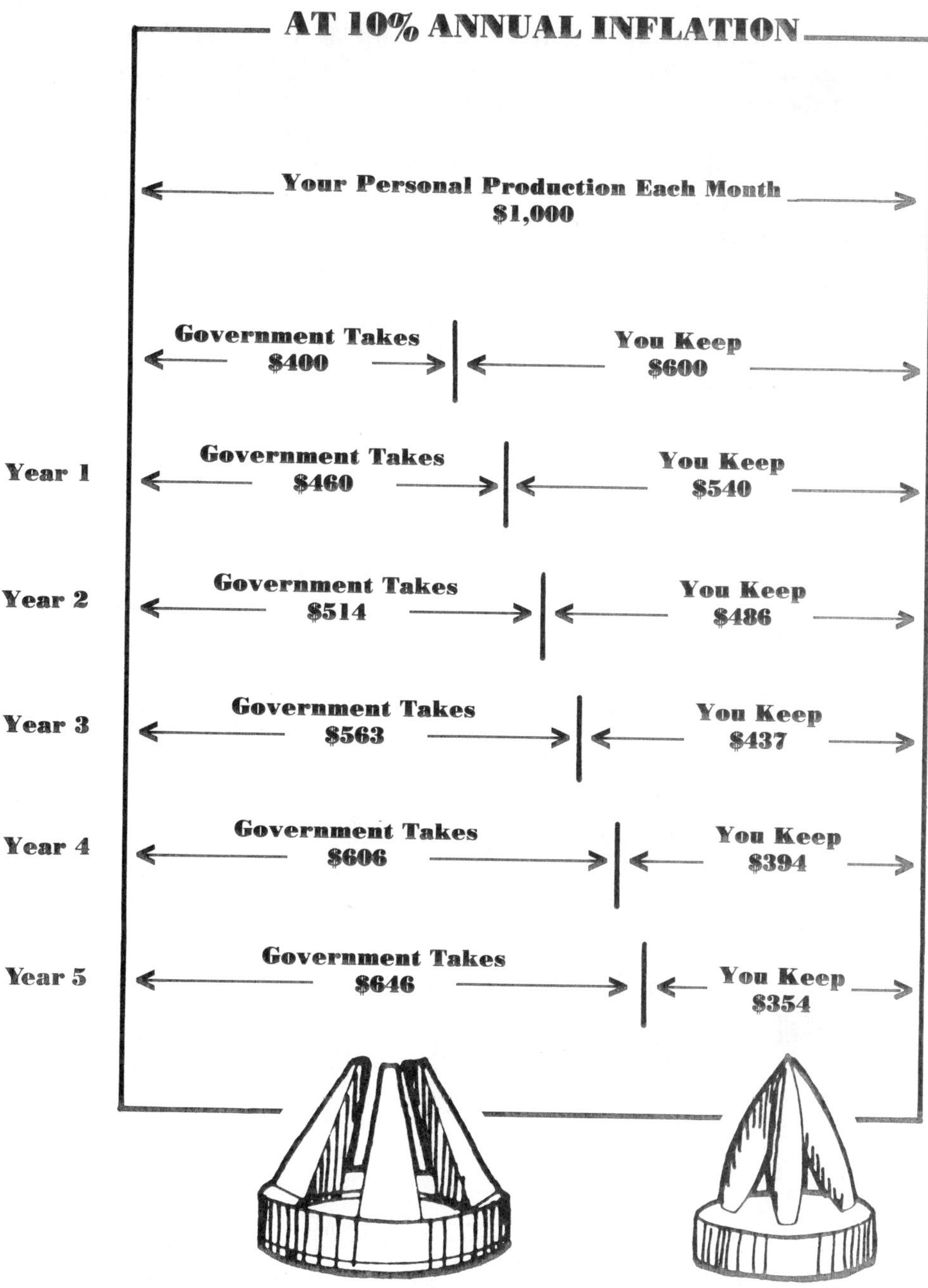

At the fifth year you keep $354. This is still called "$600," but the true value to you is $354.

The significance is that of the $1,000 you earn each month, you choose how to spend only $354. You are free to spend only 35.4 percent of your earned income just as you wish.

Who is in charge of your earnings? Sounds like an AM 64/FM 36 deal to me! The serfs of the middle ages had to pay their lords and kings one-third of their income. It appears that we have arrived at serfdom-times-two!

On the other hand, the organizations of the anti-market, choose how the remaining $646 you earned will be spent! That is not the first four months of the year that you are working for the government. That is from New Year's Day until August 23— 236 days or almost eight months. You must work until September lst to start working for you.

There is no law on the books that says the government cannot take *100 percent of what you produce.*

THE FORCEMODE

There is an especially distasteful characteristic of Piece 14. It tells us why our serfdom could be eternal. It is the effect upon Piece 11, the product/services ring, the linchpin. The character of Piece 11 is altered.

Whereas the free-market organization self-destructs when it fails to continue to produce a product or service that holds value for consumers, the anti-market organization can go on for decades without producing a good or service that satisfies the need of any market.

The anti-market Forcemode has the steady injection of tax dollars to keep it alive. These funds flow from you, Piece 1, to the adjacent Piece 5, up the leg (Piece 14) of the Forcepod, to sustain the anti-market organization at the top of the structure.

When we ask the question, "Must I fund, like it or not?" the free-market answer is "No." The anti-market answer is "Yes".

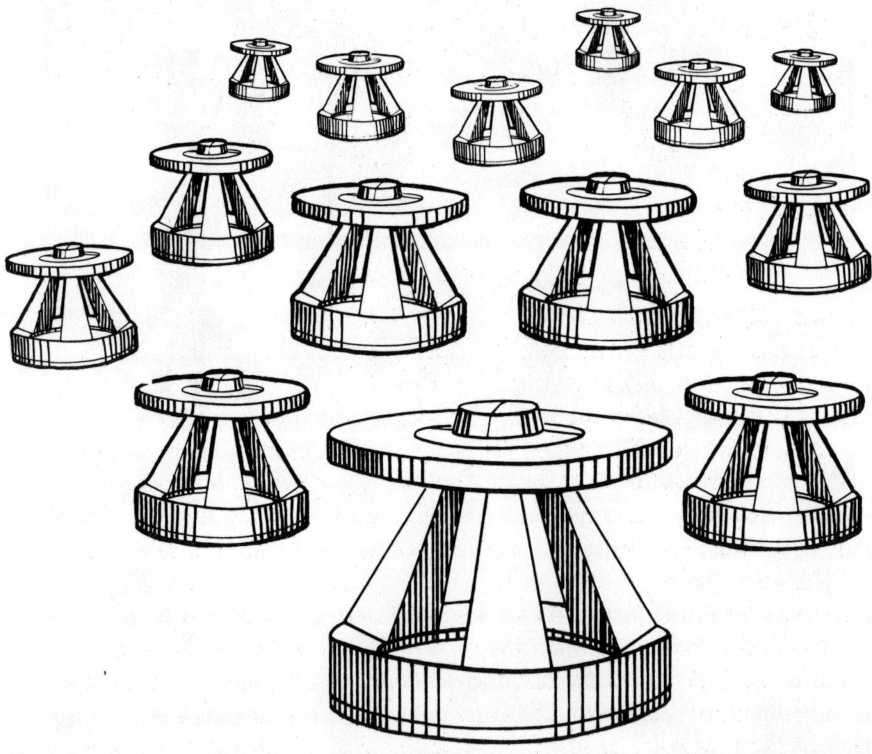

Anti-Market Orzanizations = AM Community

THE ORGANIZATIONS THAT DO NOT SELF-DESTRUCT

The government-owned organization can continue to exist because it has a direct vacuum attached to our individual pocketbooks. The net effect of this is that old governmental bureaus, no matter how ineffective, never die. As Anthony Downs puts it, "they die only when the government itself dies."

Our wooden Philomod illustrates this.

Remember when you removed Piece 11, the profitable product/service ring, from the Freemode structure? The Freemode structure collapsed. Because the organization did not produce a profitable product or service, it went bankrupt or quietly shut its doors. In this manner the free market cleanses itself and helps preserve the world's scarce resources.

Now remove Piece 11 from the Forcemode structure.

It does not collapse. It lives on.

There it stands, a structure without purpose. Piece 1, your freedom to choose, was not needed in the first place. But you, as "fleecee," certainly are. Nor could limitation & dispersion of governmental power, Piece 6, play its vital role. Now we see that Piece 11 is also unnecessary. No product is required. Whatever product or service the organization was supposed to produce either failed or has long since been forgotten. Piece 5, centralized governmental power will support this meaningless structure, feeding it your funds through Piece 14 forever.

The anti-market community lacks a self-cleansing mechanism.

Now, if the AM community has no natural method to shed its useless bureaus, while the free-market community continuously cleanses itself of its unprofitable organizations, which of these two communities will grow in number? Which will be favored by the passage of time? Anti-market force over free-market choice—the direction of tyranny? Or, free-market choice over anti-market coercion—the direction of liberty?

We don't have to be very smart to figure out that sooner or later we are going to be up to our necks in anti-market organizations!

Let's return to our ten-nation chart for 1972 and update it. The purpose is to determine the current ratio, direction, and rate of change in the AM/FM ratio.

TEN NATIONS
AM/FM RATIO
1972 - 1982

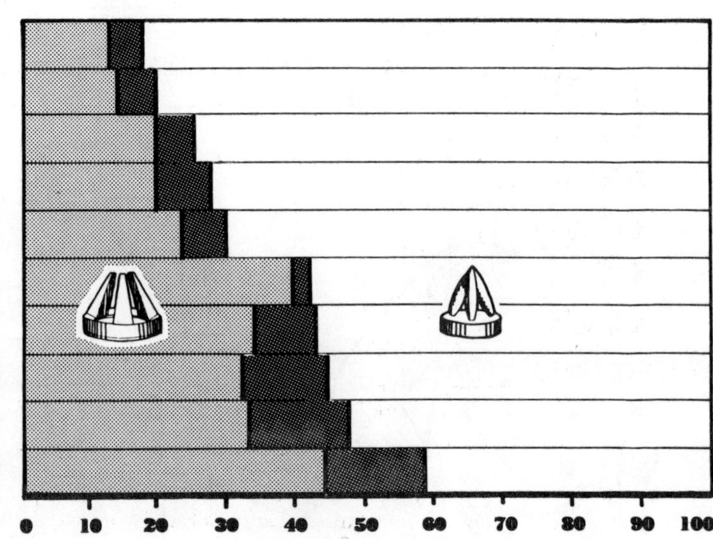

Source: same as the previous chart.

Does liberty really perish when unattended?

Ten years later, 1982, we can see how the anti-market has grown in every one of the ten nations. From 20 percent to 26 percent in the United States, a six percentage-point increase in just ten years. At the same time, our free-market community shrank from 80 percent to 74 percent!

In the Netherlands, the anti-market now controls 59 percent, the free market only 41 percent.

Before we Americans start congratulating ourselves, we should take a look at our free-market history—and more important—the acceleration in the rate of change—from Census Bureau figures over the past 100 years.

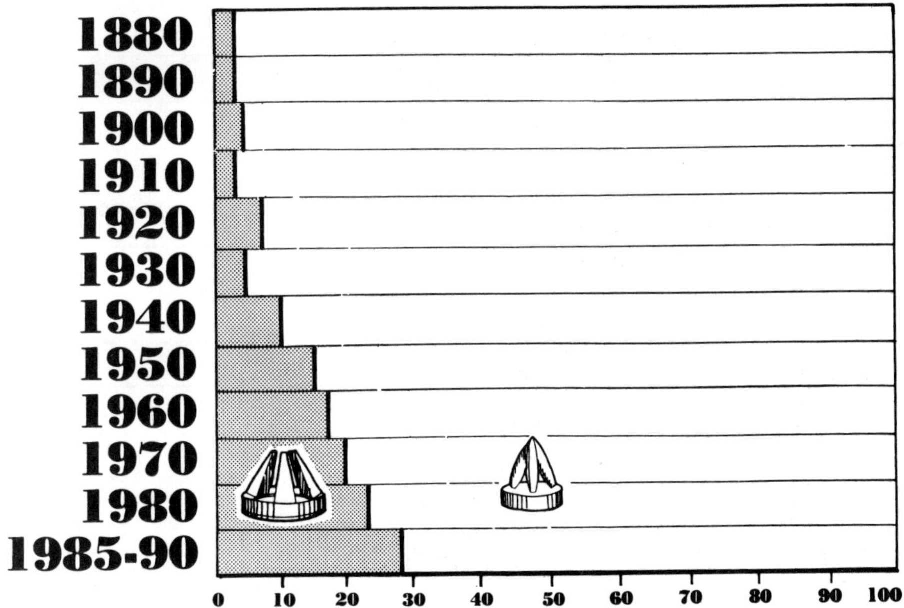

Data from Historical Statistics of the United States, Colonial Times to 1970. U.S. Department of Commerce, Bureau of Census, Vol. 1, p. 244 and Vol. 2. pp. 1114-1115.

For 300 years in the United States the free market was respected, and was unthreatened by the modest size of the anti-market. Throughout the 1800s the free market held firm at 97 to 98 percent. Ninety-eight percent of the econonic power was decentralized in the hands of the people and enterprises, all either Piece 1 or based upon Piecc 1. The anti-market was contained to only 2 to 3 percent. As recently as 1930 the anti-market's share (federal government only) was only 5 percent!

Economist Murray Rothbard, in his book *America's Great Depression*, showed how the size of government grew quickly from 1929 to 1932. The total anti-market (federal, state, and local expenditures combined) grew from 14.3 percent in 1929 to 24.8 percent in 1932—almost doubling the burden of government in four years! Of course the nation went into shock!

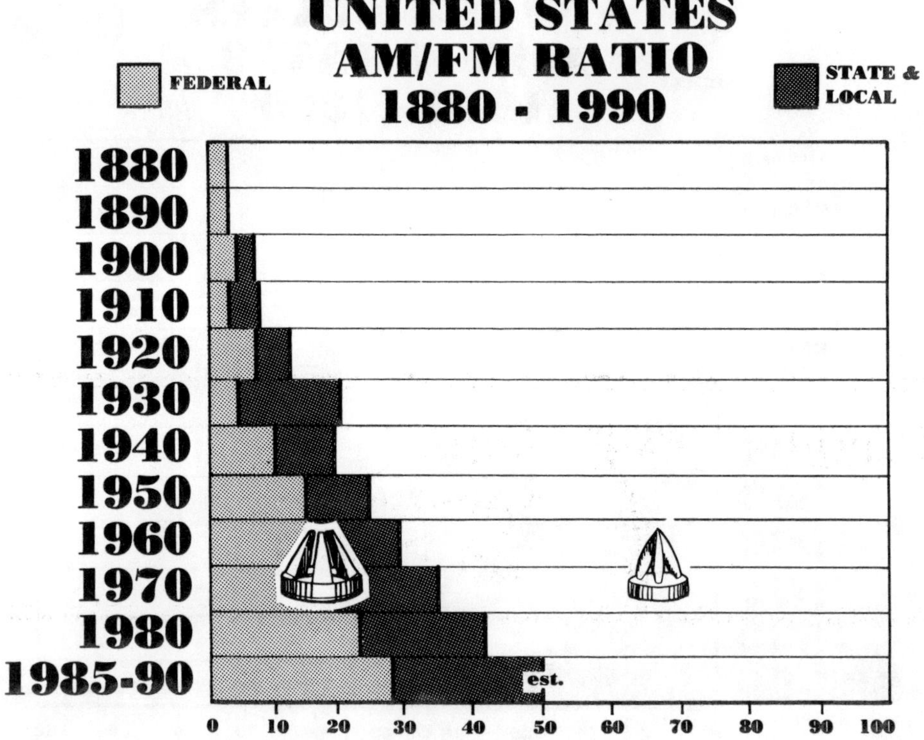

Source: same as previous chart. Additional data from Historical Statistics of the United States, Colonial Times to 1970. U.S. Department of Commerce, Bureau of the Census. "Federal, State, and Local Government Expenditure and Governmental Debt: 1902 to 1970," Vol. 2, pp. 1119-1120.

This chart includes those state and local expenditures (since 1900) as well as federal expenditures of the past 100 years. In the 100 years from 1890 to 1990 the combined anti-market will have advanced its share from less than 5 percent to an estimated 50 percent!

Government's political power is now reinforced by one-half of the nation's economic power. The potential for political tyranny is scary, and history suggests that the only spark required is a national emergency: A severe recession or inflation. A massive economic collapse ignited from abroad, resulting in major bank failures. Or an emergency related to technology, terrorism, or both. A nuclear energy plant crisis, or a terrorist with a nuclear weapon and 10 million hostages.

In the past in times of crisis, governments have appealed to their people: "Give us the emergency powers. Let us pass the laws that are needed and we will save you."

Sound unlikely? Hayek, forty years ago in the *Road to Serfdom* pointed out that "... in Germany as early as 1928, the central and local authorities directly controlled the use of more than half the national income (according to an official German estimate then, 53 percent), they controlled indirectly almost the whole economic life of the nation."

Hitler's AM organization, the National Socialist Party, needed to control only 53 percent of the economy to control totally!

Chapter 7 Tests, Spectrums, and Preludes

Since the value of freedom rests on the opportunities it provides for unforeseen and unpredictable actions, we will rarely know what we lose through a particular restriction of freedom.

Friedrich Hayek

The business of this chapter is to put our three test questions to work on a number of organizations: May I own? May I exchange? Must I fund? We get down to cases.

Then we introduce the Choice/Force Spectrum. Nothing said in this section points a finger at anyone. The cancer of coercion is in the capillaries of all of us. In this land of equality, we are equally infected.

To close the chapter on a more optimistic note we will examine "Preludes to Power." We will see that we get ourselves into these coercive messes because of our humanness. While it is human to strive to be free, it is also human to avoid risk and to disavow responsibility—shortcomings we would prefer not to hear about ourselves.

In Philadelphia in 1787, the founding fathers defined what they thought was the proper role of government. We have made a point of the fact (Chapter 5) that they established five, and only five, cabinet-rank positions under the president: state, treasury, war (and navy) now defense, attorney general, and postmaster general. The last, in 1970, was demoted from cabinet rank and became the United States Postal Service.

Nine new cabinet secretaries were formed between 1849 and 1977. Those are nine new anti-market organizations along with tens of thousands of new government personnel as support staffs.

Note that it took sixty-two years (1787 to 1849) for the government to form the Department of the Interior, a cabinet post that the founders had not thought necessary. Note also that we endured for seventy-five years without a Department of Agriculture, without price supports for farmers or food stamps.

Still, only two new cabinet positions were formed in the entire nineteenth century! As late as 1900, the total United States anti-market (federal, state, and local expenditures as a percent of the GNP) accounted for less than 5 percent. The score was still AM 5/FM 95.

A total of 116 years (1787 to 1903) went by before Commerce and Labor Departments were formed. The entire nineteenth century—the most creative, innovative, and productive century in history—evolved without a Department of Commerce, a Department of Labor, OSHA, or a minimum wage!

Then, just since 1965, five new cabinet-level departments. As many new top-level federal anti-market organizations were created in the past twenty years as were created in our nation's entire first 116 years!

The nine newest bureaus deal with: land, farming, business, labor, education, health, housing, transportation, and energy. *These are matters of commerce, not government!* The repeated acts by Great Britain to control *colonial commerce* touched off the American Revolution!

Each bureau brings the force of government into free-market functions where there was no centralized force before. Specifically, as we have seen in the previous chapter, they impose force over privately owned goods and services and into the free exchange of those properties. Many of these federal departments have corresponding agencies at the state, county, and city levels. The feds reach into our communities with branch offices of their bureaus; or the states, counties, and cities create their own antimodes. Frequently the anti-market force is applied at all four levels at the same time. Housing and transportation are examples.

TEST OF ORGANIZATIONAL STRUCTURES

Let's take a ride in my helicopter. We will be able to hover as long as we want over various organizations in the Jacksonville area and think about the structures that are within them. Jacksonville is a fine, delightful city with many nice people, beautiful beaches, great fishing and sailing, and many excellent restaurants. It is my favorite city. Twenty-five years ago my wife and I selected Jacksonville as the place we wanted to live. Its AM community is probably comparable to any other American city. I use it as an example only because I am best acquainted with it.

If we are to extend the frontiers of the community of free-market organizations, we must first get an idea of the present position of the front lines.

So that's our flight plan. Slam your door. Here we go.

Our first stop is the Maxwell House Coffee plant east of the downtown area. May I own? Yes, you can buy shares in General Foods, its parent company. You would also own a part of Post Cereals, Jello, and other foods. Am I free to exchange? Yes, the product is available in groceries. May I compete? Certainly, start your own coffee company. Must I fund this organization, whether I want to or not? No. You can help fund Folger's by buying its coffee, or buy the stock of its parent, Proctor & Gamble, if you prefer. Rating: Organization is based on Pieces 2, 3 and 4 and is therefore a Freemode.

Now we fly over to United Parcel Service. UPS delivers packages by plane and truck all over the nation. May I own? Yes, you can buy stock in UPS. May I exchange? Yes. They deliver your package; you pay them a few dollars. May I compete? Yes, Federal Express competes, as do Purolator, Emery, and the United States Postal Service. May UPS compete freely? It is not yet permitted to deliver letters. Neither is FedEx. Must I fund? No. This organization has been hampered by United States Postal Service monopolistic practices. But in spite of that, FedEx, Purolator, and UPS operate profitably without any tax funds. Rating: Organization is a Free-mode, based on Pieces 2, 3, and 4.

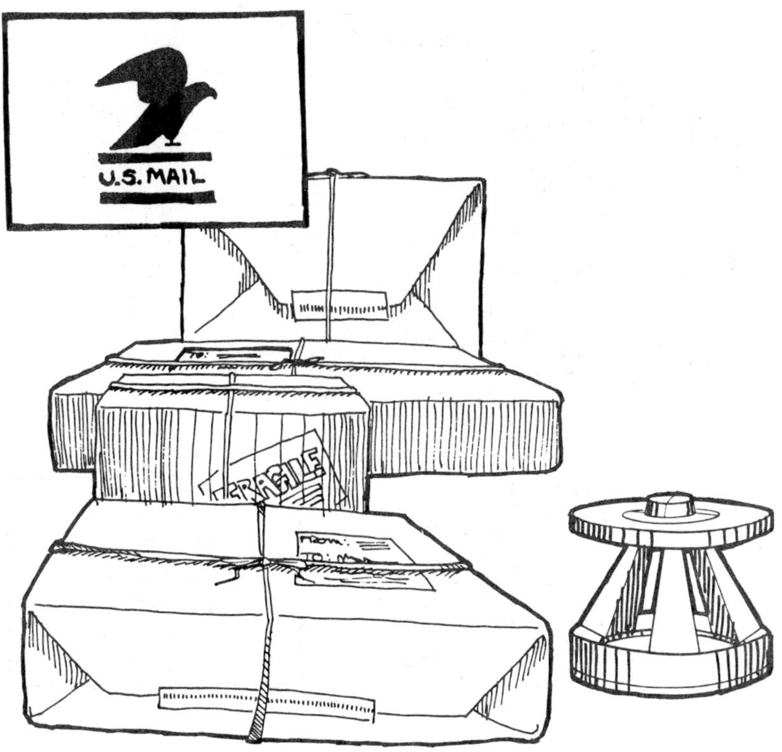

To the west of downtown we look down and see the regional branch of the United States Postal Service. May I own? No. May I compete? Yes, but not for first class mail. Must I fund? You must. Through taxation, Piece 14, you are responsible for their losses, if their operating expenses exceed revenues. Rating: With three AM legs, Pieces 12, 13, and 14, this is a Forcemode.

Here we are over a classic Georgian Presbyterian church. Who owns it? The deed to the land and building is in the name of the church itself. Its deacons manage the organization. Am I free to buy it? No, you cannot buy shares. If, for some reason, this building were no longer useful to its congregation, it is possible that they may want to sell it. May I "trade" here? Yes, but trade is not the right word. They would be glad to have you attend and join. You may enjoy considerable psychic satisfaction. In return they expect you to give of your time and financial support. Without that support, this organization would collapse. May I compete? Certainly. Start your own church. Must I fund this organization? No, all funding is voluntary. Rating: The structure of this organization is based upon Pieces 2, 3, and 4—a pure Freemode.

A few blocks away is a synagogue, a very modern building for a very old religion. Asking the same three questions, we get identical answers as for the church above. Like the Presbyterian church, this synagogue would not continue without the voluntary support of its congregation. Were it to encounter financial difficulties, we would never expect its board of directors or the Presbyterian organization to turn to the government for help—by law they cannot. Rating: Pure Freemode, resting solidly on Pieces 2, 3, and 4 and, of course, freedom to choose, Piece 1. We can see why churches and synagogues are oppressed in certain countries. Being Freepod-based, they are seen as a threat by dedicated anti-market regimes.

We're hovering above the Jacksonville Transportation Authority, the local bus system. May I own? No, it is owned by a bureau of the city. May I compete? Not directly by running other busses on the streets of the city. I might offer taxi service, for which I must buy a license from the city. Must I fund? Yes. Funding comes only partially from fares, inadequate to sustain the organization. Funding is compulsory by people from all over the nation who fund through the Department of Transportation, which subsidizes the JTA. Rating: Forcemode, based upon Pieces 12, 13, 14.

Our next stop is The People Mover, now in the planning stages, for downtown Jacksonville, 0.7 mile in length, and will cost $23 million. It will ultimately cost over $100 million. May I own? No, it will also be owned by the JTA. May I compete? No. Must I fund? Yes, the federal government sees that funds are withheld from weekly paychecks. It will fund construction of the People Mover and then its operation, which will forever be at a loss—a fact fully acknowledged from the outset. Worse yet, usage of the local public transportation system is already in a decline. Rating: Forcemode, based upon three AM legs.

We move on to KOA Kampground, the local franchise of a national ogranization. May I own? You can buy it if your offer is acceptable to the local owner. May I compete? Yes, there are other campgrounds in the area, including Hannah Park, a Hybrimode, which is owned by the city. Must I fund? No. But I am funding Hannah Park whether I am a camper or not. Rating: Freemode based upon the Freepod.

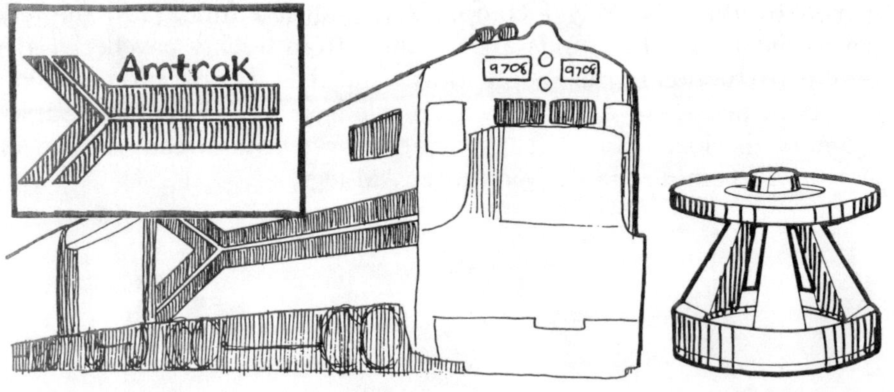

As we continue to fly over the city, we see Amtrak running through Jacksonville. May I own? No. May I compete? No. Must I fund, like it or not? Yes, through federal taxes and inflation of the currency. Would it fold without my contribution? Absolutely. The costs of operation are only partially covered by fares. Rating: A base of three square legs—Forcemode.

Next we come to Winn-Dixie, a Jacksonville-based supermarket chain. May I own? Yes, listed on the New York Stock Exchange. May I compete? Yes, Albertson's, Big Star, Pic-N-Save, and hundreds of small groceries do. Must I fund? Not if you don't want to. Buy someone else's stock, or shop elsewhere. Rating: Pure Freemode.

Below us now is Jacksonville University. A privately-endowed four-year university. May I own? It is "owned" by itself and managed by its board of trustees. Compete? Yes. Must I fund? No. Rating: Freemode.

We fly over the University of Florida at nearby Gainesville. May I own? No, it is state owned. May I compete? Yes. Must I fund? Yes, it is only partially funded through tuitions and fees. Rating: Hybrimode, based upon two legs of force (Pieces 12 and 14) and one of choice (Piece 3).

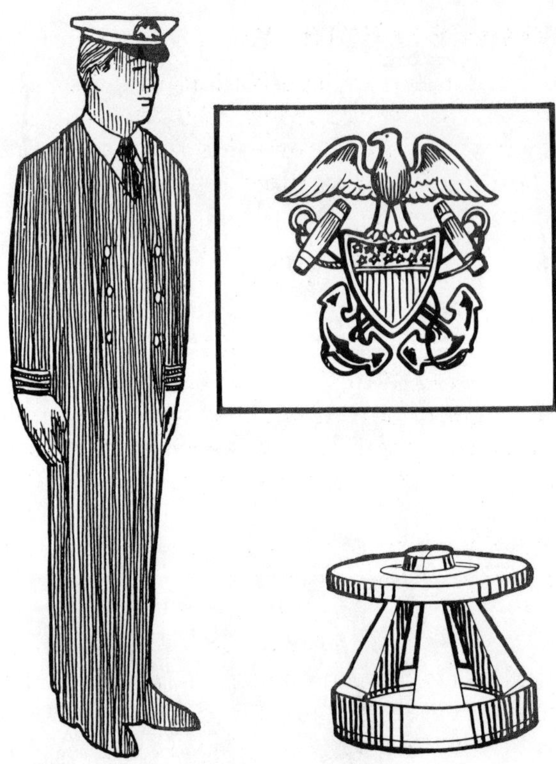

Down there where the St. Johns River runs into the ocean we see Mayport Naval Station, one of the local bases of the United States Navy, Jacksonville's biggest employer. May I own? No. May I compete? No. Must I fund? Yes. Rating: A Forcemode, representing the *proper* use of force, one of the five original cabinet offices established by the founding fathers for national defense.

Our helicopter ride has taken us on a tour of just one area, but you can see that the Jacksonvillle area is representative of the mix of Freemodes, Forcemodes, and Hybrimodes across the nation.

How in the world did commercial organizations get under the fist of all of these anti-market bureaucracies?

Ben Franklin would button his coin purse in a huff and go off to fly a kite. Washington, father of our country, would look down his long nose at his children and snort, "You're not my children, you illegitimate freeloaders!" Jefferson and his good friend Madison would go off to Monticello together to decry the sad state of their nation over a bottle of bourbon. John Adams, one of those resolute New England men of "granite and ice," would take his Abigail for a brisk walk on the Common to vent the heat of their frustrations in the cool New England air.

These people fought for our independence from the centralized tyranny of Great Britain because of its political control over colonial American commerce. Then they carefully prepared a Constitution and Bill of Rights to preserve those freedoms ... for this? A mockery! King George III, whom they detested and against whose organization they fought to be free, would laugh until he wet his white satin breeches clear through to his red velvet throne.

THE CHOICE/FORCE SPECTRUMS

We will now introduce new visualizations called the Choice/Force Spectrums. They could as easily be called the FM/AM Spectrums or the Liberty/Tyranny Spectrums. They are all three. Each of the spectrums operates on a scale of from 0 to 100 and at three interdependent levels: *individual, organizational, and national.*

We have established that residing within the borders of all nations are many AM organizations and many FM organizations. This is completely normal. It has been normal throughout man's history. To borrow from Locke and Jefferson, this truth is self-evident.

We have also discovered that it is the ratio, the direction, and the rate of change of AM to FM organizations that reveals the present profile of a nation. We can then see clearly a trend toward liberty or toward tyranny. Again we say they are the proper words; they are not typical twentieth-century euphemisms.

The indicator on the face of each spectrum shows (1) an approximation of the *current position* of the individual, organization, or nation and (2), the *direction of the thrust* of each. As individuals and organizations take actions to improve their situations, they bring about changes, and so move (albeit ever so slightly) in one direction or another; and, they exert an effect upon their nation (albeit ever so slowly) in the same direction.

If we were to conduct a sidewalk survey and ask average Joe American to position himself on the Choice/Force Spectrum, he would—almost to a person—choose to ally himself more closely with freedom of choice rather than force. The thrust of his personal preference would be toward even more freedom of choice if possible.

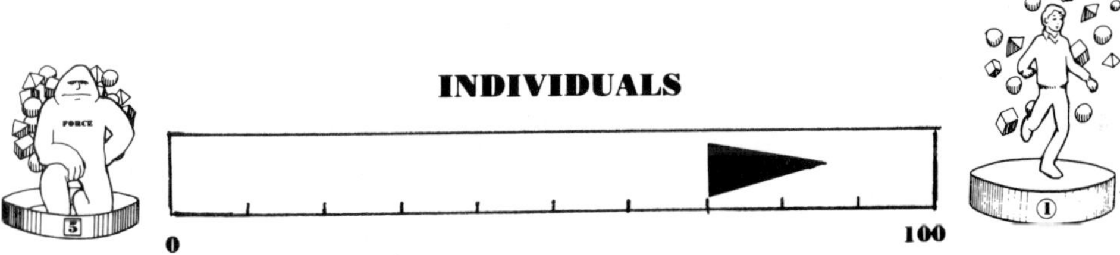

When this individual starts his own enterprise, he founds it on the principles of the freedoms to own, exchange, and fund. Since only individuals make choices, he makes the choices for his new enterprise, placing it more or less where he chose to be on the spectrum. The thrust of both is toward choice.

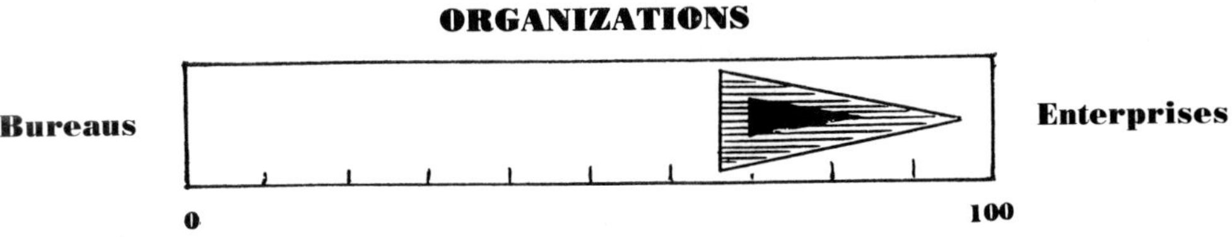

We have seen that individuals with common interests, occupations, and goals tend to form associations and organizations. In working toward the solutions of economic, political, or social problems, many organizations show a bias toward solutions based upon force rather than choice. And, as some organizations grow and age, their positions and their thrusts—originally oriented toward a Freepod structure—move in the direction of a Forcepod structure. They move in the opposite direction now, because individuals within them choose to do so.

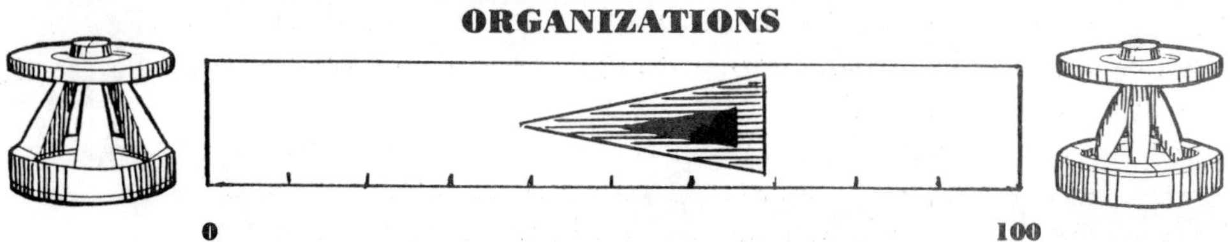

Just as the organization is moved in the direction chosen by the individual, a nation moves in the direction set by its organizations. An increase in the community of organizations whose thrusts are toward force can alter the thrust of a nation.

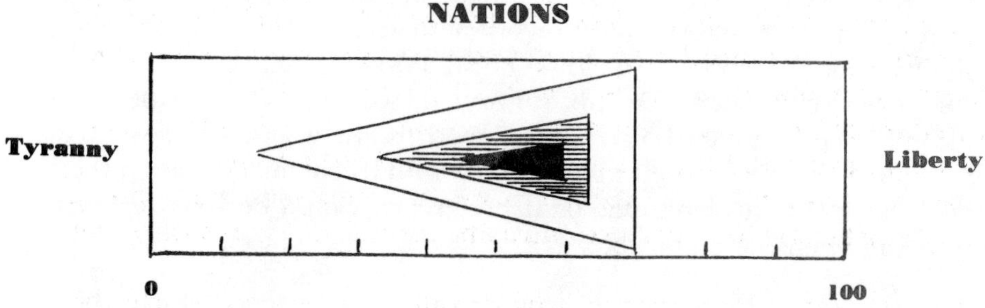

Why did we expect our nation to move in the direction of liberty, when the thrust of so many of our organizations has been in the opposite direction? Milton Friedman wrote, "Bureaucrats have not usurped power. They have not deliberately engaged in any kind of conspiracy to subvert the democratic process. Power has been thrust upon them."

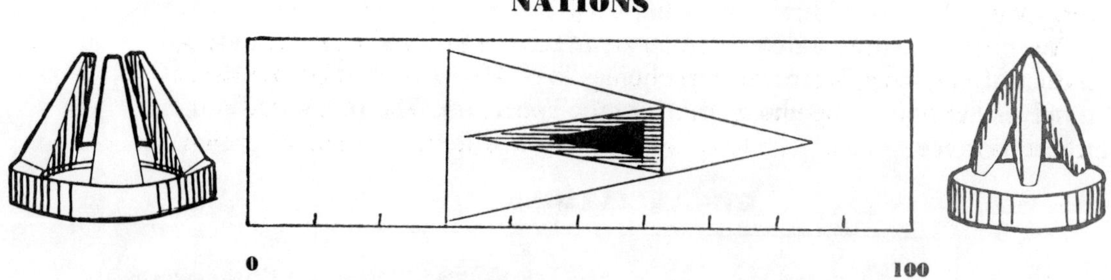

In this subtle manner, it is possible for the individual (who began with a preference for choice) *to work innocently and unknowingly toward the ultimate destruction of his own liberty*.

We as a nation have gone far in the direction Jefferson envisioned. He would never have imagined—even in his most creative-inferno-like moments—the magnificence of our success in setting the freedom example for the rest of the world. As Anne Robert Turgot wrote about us in 1778, "This people is the hope of the human race. It may become the model."

We have. And yet we have brought down the coercion of the anti-market upon ourselves.

Before we see how we can pick up on Jefferson's leading edge of freedom, sharpening our working tools and utilizing our symbols and models, we need to look in our mirrors.

In order to get some sort of handle on how this curious mechanism of the spectrums works, it is necessary to go back again to ourselves as individuals. What we say and what we do are not always the same.

We are such *ambivalent* creatures. We can fool ourselves; do it all the time. We can make a statement with the greatest assurance and then contradict ourselves immediately after. Moreover, we can do it without realizing it.

To illustrate, let's ask Joe American, who believes in freedom of choice, four questions. What, for example, is his attitude toward private ownership of guns? Toward pets running loose in the neighborhood? Toward the construction of a coal-fired generating plant two miles from his home? Toward import quotas on Japanese cars?

We find that he favors owning guns for his own protection (choice), but he thinks "Saturday night specials" should be outlawed (force).

He favors having his cat run free (choice), but he thinks there should be a law against dogs running loose and using his front lawn as their toilet (force).

He favors cheap energy produced by private utilities (choice). On the other hand, he has just signed a petition that demands that the new power plant be located somewhere else (force).

He is all for a competitive auto industry (choice), but he thinks a quota on Japanese cars is a good idea to protect American workers (force).

On each issue he has contradicted himself without blinking an eye. He has not suspected that he has been in the least inconsistent. He has given "reasonable" answers to simple questions dealing with his personal preferences (CC-5).

We need to be aware of this perfectly natural human trait, this normal, emotional, aggravating, human tendency to be inconsistent, to contradict ourselves without suspecting that we are doing so, and to bristle with indignation if someone should be so rude as to bring this to our attention!

PRELUDES TO POWER

In fact, even the noblest politicians and civil servants can no longer be expected to resist the public clamor for social benefits and welfare.

Hans F. Sennholz

In Chapter 1, we identified the ten CC's and the eight CP's as the components of free choice. Now we will explore the twelve PP's, the precursors of power. Forcemodes are formed as result of a dozen perfectly normal human feelings:

1. Love of power
2. Tendency to band together
3. Urge to organize
4. Desire to follow a charismatic leader
5. Intolerance for the unique
6. Feelings of guilt and envy
7. Desire to share
8. Do-gooders seeking mandates
9. Something for nothing
10. A sense of fairness
11. Fear of unknowns and uncertainties
12. Repugnance for responsibility

If there are others in addition to these twelve, let's ignore them.

After we acquaint ourselves with these beginnings, which we call "Preludes to Power," we may become more aware of the perils to liberty. We will see and hear early warnings we could not sense heretofore. We will see how seeds are planted. We will improve our opportunities to impede, should we choose, the early splitting and growth of the coercive cells.

Love of Power

When a bully blocks our path on a city sidewalk, he still leaves us choices. We can walk around him, back down, or deck him. The choices he gives us are in reality our secondary choices. Our primary choice, which he has denied us, was to walk straight ahead. Here we have a relationship to (CC-3)—we cannot achieve the best outcome because the best alternative is denied us.

Coercion is a subtler force but with the same outcome.

"Coercion occurs," wrote Hayek, "when one man's actions are made to serve another man's will, not for his own but for the other's purpose ... Coercion is evil precisely because it eliminates an individual as a thinking and valuing person and makes him a bare tool in the achievement of the ends of another."

Hayek uses these examples: If someone guides our hand to force us to write our signature, that is physical coercion. If someone presses our finger to the trigger of a gun, that is violent coercion. When someone manipulates our mind so that we are apparently expressing our will, but in reality we express his, that is coercion.

Someone offers us alternatives but has so manipulated us that the action we take is the least painful one. Someone controls the circumstances of our environment in such a way that we are forced to act, not according to our plan, but according to his.

Free societies meet the problem of the bully by conferring on the state a monopoly on the use of force. Piece 5 plays its proper role in providing a policeman with his billy. General rules are provided at the same time to ensure that he use his billy only to defend. In addition, the state, having supplied the policeman to protect us, expects that we as private persons will not resort to coercion ourselves.

Now comes the good citizen who says, "We have reduced the number of bullies on the sidewalk. The policeman is there. I find it offensive that men are jogging without shirts. Why don't we have an ordinance to prohibit jogging without shirts (The city of Palm Beach has such an ordinance.) All the policeman has to do is watch for such joggers. And while he's about it, have him watch for girls who are loitering on street corners, smiling at the men who jog by."

And it is done. Jogging, shirtless men, and smiling, loitering women join the likes of bullies who block the sidewalk. The good citizen who pushed for the ordinance is pleased with a sense of power. One man's and one woman's actions are made to serve the will of another. The role of the policeman has been expanded to include offense against selected citizens as well as the defense of all.

Hayek, in the *Constitution of Liberty*, traces the growing permissiveness toward coercion through the laws of Europe and America in the latter half of the nineteenth century. Some of the elements are present in the other preludes to power ...

Tendency to Band Together

Like Cro-Magnon families huddled around the fire in their dreary cave, we band together. Persons of similar tastes and occupations gravitate toward one another. Even before they meet in person, each understands many of the pleasures and problems of the other. They have similar subjective value preferences (CC-5). Upon meeting they benefit from trading experiences. They continue their career education through meetings, seminars, and conventions. They band together in trade and professinal associations. They charge dues in return for memberships. (There are over 1,400 such nationwide associations in the United States.) They set professional standards. Soon they reach a critical mass. They have "clout." The group seeks a lobbyist in Tallahassee and then one in Washington, to represent its interests.

Then their colors change. From being a *self-educating, self-regulating* body they become a *monopoly-seeking* body. "Some people practicing our profession are improperly trained," they tell their legislative committees. "These unskilled persons are a threat to the health and safety of the citizens. We are here to suggest laws that will assure the safety of the citizenry." At least that's the way it will go into the committee minutes, which become a matter of public record.

Better they tell it the way it is. The legislators were not born yesterday; they see through the scam. "Mr. Chairman, Committee members, there are too many people in our profession. We want laws to limit entry into our markets." Economic movement, historian Arnold Toynbee said, precedes governmental formation. The entrepreneurial artisans and professionals were pleased when they discovered exciting new markets. They created goods and services and competed vigorously. Then saturation. The more creative and better organized prospered. Those of less talent began to hurt. They react by planting the seeds of coercion in the committees on business regulation within the state legislatures. The result: new Pieces 13 sprout from old Piece 5.

Our Urge to Organize

Now the state association has its desired laws and its lobbyist in the state capital. Needed next are federal laws. "I remember old George Whatsisname," cries an association member. "You remember George. He practiced law down on Spruce Street. He was a member of congress and now he has a law practice in Washington. Let's go see if old George can help us out."

So the Tallahassee scenario is repeated in Washington, aided and abetted by committees from forty-nine other states. Piece 13 on the state level now locks out competition on the federal level Piece 13. Good old George has another client, so now he has more clout, because he represents more voters back home than he did before.

Old George and the 7,000 other lobbyists in the nation's capital know about power. Old George knows how blocs work. He lobbies the interests of his associations. These interests position Old George very simply. He is either for or against. He finds other lobbyists who are "for" a piece of legislation, and he joins forces. He finds others who are "against" other legislation, and again he joins forces. These blocs exert mass pressure on senators and representatives. The blocs then demand federal funding of their associations' interests. Pieces 14, new tax laws, now grow from Piece 5 and alongside Piece 13.

Soon a bureau is formed. It is needed to administer all the regulations of the associations. A new Piece 12 joins its fellow antipodal legs. An adminstrator of the bureau is appointed. He hires a staff. And we have a new anti-market organization complete with anti-preneurial Pieces 7, 8, 9, 10, providing a new coercive service, Piece 11, which only one voter in a thousand wants.

Desire to Follow a Charismatic Leader

A bureau may also be formed, Anthony Downs tells us, through the personal devotion of a group to a charismatic leader. Ralph Nader and the field of safety come to mind. The genesis is different from those bureaus beginning through trade associations.

The basis is frequently ideological, a group of persons espousing a particular anti-market policy, such as environmentalism; or a policy such as animal rights, right-to-life, or right-to whatever is in vogue that decade. He who leads through charisma possesses some of the entrepreneurial qualities of Pieces 7 and 8. But his objectives are antipodean. *He's* going for an organization based on Pieces 12, 13, and 14; *not* 2, 3, and 4.

Initially, Downs says, such a bureau is dominated either by zealots or advocates. Early on, it goes through a period of rapid growth, while it is in the eye of the press and public. It must immediately begin seeking sources of external support in order to survive. Then, once placed under one of the cabinet bureaucracies and funded from the public coffers, it hunkers down for eternity. Unceasingly it will seek to expand its influence through the regulation of any economic matter even loosely associated with its sphere of responsibility.

Intolerance for the Unique

We learned about this human trait in Chapter 4. When the inflamed creative mind (Piece 7) interfaces with the contented ones (Piece 8). Whatever is unique is at risk.

The creative mind asks, "Why doesn't everybody like what I do?" The contented ones ask, "Why isn't everyone like us?"

The great historian/philosopher Will Durant had words to say about the contented ones. "Contented people are usually those who adopt without question the manners, customs, morals, vocabulary and grammar of their group, becoming indistinguishable molecules in the social mass, and sinking into a restful peace of self-surrender that rivals the lassitude of love … In the final result a large population becomes almost an immovable body; the natural conservatism of society outruns the chauvinism of the state."

Feelings of Guilt and Envy

The guilt-envy syndrome is the subject of a thousand psychology books, a foolproof formula for the soapbox orator in Hyde Park or Washington Square: There are those who have everything and feel guilty; there are those who have nothing and are envious. The two work hand-in-hand to form Forcemodes. The soap box orator uses the feelings as a weapon: Increase the envy of the have-nots; increase the guilt of the haves.

Mises explores the phenomenom in terms of American workers. Low-paid faculty professors despise the alumni who are more interested in the high-paid football coach than in scholastic excellence.

The white-collar worker versus the boss. The worker sits at a desk; so does his boss. He works with papers, reading and writing; so does his boss. Both work by their brains. Yet the worker is envious, because he makes $300 a week; his boss makes $3,000.

White collar versus blue. White works with his mind. Blue with his hands. White does not see that the papers he works with are routine, requiring only basic training; that blue, "uneducated," is a skilled technician or mechanic working with intricate machinery and equipment. White, inside and near the bosses, envies the higher pay of blue out there in the plant.

"In a society based on caste and status," Mises asserts, "the individual can ascribe adverse fate to conditions beyond his control ... His wife cannot find fault with his station."

It is quite different in the free market, where everyone's station in life depends on his own doing. "Why do you make so little," the wife nags. "Look at your friend, Tony. Why aren't you in charge of the plant now instead of Tony? You had the same choices." What she harps on, in effect, is "Why aren't you smarter?" Envy. Unfamiliar with the way the free market works, she thinks that enterprise automatically generates profits.

And then there is guilt. Typical is the son of an extremely wealthy family who goes into politics. Show him a cause; he'll form a bureau and fund it. The rich son sees only the injustices of the free market, none of the rewards that more than compensate for its few shortcomings. "There is plenty of everything for everybody," he says. "All we have to do is redistribute it." *That goods and services must first be produced* before they can be distributed never enters his mind, because he never had to produce any. Openly philanthropic toward the "underpriveleged and oppressed," he develops an expertise in distributing your wealth, not his.

Centralized anti-market power? He dotes on it. He can never see that the free-market system "grants to each the opportunity to attain that which can be attained by only a few."

Desire to Share

Robert LeFevre, an expert on the philosophy of property and ownership, also has some strong opinions about sharing. "If we own nothing, then we can share nothing. This is nowhere more clearly shown than when we consider man's enormous drive to act as a host .... A man acquires a home ... he can hardly wait to invite his friends so they may see what he owns. He wants to feed them ... to display objects of art he has acquired ... and in many way obtain the satisfactions that can come only through this process .... It is probable that this urge to share is one of the dominating emotions which grip virtually all holders of political office. Politicians are so eager to share that they are willing to take property not belonging to them so they can bask in the glow of having given it away."

Do-Gooders Seeking Mandates

"There ought to be a law..." If ever there was a dead giveaway of coercion, this phrase is it. *Entrepreneurs seek solutions in markets. Lawyers seek solutions in laws.* John Stuart Mill wrote about the good of others. The good of others is a common denominator in the profit seeker and the parliamentary do-gooder. The uncommon denominator is that the profit seeker seeks rewards through *risk*. The do-gooder seeks psychic satisfaction through making it *mandatory*.

An ancient Chinese proverb states that when a nation begins to have many laws, it is slipping into senility. Each day 50,000 words of new regulations, codes, laws, and interpretations of the law come out of Washington, D.C.

Arnold Toynbee, the historian, talked about the "Dinosaur effect." Governments fall because they grow so big they can no longer support themselves.

Something for Nothing

"But it doesn't cost anything!"

Allan Meltzer, professor of economics at Carnegie-Mellon Institute, says governments grow "because the benefits are concentrated and the costs are diffused." The $100 million downtown people-mover is promoted by the mayor as "free," meaning it is funded by the federal government. Right. One-hundred million taxpayers need pay only $1 each. Wrong. Overlooked is the fact that every congressional district has hundreds of $100 million boondoggles.

A plausible argument could be made that the average citizen believes that these goodies come straight from heaven. The mayors, governors, representatives and senators are nothing less than archangels acting as emissaries.

Frederick Lewis Allen calls it "the Extraordinary Delusion." We need only to remember (CC-4): every choice has a cost.

A Sense of Fairness

"You did it for them. Now do it for me."

Choices have primary and secondary consequences (CC-8). Once people learn how to provide for themselves through legislating in the anti-market rather than the choices of the free market, the line begins to form.

After the taxpayer has observed the "transfer process" long enough, he reacts. Who can blame him if his reaction is: "I'm tired of paying the bill. I want my share." The other reaction to "unfair" treatment is: "I'm not paying any more," and he enters the underground economy. In the United States it is estimated that $100 to $200 billion in business is done "off the books" annually!

Fear of Unknowns and Uncertainties

Jefferson felt that simplified government, hand-in-hand with good public education, would ensure that the American would make good choices. Now government itself has become complex and all-powerful. The tax laws are an example. Greek to the common man, the codes are so complex that three CPAs can have three different interpretations of the same tax code, and the IRS a fourth. Thousands of codes and regulations disrupt the natural flow of capital, the normal supply and demand of vital markets. A two-year forecast becomes a guess; a ten-year forecast, an impossibility. The best economists can no longer forecast the economy. It is becoming a hilarious sideshow, greatly increasing the risks of producing.

The common man, bewildered by unknowns and made immobile by uncertainty, needs all the help he can get, so he turns to government.

"Insure my declining years," he pleads. Social Security is born.

"Instruct my children." Departments of Education are born.

"Provide me with recreation." The United States Park Service and local Departments of Recreation are founded.

"Heal me, for I am ill." Medicare is spawned.

"Protect the income from my crop." The Department of Agriculture pays the Georgia farmer to grow peanuts.

"Protect my savings." The FDIC and FDLIC are born.

"Build me an apartment." HUD complies.

Laughable? 50.2 percent of all American families are now dependent on the government! Most of these get some sort of green government check direct each month. Others work for organizations that would collapse without the business or supports their organizations get from government.

That is why I say that the cancer is spreading within the cells of all of us. We are transgressors. We condone coercive government. We are against all forms of centralized governmental power *except for the bureau that mails us our green check*. Our "untouchable entitlements." You and I expect too much of government. If we expect the anti-market to care for us from birth to death, its legislators will be incapable—as they have proven—of saying no. As we relinquish our free-market responsibility for ourselves, we abandon liberty.

Repugnance for Responsibility

We alone are responsible for our choices (CC-9). That's where it begins. That's where Jefferson, Washington, and Madison placed it.

Madison wrote, "The prescriptions in favor of liberty ought to be leveled against that quarter where the highest danger lies, namely, that which possesses the highest prerogative of power. But this is not found in either the Executive or the Legislative Department of the Government, but in the body of the people, operating by the majority against the minority."

Historian Will Durant wrote: "Apparently it is not democracy alone that is a failure; it is ourselves. We forgot to make ourselves intelligent when we made ourselves sovereign. We thought there was power in numbers, and we found only mediocrity. The larger the number of voters, the more ordinary must be the man or the qualities that will appeal to them."

Chapter 8   The Impact of Coercion

> *As soon as government management begins it upsets the natural equilibrium of industrial relations, and each interference only requires further bureaucratic control until the end is the tyranny of the totalitarian state.*
>
> Adam Smith (1776)

In this chapter we will explore briefly the effects of coercion nationally, organizationally, and individually. We will see (1) an anti-market community out of control, (2) a national burden of debt encumbering several generations, (3) the impacts upon bureaus, enterprises and individuals, and (4) the impact upon nations.

The AM: A Community Out of Control

The anti-market strives constantly to extend its control over the *free* market, yet it cannot control *itself*. The anti-market's control over the free market has grown over the last several years at a rate of a percentage point each year (Chapter 6). With no workable mechanism to cleanse itself of ineffective organizations, the anti-market now rages out of control, a wildfire of waste. We the FM are being suffocated by its smoke.

The United States government currently has an acknowledged national debt of about $1.5 trillion. Additional contingent anti-market liabilities amount to $5 to $6 trillion. Contingent liabilities are those government promises to pay in case of default, retirement, or other circumstances. Examples are private-loan guarantees such as FHA and VA mortgages, the farm credit insurance fund, small business loans, Export-Import bank loans, REA loans, and the student-loan insurance fund. Insurance liabilities include: bank and savings and loan deposits, and credit-union deposit insurance, riot insurance, nuclear regulatory insurance, flood insurance, and unfunded social security commitments.

Do you know how much $7 trillion is?

A stack of one thousand $100 bills is about 7.5 inches thick. A million dollars in $100 bills will stack about as tall as Thomas Jefferson, say 6-foot-3. A billion bucks in $100 bills will stack one thousand times as high: 6,350 feet—over a mile.

To illustrate, the tallest building in the world is the Sears Tower in Chicago—1,454 feet tall. It would take four stacks of $100 bills that tall to construct a billion-dollar stack, and you would have a lot left over. When we stack $100 bills this high, they become uncontrollably wobbly, so let's lay them down, beginning at the base of the Sears Building, on the center-line of Interstate Highway 80, in tight stacks in the direction of New York.

Eastward on I-80 through Elkhart, Toledo, and Youngstown. On into Pennsylvania, through Beech Creek, Berwick, and Stroudsberg. Across the New Jersey line and the Hudson River into the Big Apple. Still we have come only 802 miles! To complete our trillion-dollar stack of $100 bills, we must go another 382 miles south on I-95 to a point twenty miles south of Norfolk, Virginia—coincidentally, an area named the Great Dismal Swamp.

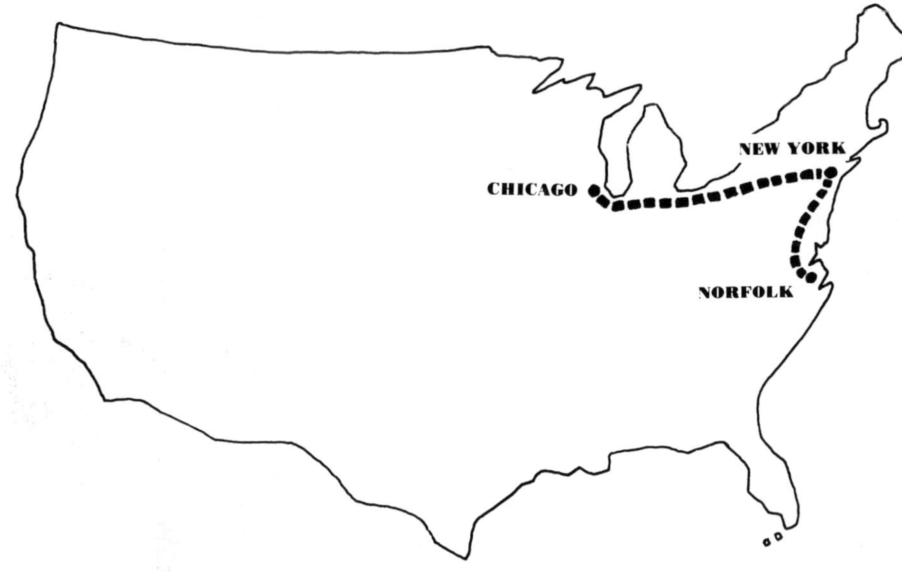

That journey illustrates only the first trillion dollars. Our federal government has committed us for seven trillion.

That sum is the *shortfall* between the wealth we have *actually produced* and *the entitlements we have legislated* to ourselves.

A Burden on Unborn Generations

The total burden of revealed and concealed federal commitments amounts to about $30,000 for every man, woman, and child in the United States. If you have a family of four, your share of these federal obligations is $120,000.

By Jefferson's definition, our "land does not belong to the living but to the dead" (Chapter 5). Today's 18-year-old American male can expect to live to age 71. You 18-year-olds have been burdened with $30,000 in present and future government obligations. To clear the obligation during your lifetime, you have about fifty-three years.

Your grandparents—but more specifically—your parents have "bound" your future. As you have seen from our charts in Chapter 6, little of this debt was incurred before 1900. Most of it has accrued since 1930, and since the 1960s it has accelerated in an uncontrolled wildfire.

We who are thirty-eight and fifty-eight have acted irresponsibly. Many of our children hold us accountable. We were supposed to be responsible for ourselves (CC-9). Our parents, in neglecting to tell us about the characteristics of choice, did not teach us this. We too have our $30,000-per-person share of the national debt, and, with the fewer years left in our lifetimes, it is even less likely that we will clear our own ledgers.

In Chapter 10 we will explore the opportunity to make amends. *We will have the opportunity to break out of this generation-to-generation cycle that has neglected free-market principles.* We will see that we can fight the wildfire quite effectively.

IMPACT UPON BUREAUS, ENTERPRISES, AND INDIVIDUALS

Impact Upon Bureaus

Organizations perched atop Forcepods differ from those based upon Freepods. The substance of each of the pieces atop the Forcepod is altered from its norm as we observed it in the enterprise. The alterations in substance reflect the character of the three square legs:

- Public Ownership
- Controlled Markets
- Forced Funding

To make it easier to understand what happens to the bureau, we can make a further refinement in the "shorthand" of *Structures*. Pieces 1 through 11 (with the exception of Piece 5) are free-market concepts. Their numerals in our illustrations are enclosed in circles. The numerals of anti-market pieces are enclosed in squares.

If we were to write these piece numbers in freehand on a blackboard, we could employ the "shorthand" of enclosing these numbers in circles or squares, but this cannot be done in a line of type. So we need to introduce an additional identifying device. Wherever it might assist in communication, numbers of free-market pieces can be placed in parentheses like this—Piece (1), or simply (1). Numbers for the four anti-market pieces can be placed in brackets—Piece <5>, for example, or merely <5>.

We learned in Chapter 4 that creativity (7) responds poorly to coercion. We observed that the creative flame is fragile. It can be snuffed by removing any of its stimulants: motivation, input, or respite. The three square AM legs can alter considerably the quality of creativity within the bureaucratic organization atop them. There can be a noticeable difference in motivation from that seen in enterprise. Since monetary incentives are usually lacking in the tool kit of the bureau head, he has fewer choices with which to work than his free-market-manager counterpart. Since the official must operate within many constraints of governmental policy, the chances for unusual input are reduced. Bureau policy frowns on the extraordinary. "Don't rock the boat," the bureaucrat tells his people. And there may even be less opportunity for respite, the retreat from routine that refreshes and stimulates the disorderly, subconsious mind.

Our refined shorthand illustrates the subtle alterations in character: a creative and innovative (7) becomes a less creative, less innovative <7>!

The quality of management, Piece (8), is altered by the AM legs to become <8>. Anthony Downs, in his excellent work, *Inside Bureaucracy*, explains the subtle differences that occur in the bureaucratic organization.

- Officials tend to distort information passed upward in the hierarchy, exaggerating data that reflect favorably upon themselves, minimizing data that may reveal personal shortcomings.
- The bureau head will be biased toward policies that advance his own interests, will drag his feet on carrying out all other policies.
- Each official will vary in the degree to which he carries out directives from above. Subordinates will zealously expedite some directives; shun or ignore others.

Downs suggests why biases are greater in bureaus than in profit-making firms: " ... the existence of profits as an objective measure of performance provides at least some way of detecting strong biases among subordinates ... thus limiting the amount of bias members believe they can safely embody in their actions."

Management as Piece <8> shies away from risk and uncertainty to a much greater degree than (8) in the enterprise. Fearing censure, managers within anti-market organizations are extremely reluctant to pick up unique, innovative ideas and run with them. We have used the FDA as a good example of this. It prefers to embrace only proven ideas that are acceptable to the majority. Without the motivation for profit—or the clear-cut objectives which it demands—management loses its inquisitive thrust.

Pieces (7) and (8) combined spell "entrepreneur". Pieces <7> and <8> together spell "anti-preneur".

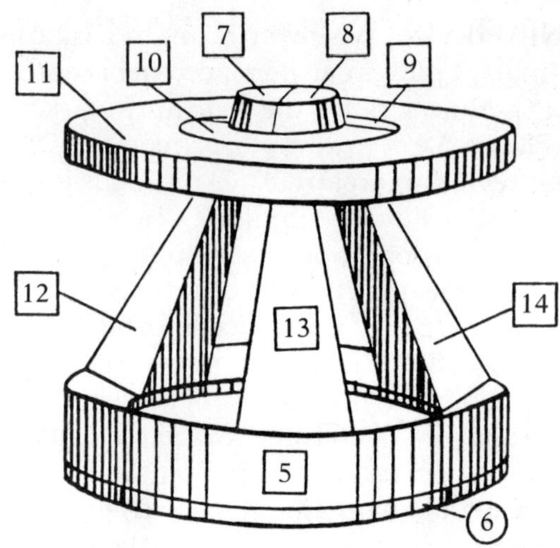

As innovation declines, costs usually increase. Human resources <9> and property resources <10> are squandered. Funding flows into the organization from <14>, which mandates that we fund it through the taxes we pay. As a result, the profitable, successful product (11) may become the shoddy output <11> of an organization without fear of dying. Or there may be no output at all. The structure will not collapse. With mandatory funding, no one can "pull the plug."

Long story short, the organization now has all the classic symptoms of bureaucracy.

Impact Upon the FM Organization and the Individual

As the billions the anti-market spends grow into trillions, we grow numb. Our capacity to understand is exceded. We suffer overload. Even the press gets weary of reporting the waste. From 1975 to 1985 I have watched the subject of government waste get less and less publicity. No sustained public enthusiasm can be generated, for example, for the recommendations of the Grace Commission. Overloaded, our attitude becomes a mixture of political helplessness and economic uncertainty.

The founding fathers thought that government should be understandable by the people. Such was the reason for Piece 6, to limit and disperse centralized power. With Jefferson in particular, this was to go hand in hand with an educated, informed electorate. How can we regain understanding and control over our lives?

Nothing happens until we are aware (CP-1). Let us define the problem (CP-2) as this: We feel politically helpless and economically threatened. Our analysis (CP-3) suggests that government is no longer understandable nor responsive. And—because government now dominates and disrupts the economy—the economy too has become non-understandable. We are at that point once again in our history when we say "Enough"! Before we decide what action is best, we need to collect and create our alternatives (CP-4).

The most important question to ask yourself is this: "What is this AM/FM conflict doing to me?" To find some answers to that question, our diagram entitled "Planning for the AM/FM Database" illustrates the principles that may be employed.

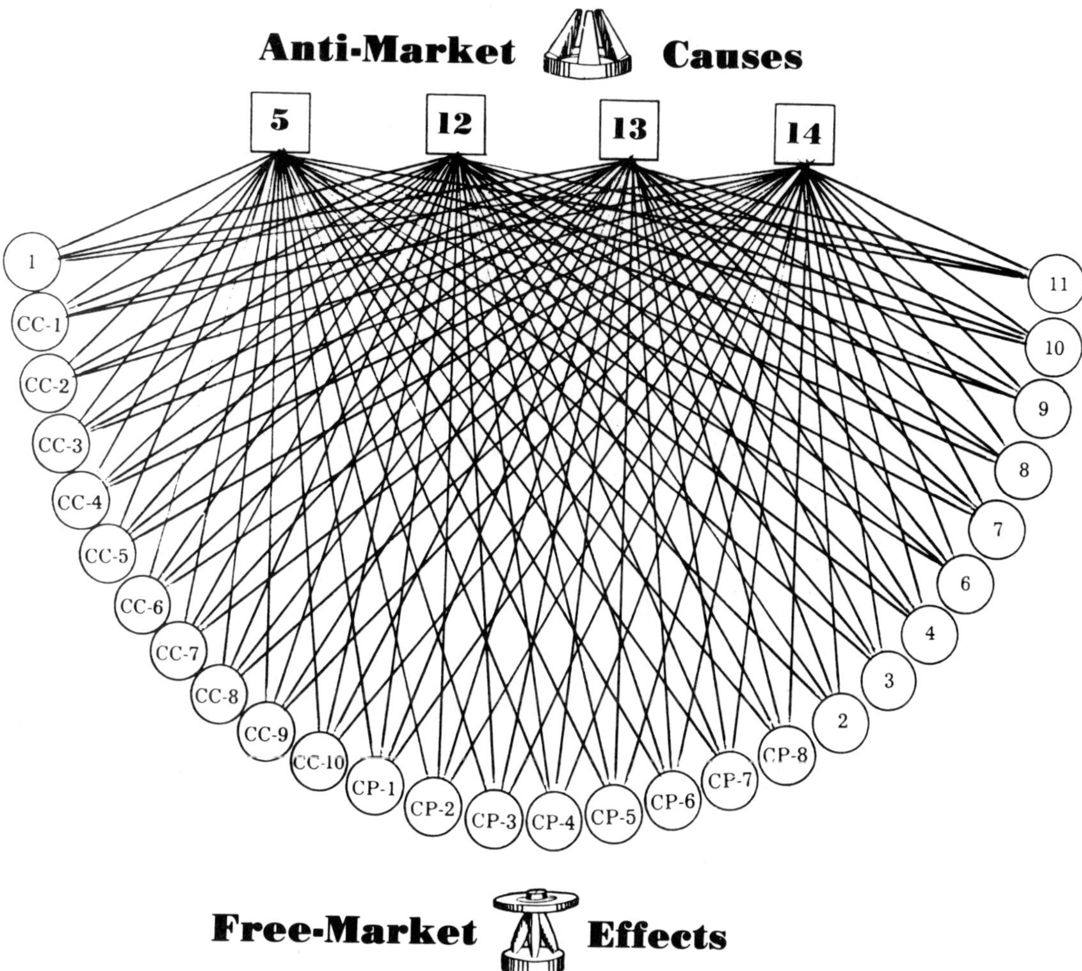

This is a method for pinpointing the anti-market causes that affect you and/or the organizations of which you are a part. Four pieces, 5, 12, 13, and 14 are the causes. The purpose is to reflect upon and compile a list of your personal "enoughs"—the various ways in which centralized power, public ownership, controlled markets, and forced funding affect your:

- Freedom to choose (Piece 1) and more specifically your freedoms:
- To utilize without constraints any or all of those characteristics of choice (CC-1 through CC-10) that might help you understand and improve your personal situation or your organization's situation
- To go through an orderly, reasoning choosing process (CP-1 through CP-8) without coercion from others, to improve your own or your organization's situation
- Freedom to own (Piece 2), sovereign rights to yourself, your productivity, and your rightfully acquired property, to be used in any way you wish as long as you do not infringe on the property rights of others
- Freedom to exchange (Piece 3) in competitive markets according to your own value preferences, without the preferences of others being superimposed
- Freedom to fund (Piece 4) or not to fund, should you choose, your own and other organizations
- Freedom to utilize the creative process (Piece 7) most effectively (input, motivation, and respite) to improve your own situation or that of your organization
- Freedom to utilize good management practices (Piece 8) to implement ideas through other people
- To work with and through other people (Piece 9) to accomplish the objectives of your organization
- Freedom to employ property resources (Piece 10) as necessary to bring forth a profitable product or service (Piece 11), as long as the use of those properties do not infringe on the rights of others

You can start your database by using a worksheet patterned after the diagram below. Trace each specific cause from its originating AM piece at the top of the diagram. Consider each FM piece, (CC), or (CP) in the line below that has been affected. We suggest a separate worksheet for each cause. Even better, since each concept in our Philomod is identified by number, you can enter this information by identifying code (piece numbers) into a computer program. *For the first time, it should be possible to begin building a comprehensive AM/FM database of causes, effects, and alternative courses of action (CP-4).*

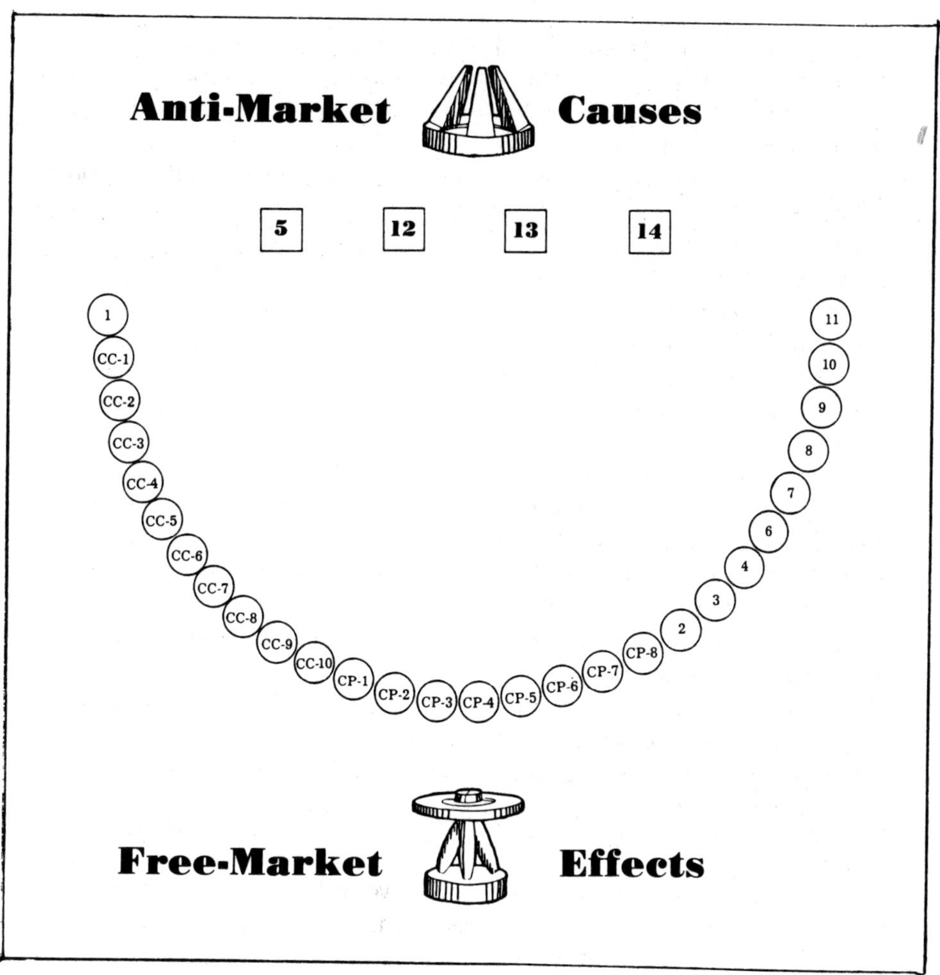

This is one of the advantages of a *model* that serves as a *standard* (see Chapter 2). Studies of the anti-market and its impact on the free market can now be recorded in a uniform "language"—the terminology of our Philomod. Those who are interested in protecting and perpetuating free-market concepts can now begin storing information on the AM and FM. Personal databases can be tied together to provide a community databank. These can eventually be linked to function as local, state, and national databanks. The databank will enable us to better understand the thousands of ways in which the anti-market antagonists impact the free market.

A group or FM organization with an AM problem in Scottsdale, for example, could request alternative solutions over a databank hotline. Within minutes, suggestions and alternative solutions that proved valuable in Seattle, Syracuse, and Sioux City, could be beamed back to Scottsdale. Just as legislators in one state capital borrow ideas for new laws from another, free-market groups could better formulate their own strategies and defenses.

As we will see in Chapter 10, it is now within our grasp to begin an effective campaign to reverse a three-generation trend and restore a sensible balance to the AM/FM ratio.

In earlier chapters we have provided a number of examples of the damage the anti-market can do to the free market. I would like to provide three cases that have caused me personal concern. One of my "Enoughs" is a local example, one is federal, and one is state.

Case #1, The Downtown Rejuvenation

Twice within the past twenty years the city has torn up the street in front of the store my brother and I own. We lease it to a well-known chain. Wonderful tenants. The city, spurred by a group trying to "bring back the downtown," tears up the streets and sidewalks in order to remodel "to compete with the neighborhood malls." Instead, during each of the one-year periods of renovation three or four more stores on the main street close their doors permanently. The properties remain empty, never to be leased again. Those businesses that are able to remain open lose half their annual gross revenues.

This is my first personal "enough". The specific antagonist? The city planning commission was trying to improve the situation (CC-1), but did not involve downtown landlords in its analysis of the problem (CP-3) or its decision (CP-5). As a result, the commission brought Piece 13 into play, an anti-market disruption of trade. The coercion affects Piece 3, freedom to trade, and Piece 4, reduction of funding to the store through a drop in profits. Secondary consequences (CC-8) had not been considered. The remodeling twenty years before accomplished nothing and drove several downtown merchants out of business. There has also been an increase in our personal risks and uncertainties (CC-7).

Case #2, The Beach Refurbishment

On the editorial page this day: three letters from owners of beachfront property. They want to know when the Army Corps of Engineers is going to complete pumping sand from offshore to fill in the eroded beach. This "refurbishing" was carried out four years ago at a cost of several million dollars. At that time, with the first winter Atlantic storm, all the newly filled beach washed out to sea. An absolutely futile attempt to fight mother nature.

This case is my second "enough." The antagonist is an anti-market federal bureau. It is being asked to provide a useless service *11* that could only have been repeated because of Piece 14, mandatory funding. Those coerced? All of us. The cost, spread over millions of taxpayers, was only a few cents each. But those were funds that were lost to our use forever. Our freedom to improve our situation (CC-1), according to our own value preferences (CC-5), has been impaired to the extent of those few cents. The catch, of course, is the multiplication of those few cents by all the other wasteful services of other AM bureaus in other areas of the nation.

Case #3, Tourism Promotion

In the early 1970s I participated in upgrading our state Department of Tourism to the Florida Division of Tourism. In 1975, I was appointed one of the nine charter commissioners of the Division of Tourism. All of this was brought about by our years of lobbying the state legislators with such functions as "Tourism Day." One of the effects of the Commission's efforts was a county-option "tourism tax" added to restaurant tabs and motel bills. The purpose was to raise more money so that Florida could advertise its benefits to the world.

During these same years I was intensifying my studies of the free market, designing the wooden model, and accumulating the information and materials that would ultimately become this book. I felt a growing sense of uneasiness. What was I doing, I asked myself, writing about the free market with one hand while fighting for a larger Florida tourism budget with the other? I was involved in the coercive process! I had personally helped build a bureau! I myself was a transgressor! "Enough!" The upshot was that I quietly withdrew from the Florida Tourism Commission.

What are some causes that reduce *your* freedoms to choose, to own, to trade, and to fund? Allow me to help set your mind in motion, to provide some tips on where to look.

Letters to the Editor that ask, in essence, "Why isn't there a law to prohibit ...?" "Why doesn't someone ...?" "Why can't the city ...?" "Why doesn't the state legislature ...?"

Watch the newspapers when your state legislature is in session. Observe which proposed new legislation gets most attention, and reflect on this. Whose freedoms are being threatened, and which freedoms specifically? Notice how much time your legislators take looking for *new* sources of revenue, rather than ways to *reduce* the anti-market bureaus they have created already.

Listen to the anchormen and the capital correspondent on the evening news. What new "causes" are they promoting this day? Which group does the station's editorialist think is newly disadvantaged?

When the TV news camera focuses your attention on a picket line with placards, what do the placards say? Do they support our freedom to own (Piece 2)? Are they supportive of our sovereign rights over our bodies, of our exclusive right to property that we have produced and/or rightfully acquired?

Let the Philomod be your guide. Which of the square legs is someone trying to reinforce? Which parts of your personal pedestal (Piece 1), or the Freepod, or the enterprise at the top, are most likely to have their freedoms curtailed. Which of these freedoms are important to you? You are building your database of "Enoughs!"

Get started on your own list of "Enoughs!" It will become part of your personal declaration of independence, leading to a constitution (plan). We will address your plan in Chapter 9, and will return to computer programming of the database in Chapter 10.

IMPACT UPON A NATION

Every society is a blend of AM and FM organizations. Free-market organizations are sustained only by the quality of their creativity, their management, and their people. Anti-market organizations can be sustained by four forces: the three square legs and the ring of centralized government power that allows them their footing.

When the free society shows an accelerating growth in its AM community, it is dangerously out of balance and out of control. *The nation that is burdened by debt is more vulnerable to economic or political crises.* Consider the individuals or families that are always heavily in debt. Are they not poorly prepared to meet emergencies? Consider the business organization that is burdened by debt. Where are its financial reserves upon which to fall back in bad years?

To redirect its thrust toward liberty, the nation must reduce its ratio of AM to FM organizations.

Eight symptoms become manifest when the current ratio weighs too heavily in favor of the anti-market community:

- Inability of the government system to operate within its income
- High rates of taxation and/or inflation
- A change in the psychology of the people, an erosion of the national will
- Brain drain: the emigration of key scientific and professional people
- A slowdown in technology and purely scientific advances
- A lower tax morality, increased tax cheating, increased barter, growth in the underground economy
- Risk capital drain: the flight of capital to more productive areas
- A decrease in productive capacity and economic growth

PART IV
THE STRUCTURE OF CHANGE

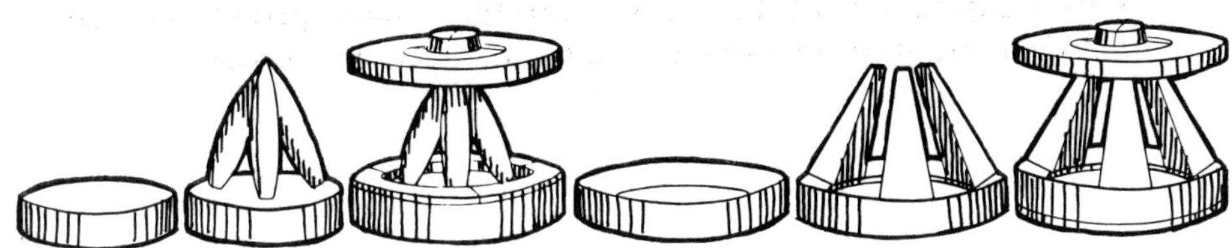

On liberty then I would say that, in the whole plenitude of its extent, it is unobstructed action according to our will, but rightful liberty is unobstructed action according to our will within limits drawn around us by the equal rights of others. I do not add 'within the limits of the law,' because law is often the tyrant's will, and always so when it violates the rights of an individual.

Thomas Jefferson

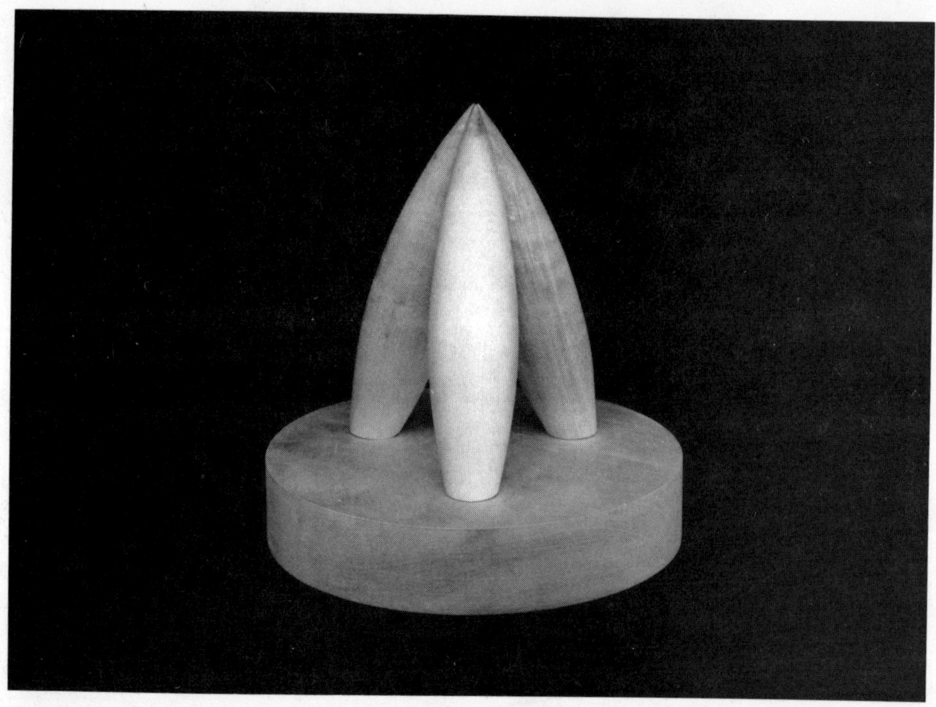

Our symbol

is our model

is our structure

of our philosophy

of Liberty.

That should make sense to you now. It would have been meaningless before you began reading *Structures*. I suggested at the beginning, remember, that you not skip to the last chapter to see how our story turns out.

THE *STRUCTURES* ADVOCACY

1. *We advocate much less government*—much less than anyone has advocated since Thomas Jefferson and James Madison. The opportune time is now. In 1987 our country will celebrate the 200th anniversary of the Philadelphia Constitutional Convention. Entrepreneurs can play a part, helping remind others of the *substance* of that historic event.

2. *We advocate the structural concept of entrepreneurism and liberty—*
marketed internationally by entrepreneurs. Entrepreneurs are the leading
edge of freedom. We play the leading roles in a community based upon the
freedoms to choose, own, trade, and fund. We have not attended to liberty,
which is perishable. We have not taught our families about choices and
free-market principles. Now our position is endangered.

Structures and the Philomod provide new, transnational symbols and models to define the philosophy of liberty and its antithesis. These fresh symbols/models are nonaligned with political parties and nations. They are detached and disassociated from the old threadbare labels. The images they were designed to convey are unique. In addition our models provide standardized terminology with which databases can be built.

There are over 12 million entrepreneurs in the United States; 600,000 have net worths of $1 million or more. Can such a group bring about change? Our group has outstanding and unifying strengths. We have (1) a common, threatening antagonist, (2) a clearly-defined objective, (3) a non-pareil pool of creative and innovative talent, (4) a majority of the management skills, (5) great financial resources, (6) the educational tools, and (7) the number of people—the clout—it takes to be effective. Which of the nation's recognized voting blocs has as many strengths as we do?

Voting Blocs

Asians	2.5 million
Farmers (20 or older)	3.1 million
Jews	4.7 million
Hispanics	9.0 million
Homosexuals	17.0 million
Union members	18.0 million
Blacks	19.0 million
Elderly (65 or older)	28.2 million
Young (18-24)	29.0 million
Evangelical Christians	40.0 million
Women	91.0 million

ANTICIPATING SOME OBVIOUS QUESTIONS

People will try to pigeonhole *Structures*. And, if you form a *Structures* discussion group or club, which we recommend, they will try to pigeonhole that. More particularly they may try to hang the label of some political party on your *Structures* group. It is the normal, human response to something new. It is easier to associate with the old than to recognize the unique.

So what does your group stand for? Simply this:

"We are both economic and political. Every organization, like it or not, must be. We are for *economic freedom*. We are *for political power limitation*. We are *against economic controls*. We are *against unchecked centralized political power*. Now you know what we are for and what we are against."

Another way in which people will try to label your discussion group or club will be to ask who is "the leader." With whom do we identify ourselves?

The answer to that one is simply this:

"Our political philosophy is Jefferson's and Madison's. Our economic philosophy is that of Friedrich Hayek and Milton Friedman. The first wrote the Declaration of Independence. The second was called "father of the Constitution." Our economist-mentors were awarded the Nobel prize in economics in 1974 and 1976, respectively." (See Appendix C.)

Some may contend that your discussion group is out to replace the flag and other classic, patriotic American symbols. Nonsense. Our symbols/

models are meant only to supplement and complement the classic symbols of our American heritage—our flag, the Statue of Liberty, and the Liberty Bell. These symbols are exclusively American with the possible exception of the Statue of Liberty. Its meaning to the oppressed worldwide is especially powerful. Our classic patriotic symbols have their meanings well established in our minds and emotions. The Freepod and Freemode, the FM symbols of *Structures*, are designed only to give added *substance* to our classic symbols.

Because they have been designed to be nonpartisan and nonnationalistic, the Freepod and Freemode can also supplement and complement any other national flags that support the philosophy of liberty.

The Statue of Liberty was dedicated in 1886. By the 1980s the grand old lady showed her deterioration. After her restoration we celebrated her 100th birthday with skyrockets, speeches, and sailing ships.

Our fourth chart in Chapter 6 illustrates another form of deterioration during the same 100 years. Free-market *principles* have also been exposed to a lot of foul weather.

Year 1886. Score: AM 5 / FM 95
Year 1986. Score: AM 50 / FM 50

In the AM/FM contest in America, the "series" stands tied at 50/50. *The free market has not advanced its position in 100 years.*

I doubt that entrepreneurs would put up with such a losing streak on any *other* playing field!

The *principles* of liberty now deserve *their* complete restoration.

Chapter 9 Universals and Awareness

The enumeration in the Constitution, of certain rights, shall not be construed to deny or disparage others retained by the people.

The powers not delegated to the United States by the Constitution, nor prohibited by it to the States, are reserved for the states respectively, or to the people.

Amendments IX and X
Bill of Rights

If we are to decrease the centralized power of government, we need to do so through attention to dispersion and limitation and by increasing our own participation as individuals. In other words, *strengthen (1) and (6) to weaken [5].*

Searching for Universals

Our Declaration of Independence, Constitution, and Bill of Rights have provided a shining example for the freedom documents of other emerging nations.

The challenge is to *continue to extend the principles* of our documents. Although we cannot "export" our Declaration, Constitution, and Bill of

Rights per se, we *can* export the structure of liberty that *represents* their substance.

Our first requirement is that these "universals" work at home. This means that they must be perceived as compatible and consistent with our own laws, as well as supportive of our flag and other established patriotic symbols.

Second, we require universals that will work abroad. Our symbols/models/structures must be perceived as acceptable by free non-Americans—compatible and consistent with the laws of their free countries, and complementary and supplementary to their flags. In this manner we stand to strengthen the free-market sense of community among the free-market organizations within all nations.

The following universals are an extention of the *Structures* Advocacy. (If Friedrich Hayek had not already used the phrase as the title for his magnum opus, I might have suggested that the following be called "The Constitution of Liberty.")

Five Universals of Liberty

1. *A nation must value nothing more highly than liberty.*

Liberty is defined as our individual freedom to choose, Piece 1. It is an assurance that we may employ a reasonable choosing process (CP-1 through CP-8), taking into consideration the characteristics of choice (CC-1 through CC-10); and that we may do this without coercion from others. We have the right to pursue happiness in our own way—a right, in the case of Americans, guaranteed by the Declaration and Bill of Rights—to improve our individual situation as we see it at the time. To accomplish our task, we require the freedoms to choose, own, exchange, and fund, Pieces 1, 2, 3, and 4.

2. *Every nation harbors two communities.*

The tasks of the modern world are accomplished through organizations. Some are based upon the principles of free choice (the Freepod), which we view as the protagonists, the heroes. Other organizations are based upon force (the Forcepod), which we view as necessary antagonists. There are, then, an international community of free-market organizations and various communities of anti-market organizations. They represent the historic and ongoing AM/FM contest—a conflict that will always exist.

In the nation that embraces liberty, there is a healthy balance between FM and AM organizations. When the tide of public opinion and the thrusts of its organizations are directed too long in favor of the anti-market, a nation will show several specific symptoms of socio-economic illness. First among these is the government's inability to operate within its income.

3. *Time favors tyranny; liberty unattended perishes.*

Why bother ourselves about tyranny? Are we not protected by our Constitution and Bill of Rights? Indeed we are. But there is one good reason to be concerned on a continuing basis. Liberty unattended can indeed perish.

The Philomod demonstrates the way in which ineffective free-market organizations die their deserved deaths. It dramatizes how useless anti-market organizations can remain standing, sustained by forced funding. If the protagonists in the contest are *mortal* and the antagonists are *immortal,* which will survive? Which will ultimately dominate?

Woodrow Wilson, twenty-eighth president of the United States, left us this crisp counsel: "Liberty has never come from government. Liberty has always come from the subjects of it. The history of liberty is the history of resistance. The history of liberty is a history of limitations of governmental power, not the increase of it."

4. *AM organizations are enduring, transitional or temporary.*

Enduring anti-market organizations, by their intrinsic natures, lack the capability to become free-market organizations. They are our armed services and police departments, and they have a proper monopoly on the use of force. They are responsible for providing their services to the people in an accountable manner.

Transitional anti-market organizations have inherent features that make it feasible for them to "cross over" to become free-market organizations. It is in the best interest of the nation's liberty that these be privatized, upgraded from a Forcepod base to a Freepod base at the earliest possible opportunity—one leg at a time if necessary. Piece 2 replacing 12, Piece 3 replacing 13, and Piece 4 replacing 14. These organizations, then, are in a transitional mode. They will strive to become privately owned, competitive, and profitable, that is, tax-producing, rather than tax-consuming.

Temporary anti-market organizations are oriented primarily or exclusively to the control and regulation of free-market organizations. Many such Forcemodes are long overdue to be phased out of existence. All new AM organizations should be given only a limited legal life (frequently called "sunset laws"), keyed to the shortest time span necessary to accomplish a specific task, never allowed to live indefinitely or to expand their jurisdiction into other areas.

5. *Only individuals make choices.*

Only individuals make choices about organizations. We define (CP-2), we analyze (CP-3), we search (CP-4), we decide (CP-5), then take action (CP-7) to improve the situation. We can alter organizations—both ours and others. We can change them so that their thrust embraces the principles of liberty. To change our own organizations, we begin by asking the questions: Am I a transgressor? Am I in some way contributing to the coercive process? Am I producing wealth (goods and/or services)? Or, have I been asking that wealth be legislated to me?

Liberty cannot be delegated to a committee.

We can also bring about changes in other people's organizations. We can cause them to feel uneasy, so that they ask themselves the same questions. We can refuse—as well as choose—to own their organizations, to exchange with them, or to fund them. Such actions are part of the substance of these four freedoms.

The five Universals may be condensed and stated as a unified theory of Liberty:

$$FM > AM = L$$

When the free market is significantly greater than the anti-market and is moving in the FM direction, we are blessed with liberty.

And that theorem has its opposite:

$$AM > FM = T$$

When the anti-market becomes greater than the free market and is moving in the AM direction, we are trending toward tyranny.

LEVELS OF AWARENESS

Each will respond to this book in his own way, according to his own individual value preferences. Nothing happens until there is awareness (CP-1). Levels of response will fall into these general areas:

- *Personal awareness* increases; a decision is made to try some of the book's ideas to improve personal situations that have caused uneasiness.
- *Vertical awareness*; we begin to share the learning process with those with whom we are most comfortable; usually family and close friends— our "private forum" (the remainder of Chapter 9 provides examples)
- *Horizontal awareness*; we feel we are ready to move to a public forum (1) through the formation of, or participation in, a small Structures discussion group, (2) going further, we may want to supplement our income—and enjoy a psychic reward—by selling the book and model, (3) we decide to investigate the entrepreneurial opportunities of an exclusive Philomod Corporation distributorship, and/or (4) we inquire about becoming a licensee for products to be added to the Philomod Corporation product line (Chapter 10 explains)

SPREADING AWARENESS VERTICALLY

When we mention a book to someone, the natural response is, "What's it about?"

When someone sees the Philomod for the first time, the natural response is, "OK. What the hell is it?"

There are two standard answers to these normal questions:

"*Structures?* What's it about?"

"It's the most powerful argument for the free market in 200 years."

"A Philomod? What is that?"

"In the pursuit-of-happiness puzzle, a Philomod puts some of the pieces in place."

The third question most commonly asked is: "Who's the book aimed at?" The answer is "Ages 18, 38, and 58, the three most decisive times in our lives."

But there are better answers than these. Always better are answers that relate to the interests of the person who asked the question.

STRUCTURES AS A HOW-TO BOOK

"I have a book I think you'd enjoy."

"What's it about?" she asks.

"It's about making choices, creative ideas, models, success ... has to do with happiness."

The way you answer the question can arouse her interest or turn her off. Close behind sports, romance, sex, and mayhem, the subjects that people are likely to be interested in are "how-to" books. Most of us will turn and run from books about politics, economics, or philosophy. When you want to find out how others will react to *Structures*, those are probably good words to avoid.

First, *Structures* is about how to make quality decisions. This is related to reasoning. This subject may appeal more to your friends or relatives who see themselves as reasoning-type personalities.

Second, the book is about how to improve your creativity. This aspect may appeal more to your intuitive or creative friends. But administrators may also be seeking ways to improve creativity in their organizations. Introduce them to the triangle of creativity: the input, respite, and motivation that feed our creative flames.

To those interested in computers and programming, you might point out the third how-to: the book and model form a foundation for the first logical, programmable database for the collection, organization, and dissemination of free-market thoughts and ideas.

You will want others to read *Structures*, because you will want to discuss with them the ideas presented in the book. Take your time. Begin with people who are close to you. Become comfortable with your new knowledge within your private forum. Vertical awareness usually precedes horizontal awareness. (See Appendix B.)

Many people are likely to be disinterested in mathematical economics but highly receptive to *human* economics.

"Will *Structures* help me balance my checkbook?" one of my wife's friends asked.

"No," I answered, "*Structures* is a look at the human side of economics. Much more interesting and more your kind of thing."

THREE DECISIVE AGES

Life is a mountain climb. When you are 18, down in the green valley, you think a lot about how you will approach your mountain. By 38, you are at your highest advance camp, huddled in your small tent amidst the swirling snow and screaming winds, ready for the push to the summit. At 58, you are at the peak.

Why are ages 18, 38, and 58 the optimal times to pause, take stock, and plan? Each is two years before a great but different twenty years. Each in its way is a threshold. Each is a choice time for major choices. It is *your* life. *Optimal outcomes can require two years.*

Upon Reaching Age 18

According to a recent *U.S. News & World Report* article, "youth is looking for a cause." We have a cause: *to market the free market,* to promote the structure of liberty. Think about it. Liberty is perishable. It could use a few dedicated souls.

Ayn Rand wrote, "Young people do seek a comprehensive view of life, i.e., a philosophy; they do seek meaning, purpose, ideals—and most of them take what they get. It is in their teens and early twenties that most people seek philosophical answers and set their premises, for good or evil, for the rest of their lives. Some never reach that stage; some never give up the quest; but the majority are open to the voice of philosophy for a few brief years."

Youth is also seeking independence. Youth will hasten its independence by demonstrating its ability to make reasoned decisions. The three big choices remain just ahead: spouse, vocation, and location. These three choices are the most likely to make or break your pursuit of happiness. If you can construct this tripod to your satisfaction, the synergistic benefits will be a daily delight. Choose the best spouse, the best occupation, and the best place to live, and you have about 98 percent of the pursuit of happiness in your hip pocket.

If you live in a dying geographical area, leave tomorrow, if not today. "He who hesitates is not only lost, he's six miles from the next exit." Go where the action is in your chosen field. If you are there physically, you will begin making contacts and associations. Chances are you won't find those by sending out résumés. Opportunity never knocks; it slips up quietly out of the fog and stands three yards behind you. You are the one to do the knocking—on the doors of businesses and other organizations that are doing what you want to do.

If you like the ideas in *Structures*, discuss them with your parents and grandparents.

Upon Reaching Age 38

What are you aiming for, 38? Are you a corporate person who is sick of corporate life? You have two years to make the important choice: Am I going to kiss the mother corporation goodbye or, am I a corporate lifer?

According to a recent article, the most common complaint of the 40-year-old is "Why haven't I got what I expected?" Dr. Carol Nadelson of the American Psychiatric Association says "These people were told promises can be fulfilled if they worked hard. But they worked hard, and their promises weren't fulfilled."

The question is can you improve your situation. Think about (CP-4), the collection and creation of alternatives. Think about (CC-4), because the choice—whether you stay or depart—will cost you dearly. You are responsible (CC-9). If you have 70 percent happiness, perhaps that is a good situation not to change. If it ain't broke, don't fix it.

A Philomod Corporation distributorship, part-time then full-time, may be a new career alternative. We make no promises. It is not right for everyone. It certainly will not be easy. But you might want to take a look. The rewards can be both monetarily and psychologically satisfying.

Introduce *Structures* and the Philomod to your children and your parents. Use it as a tool to bridge the generation gap.

Upon Reaching Age 58

Take a year to plan 60 to 80. These are twenty years in which you have a choice. Are you going to be a burden to yourself and to those around you, or, will these be two exciting decades in which you will pursue what you have itched to do all these years? Retirement? Many entrepreneurs I know are having so much fun that they want to keep on doing it!

Time for *Structures* and the Philomod too, with your children and your grandchildren. They really don't know about choices. *You teach them.* Now you have the materials to make the political/economic/social/moral relationships a little more understandable and meaningful. Especially if your children are approaching their eighteenth and thirty-eighth birthdays. Make it a personal project. Never cease being a little bit of a teacher. You know what you'll find? As you share and discuss the ways of free choice, your horizons will expand! "There is increasing evidence that intellectual growth continues through the later years. Quality of life is critical." says Dr. Robert Butler, a geriatric specialist, "If you don't keep learning, you don't keep growing; then it becomes less exciting to stay alive."

You may enjoy such discussions so much that you will want to become a roving ambassador/sales agent for the book and model. It's a way to travel, to make new friends, to get into some lively discussions, and to supplement your income at the same time. You too might want to apply for a Philomod Corporation distributorship.

Chapter 10 — A Plan to Increase Awareness

In a free society the state does not administer the affairs of men. It administers justice among men who administer their own affairs.
Walter Lippmann

That no free government or the blessings of liberty, can be preserved to any people but ... by frequent recurrence to fundamental principles.
George Mason, 1776, Article 17, Virginia Declaration of Rights

This plan is addressed to those who want to be entrepreneurs, are entrepreneurs, and were entrepreneurs. While I will address the plan primarily to those who are presently active, it is equally applicable to all.

There are 12 million active entrepreneurs within America's borders and many additional millions outside. There are 600,000 of you American entrepreneurs who have net worths in excess of $1 million. I have a very blunt question to ask you:

You pursued happiness and found it.

What have you done for liberty?

If any group can "market the free market," it is you. In their studies of your psychological profile, in interviews with you, and in your responses to their questionnaires, Venture magazine's editors know you well. In the May, 1984 and May, 1985 issues, you told all about yourselves:

- Over a third of you held three or more jobs before you were 15.
- Almost half of you—44 percent of you men, 47 percent of you women—were firstborns. As the oldest child, you assumed a leadership role early in life
- You are at work before 8 a.m.—57 percent of you. Thirty-four percent of you are at work before 7:30.
- You make most of your business's decisions—62 percent of you. Twenty-seven percent of you make all the decisions.
- A great many of you started your own business because you felt victimized by your former employer. You found it totally frustrating to work for someone else. You were offended that you had to justify your good ideas.
- You are highly motivated. You have your fears, but you are not paralyzed by them as others are.
- You have a great deal of self-confidence and self-esteem.
- You feel that you could succeed in many types of businesses, not just one; many of you have done exactly that.
- You are unimpressed by consultants, formal learning, and advanced degrees. And yet you attend frequent seminars to keep up with or ahead of the times.
- Chances are you are an excellent salesman and marketer.
- You feel that no one really understands you.

I understand you because I am one of you. And I like you because our value preferences are in tune.

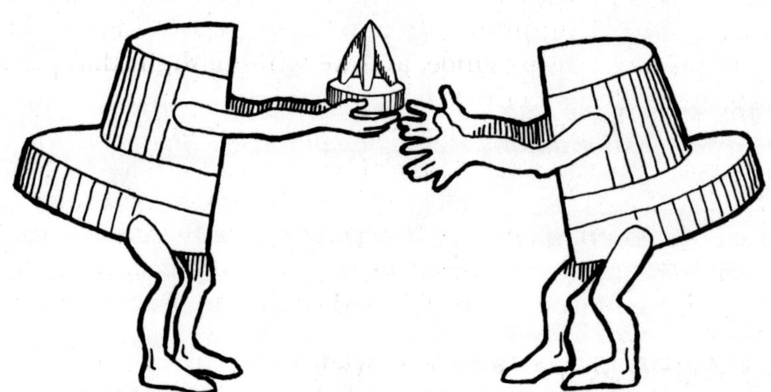

I, as the innovator, Piece 7, now approach you, as the implementor, Piece 8. You are beyond the stage of mere awareness. You are ready to put your persuasiveness into action. And I come back to my question: You pursued happiness and found it. Now what are you going to do about liberty?

I know something about you that perhaps *Venture* does not. You are a little uncomfortable, a little inarticulate with politico-economic concepts. You would not, let's say, want to talk about the philosophy of free choice before a college audience. Standing before such an audience, you would probably have a terrible case of the heebie-jeebies.

If you have done little for liberty in the past, you have had a fairly valid excuse: You have not had the proper tools.

I remember searching for the tools. I felt a sense of uneasiness. I felt that the situation required improvement even before I learned about the choosing process and the characteristics of choice. My subconscious mind kept nagging me that something was missing. What was it? What was the story I was searching for?

One of the finest books on the subject, *Restoring the American Dream*, by Robert Ringer, was published in 1979. In an interview later, Ringer revealed that he had spent a considerable sum on advertising his book but was somewhat disappointed in its level of acceptance. His experience confirmed my uneasiness that a book alone would probably leave only a limited impression in the marketplace. To achieve any degree of penetration into the American market, *a comprehensive product line would be required, backed by a well-capitalized, long-range marketing program.*

That product line and its marketing program are together now. The structures are now available, complete with the symbols and models. The supporting products can be brought on line fairly rapidly. For the first time we entrepreneurs have our act together! The timing coincides with an increased public awareness of entrepreneurs. In the past ten years the entrepreneur has come into vogue.

Structures provides you with Piece 7, the basic ideas, as well as the raw materials you need, Piece 10. You, as Piece 8, have the book, and will have the models and our other tools. Now it is up to you to add the people resources, Piece 9, stir gently, and then bring the completed product, Piece 11, profitably to market.

Only you, as founder/owner, can now take our materials, add people, and begin your own organization for liberty. Yours is the opportunity to help market a successful, profitable product/service. We have a complete business plan to use as your guide, and we will highlight that plan on the following pages. The market is *there* and *waiting*.

Our nation's 235 million individuals and millions of others are waiting for you, as an entrepreneur/ambassador, to share with them what you now believe. Liberty, I must tell you, will not be an easy sale. It may be one of the toughest challenges you ever tackled. You will be wise to prepare yourself well. Putting the anti-market back in its proper place will take time.

THE CORE OF YOUR *STRUCTURES* CLUB

Start simple. Think in terms of the three phases all founders must think through. Your *Structures* Chapter or Discussion Club will serve an educational function—first for educating yourselves, then others. And it can, if you wish to have an income generator, also serve the function of selling the book *Structures*, the model, and our other supporting products as they are brought on line.

First, start thinking about what you will state in your "Declaration." What in the anti-market have you had enough of? Just as America's founding fathers were fed up with the abuses from mother Britain in the 1770s, now you must enumerate the anti-market abuses that you are sick of in the America of the 1980s.

Second, frame your "Constitution" or general business plan. Develop your own plan, or let us provide you an outline.

Third, prepare your "Bill of Rights," the specific particulars that you want and don't want. We'll return to these in a moment.

Start simple, perhaps yourself plus two others—a "core."

Now pause for a moment and think. Who will be your Piece 7? He or she will be your creative, innovative wizard, your idea person, your gentle flame, your Thomas Jefferson.

Who will be your Piece 8? He or she will be your "people person." He is the capable organizer/administrator, your leader, your personable, pragmatic George Washington. He will organize and lead your human resources, your Pieces 9.

Who will be the person in charge of capital, your Piece 10? He or she will be your funds generator, your finder of angels, your financial pro, your Alexander Hamilton.

If you yourself are a natural Piece 8, go out and scout for your Jefferson and your Hamilton, your idea person and your money person. If you are an idea person yourself, form in your mind a list of friends who are capable administrators. Think of others who are generous contributors to their church and to philanthropic causes. Among the 12 million entrepreneurs in the United States, 600,000 of you— one in every twenty entrepreneurs— has a net worth of a million dollars or more. In America we give $75 billion a year to our churches, synagogues, and favorite philanthropies! You need venture capital. And there are risks. Your angel may find out later that your chapter was more philanthropy than investment. That's OK. Happens to all of us. Think of the good you will have done for liberty! Just be sure to pick an angel who would not be hurt by a little loss.

If you have funds that you are willing to use to start your organization rolling, then you need to find your Jefferson and your Washington. Place your requirements in front of them: "I will provide the initial funding for this if you two will develop the plans and organize the people." That's the kind of deal that's made every day, as you well know.

Your organization will be workable and flexible when these three complementary personalities are at the core—ideas, administration, and money. Three who are at ease with each other and share similar views. Three who have perhaps made a few dollars together before.

Think about close associates or friends for your core. If you are 38 or 58, recreational pals in your bowling, camping, boating, swim, tennis, or country club. Women's club and garden club friends. Business associates, your accountant, attorney, fellow civic club members. Neighborhood friends. Church or synagogue friends.

If you are 18, think about close friends, teammates, barracks buddies, classmates, fraternity brothers, class officers and leaders, and sorority sisters.

Structures as a Part of an Ongoing Club

In Chapter 7 we listed "Preludes to Power." One of those normal human traits is our tendency to band together and our urge to organize. We band together with others with similar value preferences (CC-5). The result is that we Americans are the world's greatest joiners. You name it, and we have a club for it.

- Advertising Executives Clubs
- American Legion, Disabled American Veterans, and VFW
- Associations of Business Economists
- Associations of Certified Public Accountants
- Associations of Financial Analysts
- Chambers of Commerce Free-Enterprise Committees
- Church Men's Clubs and Women's Clubs
- Computer Users Clubs, Apple, IBM, Kaypro, Tandy, etc.
- County Bar Associations, Medical and Dental Societies
- Cuban-American Clubs, Polish-American Clubs, etc.
- Data Processors Associations
- Daughters of the American Revolution
- Engineering Societies
- Investment Clubs
- Junior Achievement Clubs
- Junior Chambers of Commerce
- Junior Leagues and Junior Service Leagues
- Numismatic and Philatelic Societies
- Rotary Club, Kiwanis Clubs and others
- Sales and Marketing Executives Clubs
- Venture Capital Associations
- Women Business Owners Associations
- Young Presidents Clubs

The list goes on to total more than 1,400 nationally recognized clubs and associations in the U.S. alone! Any club that opens or closes its meetings with the pledge of allegiance or the national anthem must have a place in its heart for liberty! What about *Structures* as a program? When Dale Carnegie first published *How to Win Friends and Influence People*, it was the focal point of thousands of club programs. (Only later did the subject become formalized into a training course.)

Every club needs activities. Have you ever been club program chairman? I have. Six times that I can recall. For me they were one-year sentences to anxiety. When the newly elected club president finds a turkey to be his program chairman, he's in high cotton.

So, Mr. or Ms. Program Chairperson, what about *Structures* as a part of each program during the next year? Take a different characteristic of choice or a different piece of the Philomod to a club meeting each month. Assign someone to talk about it for five minutes immediately following the opening pledge or prayer. By the end of the year, your membership will understand the meaning of reasonable-choices-freely-arrived-at. And that equates to freedom of choice, which equates to liberty.

Then have the club members sell this book as a fund raiser!

Hardware, Software, and Ready-to-Wear

Your core group needs tools with which to work. Among the three of you, you should have ten copies of *Structures* and one or two wooden Philomods. (The Philomod model should be in production within a few months after the book. We have included mechanical drawings in Appendix A for the do-it-yourselfer.) Also, for those who prefer viewing to reading, will be our *Structures* videotape, which will tell the story of the book and the model. We believe the tape will be an easy way to share the concepts with someone whose curiosity you have aroused.

The wooden Philomod should be given a highly visible place in your home or office: on a conference table, coffee table, or the credenza behind your desk. A copy of *Structures* should be nearby. You want both to be seen, to attract attention—quietly. You want to tweak the curiosity of business associates, drop-ins, callers, and friends. The Philomod will do this well. Rotate the Philomod among the others of your core. Loan it to them to display for a few weeks at home and at work. And loan them the cassette (30 percent of American households now have VCRs). It will help make them comfortable and confident with the Philomod.

The Philomod attracts attention and questions. You will know immediately if your prospective chapter member has read *Structures*. He or she will recognize the model. Tell him you are forming a chapter. Tell him a little about it. Was he impressed with the ideas in *Structures*? Perhaps he was antagonized. Try to find out why. You will be learning how to handle objections. If he seems interested, mention your discussion group. If he is unfamiliar with the model, get into the story from the video tape—in your own words. Loan him your book and model, with the promise that it be returned within the week because you need it for someone else. Follow up as you would with any interested prospect.

Within a few months your core group can order other items from our mail-order catalog. It will describe our products, each of which will bear an illustration of the Freepod in printed, embossed, or embroidered form.

Our Three "Primary" Products

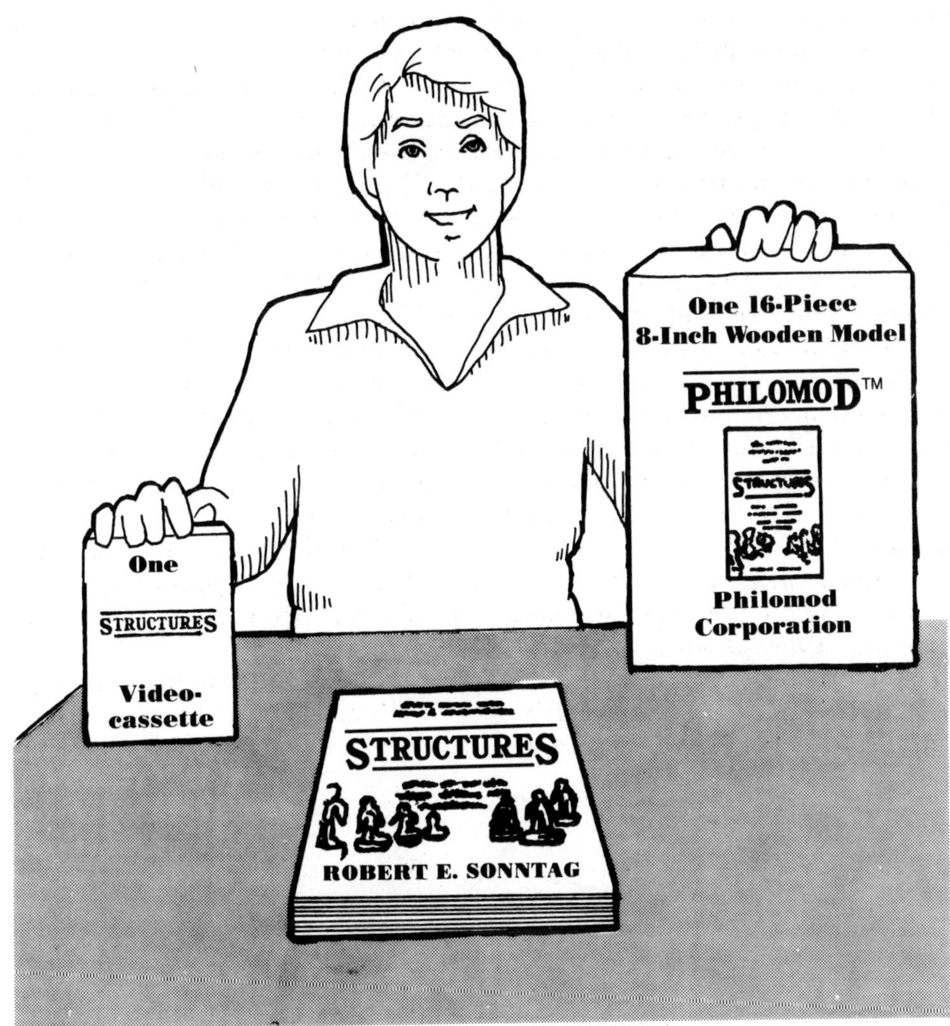

If you are of a mind to display a symbol of freedom on your tennis shirt instead of an alligator, I bring glorious tidings: a complete line of support products!

- Our book, *Structures*, hard cover
- Wooden Philomod, 8-inch diameter
- Custom leather attache case for the 8-inch Philomod
- Our vest-pocket sterling silver Philomod, 2-inch diameter
- Our introductory 128-page *Structures* comic book
- Program, 5¼-inch diskette: How To Build An AM/FM Database
- Our movie-length *Structures* videocassette
- Our audio-cassette *Structures*, a set of six one-hour tapes
- Our enlarged CC/CP Grid, 17 by 22 inches
- Men's Freepod neckties (navy, maroon, green, or gold)
- Ladies' silk scarves, same color options plus others
- Postcards and Christmas cards
- Window decals and bumper stickers
- Lapel pin, gold-filled or silver
- Our Freepod front-license tag for your car
- Our durable Freepod flags, 8″ by 12″ and 3′ by 5′
- Personalized address labels with the Freepod
- Personalized memo pads with the Freepod
- Our first-quality sports shirts, many colors and sizes
- Our hats, caps and visors for sports, men's and ladies'
- Embroidered Freepod patch, gold on navy, 3-inch diameter
- *Structures* jigsaw puzzle
- *Structures* board game
- Video game, Invasion of the Forcemodes!

(Please mail us the questionnaire in the back of this book, and help us select the products for our first catalog!)

Many are conversation starters designed to get people to ask "What is that?" or "What an interesting tie. What is that design?" Remember which items successfully attracted attention, and share them with your core group.

Sooner or later, you will want to grow from a core of three to a chapter or club of ten or fifteen. Your chapter should own about twenty books and three Philomods, so that you have enough copies to place on loan. Have on hand a small supply of those support materials you have found to be most appropriate.

Get-togethers for lunch suit some. Breakfasts together are preferred by others. Meet before or after church or after bowling, over a beer. Or around the barbecue grill. Once a month is usually adequate. There will be hot projects that will bring you together at special times. Never, never, never have meetings for the sake of having meetings—the certain kiss of death to the voluntary organization. One meeting can be built around one chapter of *Structures*; another meeting around another. And, never turn your back on those who do not like to attend meetings. Many supportive members just will not come but will prefer to contribute in other ways.

ORGANIZING YOUR *STRUCTURES* CLUB

A club member who is interested in local political news should be appointed Director of Research and Development. Your chapter's R & D person should be looking for examples of anti-market coercion as reported by the local press. These are examples of violations of someone's CC/CP rights. R & D will bring these to your meetings, and along with the ideas of others will be the basis for your Declaration, your "Enoughs!"

Don't overlook prospects who work in anti-market organizations. Some you will find to be very interested participants precisely because they are in situations that are particularly trying. They may be looking for ways out. Teachers especially are quality prospects. They are frequently frustrated by the AM system. They are usually articulate, organized, and often have funny and/or instructive stories about day-to-day foul-ups in their anti-market organizations. Economics and political science teachers will be a group you may find a little hard to read. They have had the opportunity to teach free-market principles. Check to see if they have. Let them prove themselves to you.

Avoid alliances, associations, and deals with old-line political parties. Their worn and shabby labels can do little for you. It is their complex and confusing images that you are detaching yourselves from. Yours is the fresh image. They would love to take credit for what you will do. Welcome them, but as individual, unallied participants. Explain that you are non-aligned and have sound reasons for wanting to stay that way.

Declaration, Constitution, Bill of Rights

Consider two or three projects. No more at the outset. Select them from the lists of "Enoughs!" among your members. These become a part of your Declaration. "We have had enough of X, enough of Y, and if we can do something about Z, everyone in town will be happier!" In your Constitution (your plan) set objectives and select strategies. The five Universals from Chapter 9 deserve a place in your "Constitution."

Agree on the specifics of your plan. Will you start with a series of letters to the newspaper, commenting upon coercion of an individual's CC/CP rights? An appearance by some members of the chapter before the city or county commission? (As you gain experience, you will probably want to have a chapter member as an observer at every commission meeting.) A visit to your congressman or state legislator the next time he is home? Or, all of these and more. All you are doing is getting your feet wet, learning, feeling your way in the AM/FM contest that affects our freedoms.

In your first several months be happy with the *learning* accomplishments. Your group should become comfortable in conversation using the terms from the book and model. *Structures* will be seen by many as rather radical. You are dealing with philosophy. People will have their long-standing opinions. Some will be vehement, emotional, illogical. Plant seeds. Be patient. Never force. Make friends. Loan out books and models. *Liberty is for the long haul.* Many won't recognize liberty for what it is. Many others will surprise and delight you. They will welcome you: "This is so sensible and understandable!" Such are the responses from people who can be a part of your structure.

Who are the good speakers in your group? Who are the good writers? Who is personally persuasive in one-on-one situations? Pat the backs of the members who cheerfully do the chores and run the errands that need to be done. They are the backbone of all organizations.

Horizontal and Vertical Growth

Horizontal growth means communicating with colleagues and class-mates. As a 38-year-old physician/entrepreneur, *reach out to other physicians*. As a 58-year-old farmer/entrepreneur *reach out to other farmers*. As an 18-year-old art student/entrepreneur-to-be, *seek other students* to join your chapter. As a retired traveling businessman/entrepreneur, *meet with your business colleagues*, Fraulein Hauser of Hamburg and Senor Martiñez of Madrid, when you travel abroad. Suggest that they write us about starting Philomod Corporation distributorships in their countries!

In your horizontal and vertical efforts, you will find that you will elicit three levels of response. First, those who agree with the philosophies of *Structures*, but who choose to remain passive. Save them for those situations when you need people to pack public hearings. Second, those who want to be participants and helpers in your chapter. And third, the activists, such as yourself.

Remember, some will work with you for the psychic satisfaction, for the enjoyment of doing something constructive. Others will enjoy the monetary rewards. Some persons will like the combination. Our plan helps fulfill both ambitions.

When you have your core of three—one Washington, one Jefferson, one Hamilton—and when you have an experienced and dedicated group of ten faithful souls, you may be ready to tackle a project or two. Evaluate yourselves one more time. How sound is your chapter's Declaration, Constitution, and Bill of Rights? Do you want to expand your list of "Enoughs?" Or is it better to limit them until you have had more experience? Set priorities. Which "Enoughs" have you *really* had enough of? Would tackling them require an expanded organization and plan?

Our recommendation is that you *not* expand your chapter beyond ten. Fifteen at most. Rather, when numbers are needed, form networks with other chapters. Run want ads. "*Structures* Club wishes to communicate with birds of same feather. Call Joe."

Let's say that you want to undertake the privatization of a particular local anti-market organization. (Rate this as a big, difficult, long-term challenge.) Which AM organizations in your community or state are the most vulnerable? Most poorly managed? Most arrogant? The greatest drain on the taxpayer? Offer the best free-market opportunity for privatization, to be operated for profit?

Your AM target will be protected by Pieces 5, 12, 13 and/or 14. You will be perceived as a threat to anti-market livelihoods, which means that you could need numbers of people at hearings to change protective AM codes and laws. Your Hamilton may need to raise capital for your war chest. Your Jefferson will need to prepare the package. Your Washington will flesh out your group with additional people from other clubs and direct the project.

These are projects for the experienced, however. Feel your way. Spread awareness. Watch how your chapter grows in its FM knowledge. You'll know when you're ready to tackle larger targets. Think for the long haul.

All that liberty requires is some steady attention.

It has had so little.

Entrepreneurs of the Media

We're dealing in public opinion, which changes ever so slowly. But it does change. When work on *Structures* was begun in the early seventies, entrepreneurs were a little-known breed. Each was out there slugging it out alone. "We didn't get no respect." It is better now. The climate around us has improved considerably. We have come into our own.

Public opinion is the stock in trade of the media. TV, radio, newspapers, and magazines are all working their market niches, each trying to keep its Piece 11 in place. Each giving us what they think and hope we'll buy. To survive they try to sense what is in vogue. They are looking for those opportunities "that walk ever-so-softly near them in the mist." They want to sense these subtle shapes *before* their media competitors do. They want desperately to be in tune with what we, their market, want. They pay opinion pollsters a great deal of money to find out what will be "radical chic" next.

We have news. Entrepreneurs are back in style, and we're proud. And we've got our story together this time. We know who we are and understand *the direct connection between our roots and those of our founding fathers* and the documents they wrote in Philadelphia.

We have something new for the newsmen. It is three-dimensional. It has sense-of-touch as well as sense-of-sight. Now we have the philosophy of entrepreneurship— the philosophy of freedom itself—in a wooden model that can be seen, held in the hands, shown, and shipped any place in the world.

Entrepreneurs of the media, listen. Have you been going along with anti-market editorialists, script writers, reporters, and anchormen because the free-market story was too vague, too nebulous, too unattractive as copy? Let those writers see that new ways have been found to communicate the philosophy that in 1776 was "heard round the world!"

We invite the gentle flames who create scripts, sitcoms, plays, news, and editorials—who are looking for new material— to come aboard. We have something fresh to replace the words and plots worn threadbare. "It is error alone," the Sage of Monticello wrote, "that needs the support of government. Truth can stand by itself. Subject opinion to coercion; whom will you make your inquisitors? Fallible men; men governed by bad passions, by private as well as public reasons. And why subject it to coercion? To produce uniformity. But is uniformity of opinion desirable? No more than of face and nature."

The listeners, viewers, and readers of America are ready.

Habit, Vogue and Style

Many people have voluntarily given up smoking in the past twenty years, and now they are abandoning whiskeys for lighter drinks. Many have given up pounds and waistlines through regular exercise. There's no telling what bad habits we'll give up next, nor what can slip into style. People recognize when the pressure of their peers is running against them. Behavioral changes follow attitude changes.

Slavery corrupted the owner as well as the owned. The anti-market corrupts the recipient as well as the anti-preneur.

Will Durant, one of my favorite historian-philosophers, wrote: "Every vice was once a virtue, and may become respectable again, as hatred becomes respectable in war. Brutality and greed were once necessary in the struggle for existence, and now ridiculous atavisms; man's sins are not the result of his fall; they are the relics of his rise ... There is a supply and demand in morals as well as in goods; and if the demand creates the supply more slowly in one field than in the other, it is because the soul is subtler and less tractable than the soil. But it too will receive varied seed, and produce wholesome or bitter fruit."

If it is to our economic benefit to turn away from coercion and toward choice, we will do so. Stranger things have happened. We have learned to say no to smoking. Who is to say we cannot learn to say no to the anti-market?

The score has reached a threatening AM 50 / FM 50.

Timing

The 100th anniversary of the Statue of Liberty was celebrated July 4, 1986—an exciting national party. I doubt that the 200th anniversary of the writing of the Constitution in the summer of 1987 will be the event that our 200th birthday was in July of 1976. The hype for that began years in advance. Nevertheless, we can capitalize on our connection with forthcoming events. We have the opportunity to add some *substance and support* to the hype, hoopla, and huzzas!

By 1987 we should feel good if a considerable number of copies of *Structures* are in homes, schools, businesses, colleges, and libraries. And we should feel good if there are also many Philomods about. Then, whatever publicity attends the patriotic events, our symbols, models, and structures can play their supportive role.

We are promoting a new awareness. We say again: nothing can take place before there is awareness, the first phase of the choosing process. Before you can form your group, there must be awareness of the symbols, the models, the structures, the substance.

Persuasion is a Sales Job

Let's say we would be happy—our situation beginning to improve—if by the end of 1987 there were 1.5 million copies of *Structures* distributed among the people of the United States.

Based upon 200 Philomod Corporation distributorships in the United States, each distributor area would embrace a million or more consumer prospects. Among each million of population we could expect to find about 50,000 practicing entrepreneur-prospects. (Roughly 5 percent of the population are entrepreneurs.)

If just *one out of ten* entrepreneurs owned a copy of *Structures*, that would be 1.2 million copies. If one out of a hundred of the remaining population purchased copies, that would be an additional 300,000 copies, or a total of 1.5 million books: 7,500 copies per Philomod Corporation distributor.

In our business plan for distributors, this level of sales will provide the distributor with a substantial gross revenue on the book alone. Commissions on the sales of our other products should double revenue. We cannot make guarantees. We only provide the products and the ideas. But we believe that a Philomod Corporation distributorship can soon provide a generous income.

Write Us: Philomod Corporation, Jacksonville

Send in the questionnaire in Appendix C. We will send you more information. Soon we will begin taking applications for the 200 protected United States distributorships and twenty Canadian distributorships for our Philomod Corporation product line. Tell us about the one-million-person territory you are interested in. Give us the zip codes that define that territory. We are listening.

We are also seeking additional licensees to manufacture some of the above products plus others now on our R & D drawing board. What do you manufacture that can be tied in with our group of supporting products? Contact us. We are listening.

We do expect that to qualify you as a sincere distributor prospect, you will be conversant with the ideas of *Structures* and the Philomod. You should have, at least, your core of three, all of whom are also familiar with the book and model and are as enthusiastic as yourself about the idea of marketing liberty.

I am reasonably certain that you as an entrepreneur will see that *Structures* and our other products can improve your situation.

So start building your own structure. Mail in the questionnaire today.

Appendix A

For the Do-It-Yourselfer

For those who derive pleasure from their home workshops, here is a change from birdhouses and table legs. A Philomod—a model of a philosophy. On your coffee table our model is a conversation piece. On the credenza in your office it makes a statement about the free-enterprise philosophy of its owner.

The mechanical drawings on the following pages are for an 8-inch-diameter Philomod™ Model. The drawings are one-half scale.

For a 12-inch-diameter model—excellent as a teaching aid for larger audiences—multiply all our linear measurements, diameters, and radii by 1.50. All angles will remain the same.

Just a reminder that it is standard shop practice to follow the *numbers* on mechanical drawings. Do not take your own measurements from the drawings. The drawings may be slightly inaccurate in size as a result of the printing process.

Birch or maple are the recommended materials. Also consider walnut. After all pieces have been made and fitted together, sand the finished pieces lightly by hand. To protect from warping and handprints, apply a sealer of your choice to all surfaces of your finished model. Some polyurethane sealers include stains. If you select a sealer with a stain, try it out on some scrap pieces *first*. You may wish to consider a walnut or mahogany stain to match the decor of your living room or office.

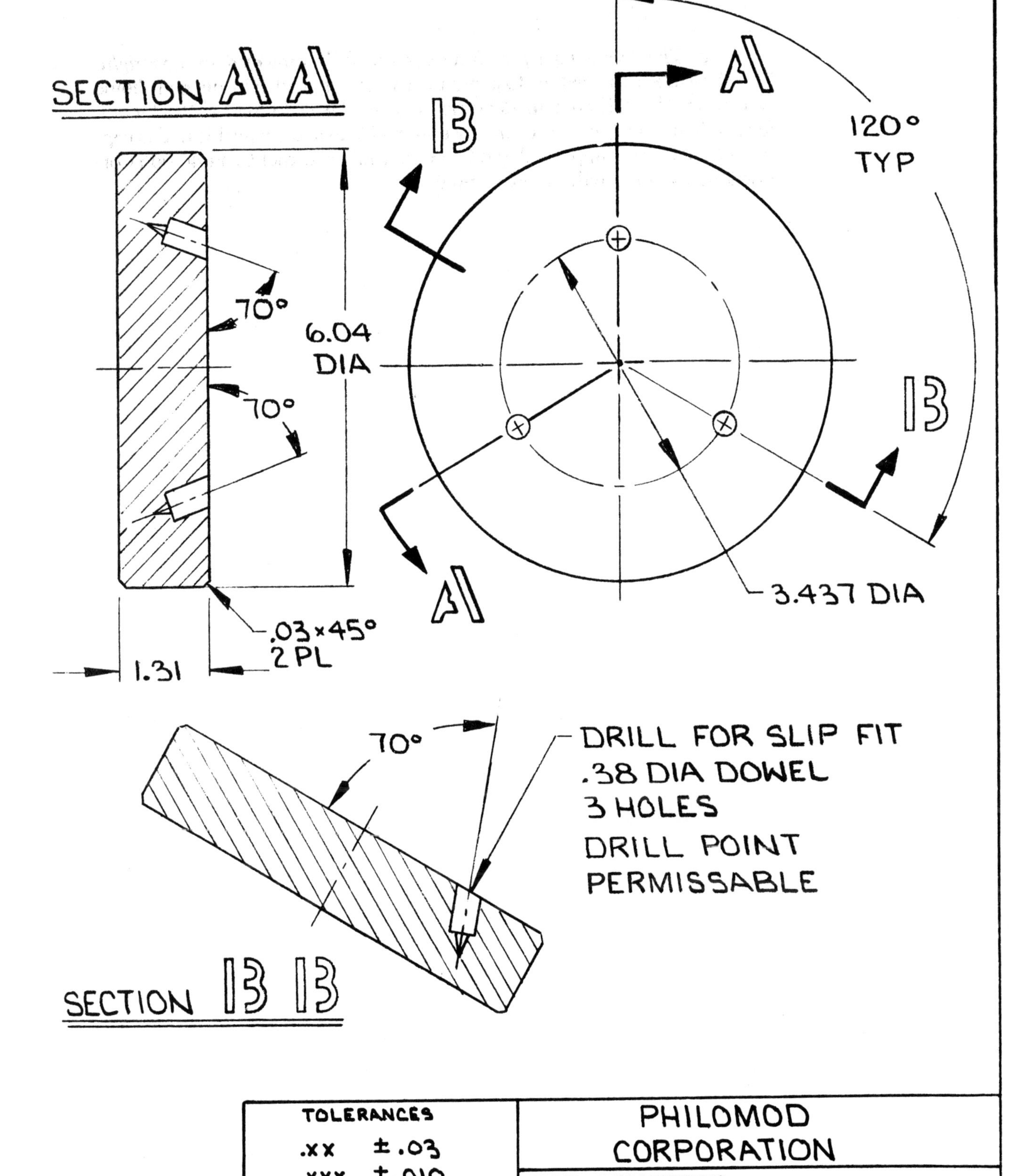

TOLERANCES		PHILOMOD CORPORATION		
.XX ±.03				
.XXX ±.010		PART DESCRIPTION		
∠ ±1°30'		PIECE 1		
MATL BIRCH OR MAPLE		DRAWN BY J. O'CONNELL	DATE 3·10·86	
		DWG NO 0000001		REV A
FINISH		SCALE 1/2	SHEET 1 OF 1	

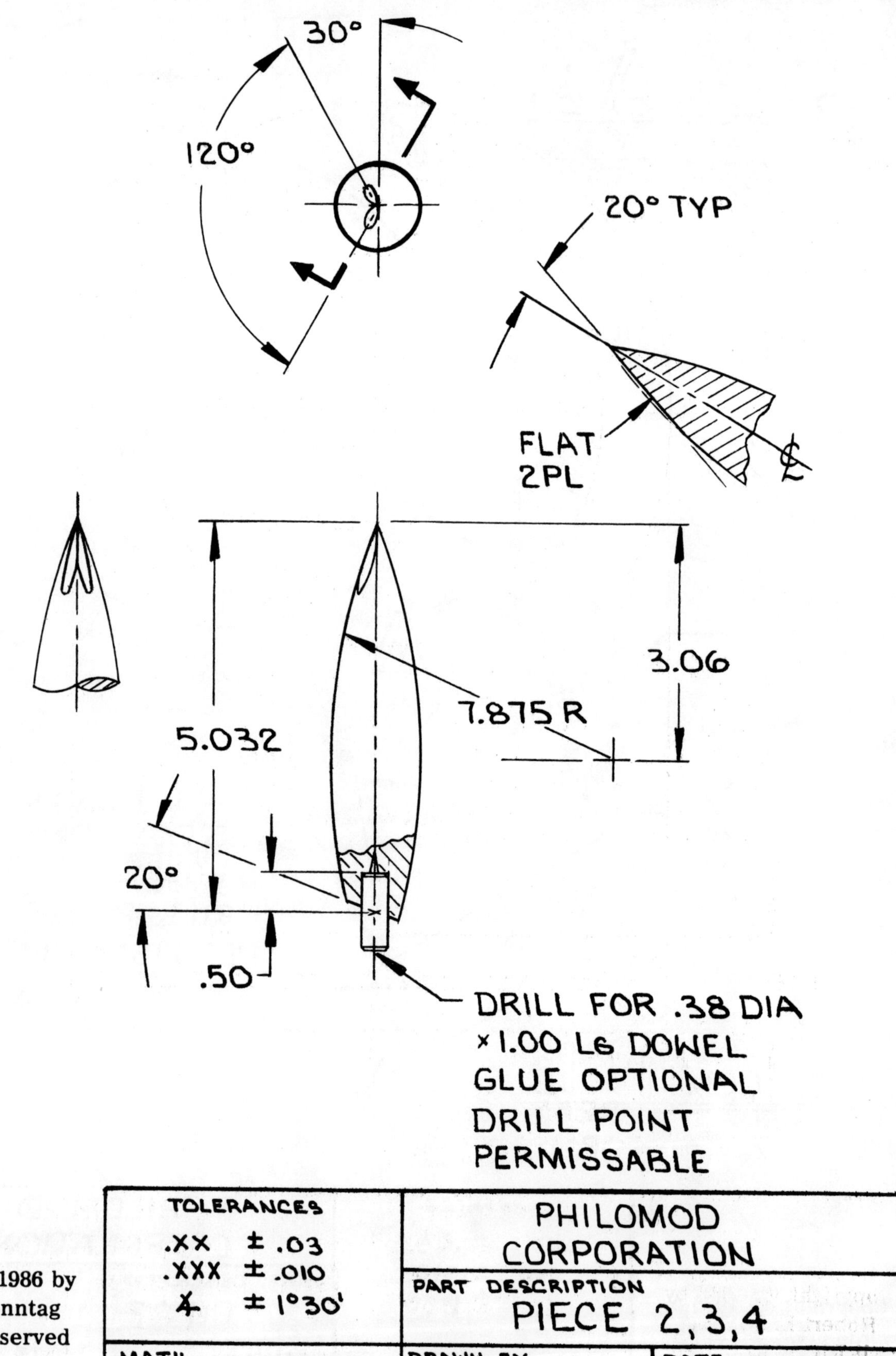

TOLERANCES	PHILOMOD CORPORATION	
.XX ± .03		
.XXX ± .010	PART DESCRIPTION	
∡ ± 1°30'	PIECE 2, 3, 4	
MAT'L. BIRCH OR MAPLE	DRAWN BY J. O'Connell	DATE 3·10·86
	DRAWING Nº 0000234	REV A
FINISH	SCALE 1/2	SHEET 1 OF 1

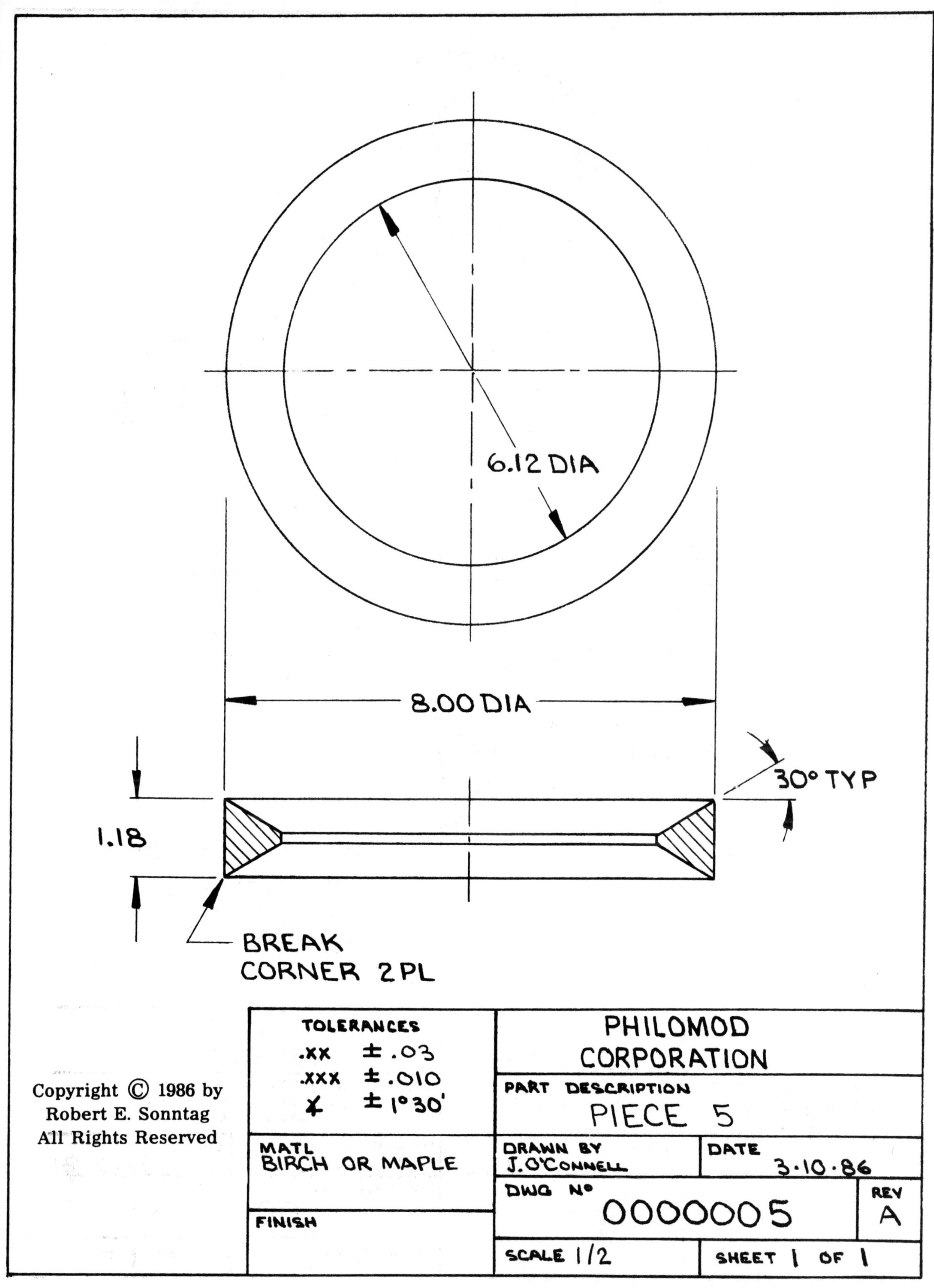

6.12 DIA
8.00 DIA
30° TYP
1.18
BREAK
CORNER 2 PL
TOLERANCES
.XX   ± .03
.XXX   ± .010
∡   ± 1°30'
MATL
BIRCH OR MAPLE
FINISH
PHILOMOD
CORPORATION
PART DESCRIPTION
PIECE 5
DRAWN BY
J. O'CONNELL
DATE
3·10·86
DWG N°
0000005
REV
A
SCALE 1/2
SHEET 1 OF 1

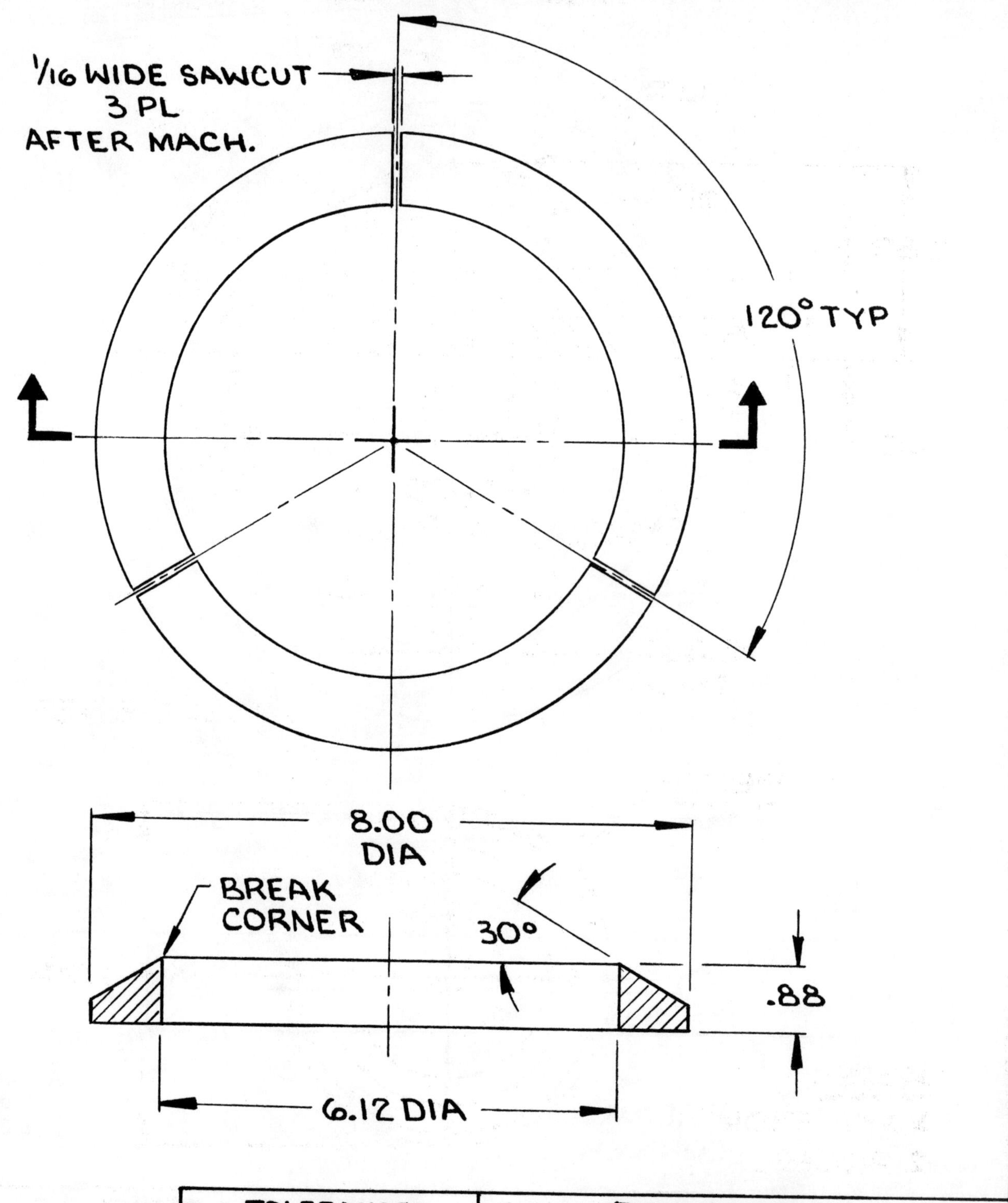

1/16 WIDE SAWCUT
3 PL
AFTER MACH.
120° TYP
8.00
DIA
BREAK
CORNER
30°
.88
6.12 DIA
TOLERANCES
.XX ± .03
.XXX ± .010
∡ ± 1°30'
PHILOMOD
CORPORATION
PART DESCRIPTION
PIECE 6
MATL
BIRCH OR MAPLE
DRAWN BY
J. O'CONNELL
DATE
3·10·86
DWG NO.
0000006
REV
A
FINISH
SCALE 1/2
SHEET 1 OF 1

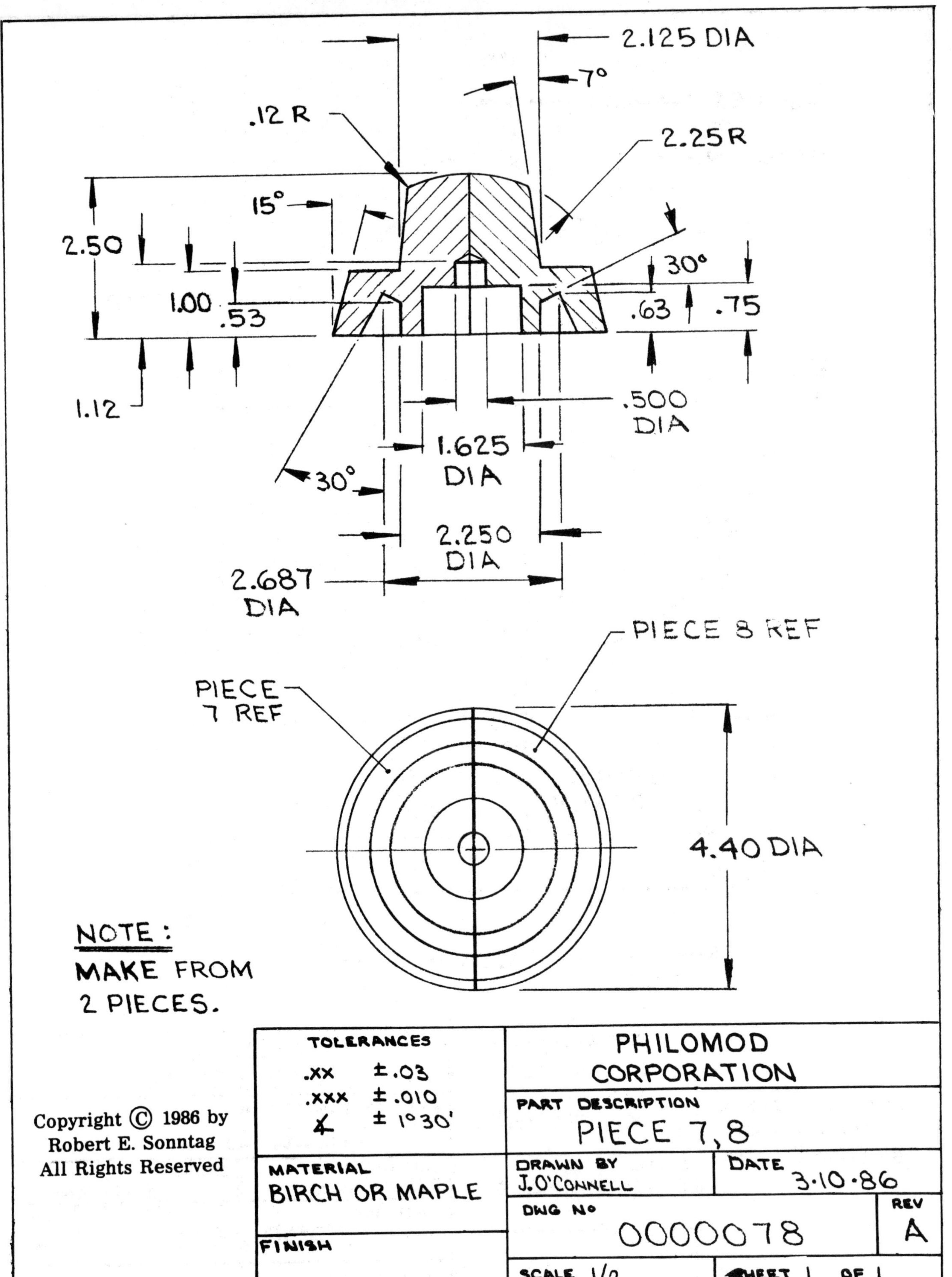

2.125 DIA
7°
.12 R
2.25 R
15°
2.50
30°
1.00
.53
.63
.75
1.12
.500
DIA
30°
1.625
DIA
2.250
DIA
2.687
DIA
PIECE 8 REF
PIECE 7 REF
4.40 DIA
NOTE :
MAKE FROM
2 PIECES.
TOLERANCES
.XX   ±.03
.XXX   ±.010
∠   ± 1° 30'
MATERIAL
BIRCH OR MAPLE
FINISH
PHILOMOD
CORPORATION
PART DESCRIPTION
PIECE 7,8
DRAWN BY
J. O'CONNELL
DATE
3·10·86
DWG NO
0000078
REV
A
SCALE 1/2
SHEET 1 OF 1

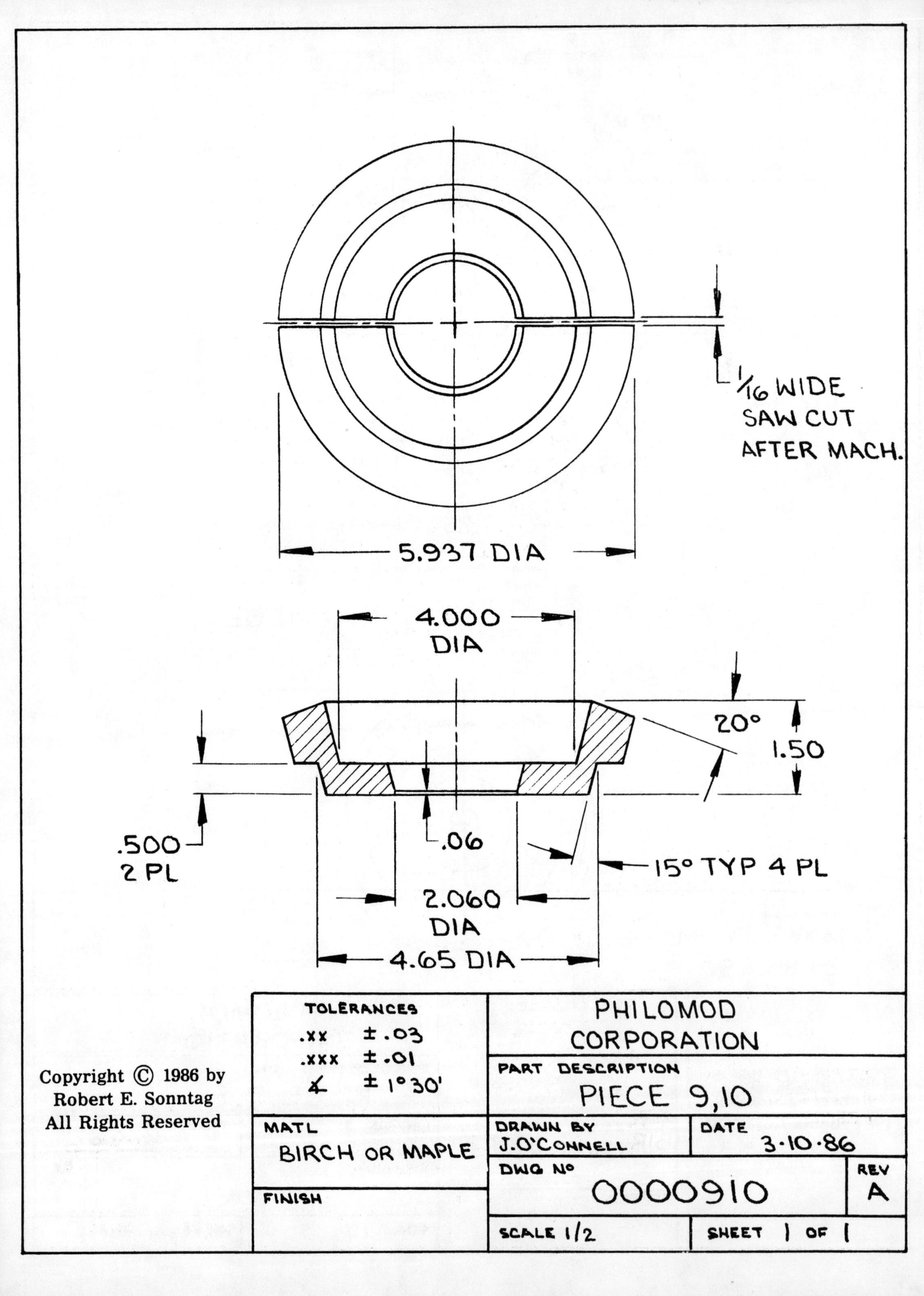

5.937 DIA
1/16 WIDE SAW CUT AFTER MACH.
4.000 DIA
20°
1.50
.500 2 PL
.06
15° TYP 4 PL
2.060 DIA
4.65 DIA
TOLERANCES
.XX   ± .03
.XXX   ± .01
∠   ± 1°30'
MATL
BIRCH OR MAPLE
FINISH
PHILOMOD CORPORATION
PART DESCRIPTION
PIECE 9,10
DRAWN BY
J. O'CONNELL
DATE
3·10·86
DWG Nº
0000910
REV
A
SCALE 1/2
SHEET 1 OF 1

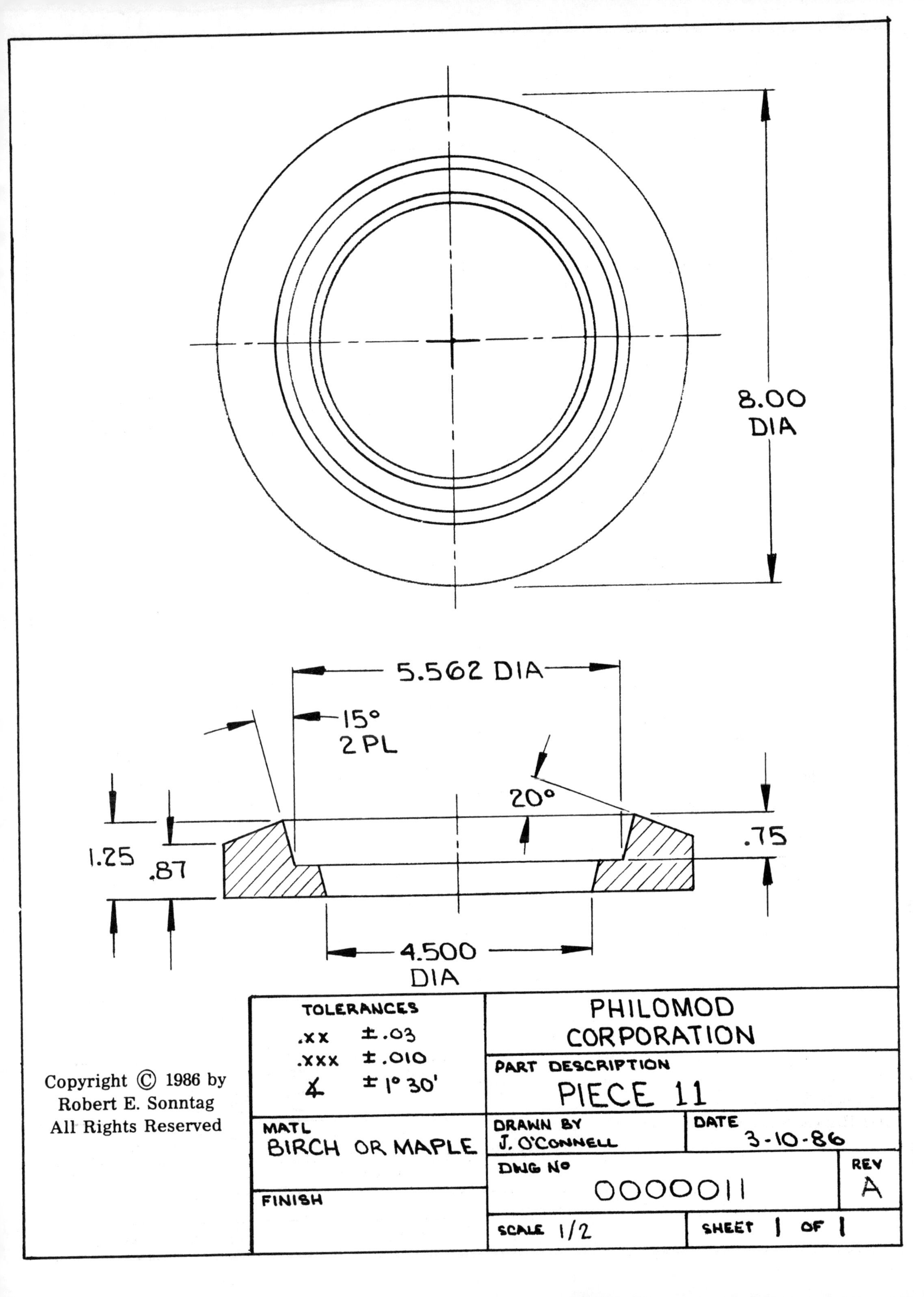

8.00
DIA
5.562 DIA
15°
2 PL
20°
.75
1.25
.87
4.500
DIA
TOLERANCES
.XX   ±.03
.XXX   ±.010
∠   ±1° 30'
MATL
BIRCH OR MAPLE
FINISH
PHILOMOD
CORPORATION
PART DESCRIPTION
PIECE 11
DRAWN BY
J. O'CONNELL
DATE
3-10-86
DWG NO
0000011
REV
A
SCALE 1/2
SHEET 1 OF 1

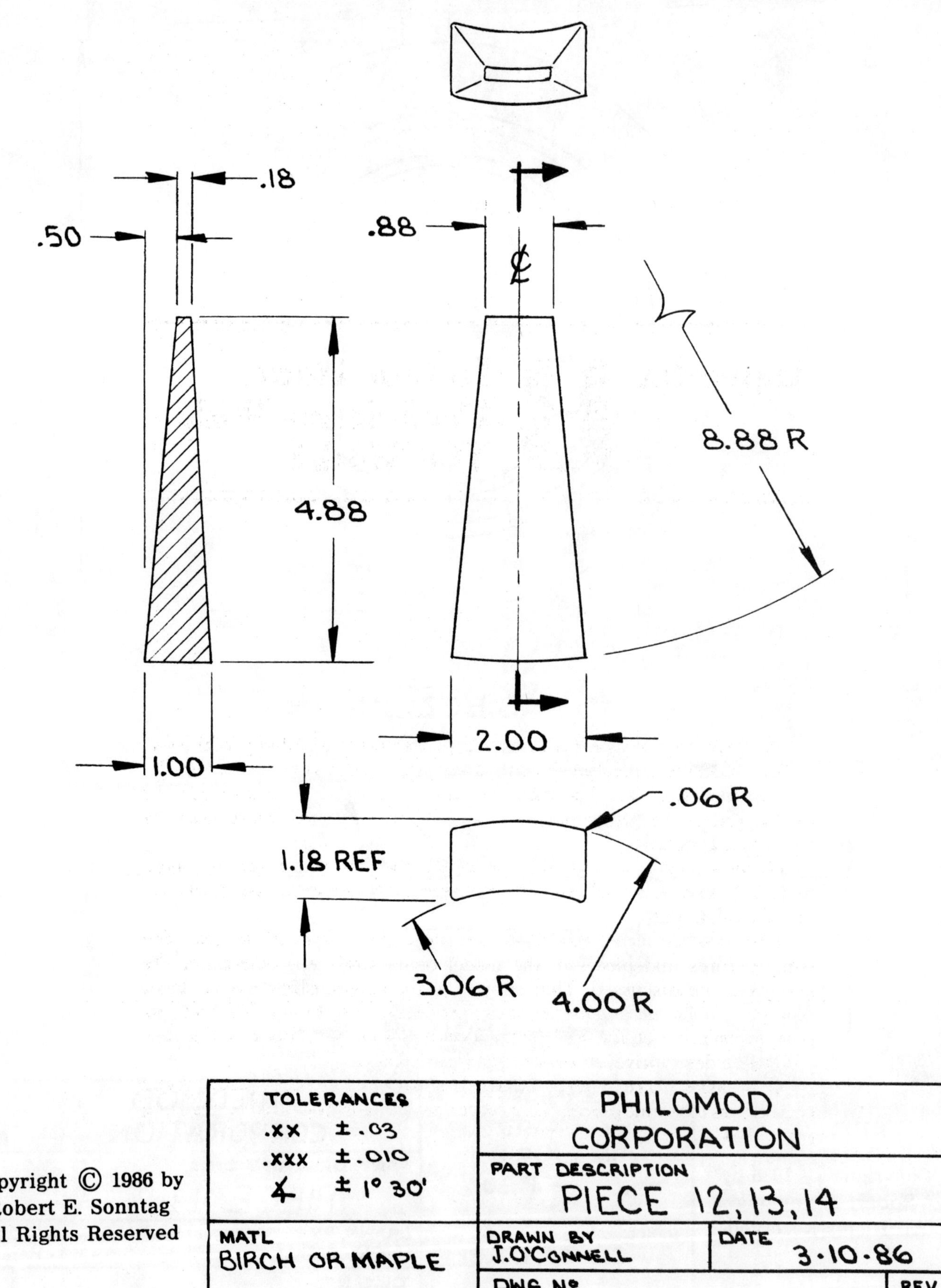

TOLERANCES		PHILOMOD CORPORATION	
.XX ±.03			
.XXX ±.010		PART DESCRIPTION	
∡ ±1° 30'		PIECE 12,13,14	
MATL BIRCH OR MAPLE		DRAWN BY J.O'CONNELL	DATE 3·10·86
		DWG № 0121314	REV A
FINISH		SCALE 1/2	SHEET 1 OF 1

Appendix B — In One Hour, Proficiency With The Model

We have been accused of inventing an executive plaything. While our wooden model is indeed pleasing in appearance and fascinating to handle, it is anything but a toy. The Philomod model is an efficient training aid. It works. The entrepreneur or executive who uses it soon appreciates its features and benefits.

(As we stated in the introduction to this book, we will make the 8-inch wooden Philomod model available commercially as soon as our book creates the demand.)

The presence of the model sets the stage for serious discussion. The substructures and pieces of the model define and departmentalize the subject to be discussed. That subject is the relationships among basic *economic, political,* and *management* principles. Used with this book, its companion product, the model introduces a new nomenclature—more precise, more descriptive, more objective, less emotional.

It is easiest to remember the numbers and names of the pieces if one remembers that nine pieces of the model deal with antithetical or *opposing* principles.

First, the model defines the six *economic* principles. These are the round legs, pieces 2, 3, and 4; and the square legs, pieces 12, 13, and 14:

- Piece 2, Freedom to Own private and productive property is the *opposite* of Piece 12, Public Ownership of productive property and the restrictions upon private ownership.
- Piece 3, Freedom to Exchange in competitive markets is the *opposite* of Piece 13, Controlled Exchange in markets that restrict freedom of entry.
- Piece 4, Freedom to Fund, or Voluntary Funding, is the *opposite* of Piece 14, Mandatory Funding, Taxation, or Inflation of the currency.

Second are the three *political* principles in the substructure made up of pieces 1, 5, and 6:

- Piece 1, Freedom to Choose is the *opposite* of Piece 5, Force, or Centralized Governmental Power.
- Piece 5, Centralized Governmental Power, is the *opposite* of Piece 6, Limitation and Dispersion of Governmental Power.
- Piece 6 protects Individual Freedom, Piece 1, by *opposing* Piece 5.

Third are the *cooperating* pieces.

The *management* principles are familiar to the entrepreneur or manager who works with them every day. These are the five pieces in the substructure at the top of the Philomod model—Pieces 7 through 11—that represent the operating organization. These pieces do *not* represent opposing principles. The enterprise succeeds only through the *cooperative interaction* of these pieces:

- Piece 7, Creativity and Innovation, is the big idea that will lead to Piece 11, and also includes all supporting ideas needed to reach that point.
- Piece 8, Management, implements the big idea through the interaction of people and the optimal mix of the property resources at hand.
- Piece 9, People Resources, produces, in concert with Piece 10, Property Resources:
- Piece 11, the Profitable Good or Service—the linchpin that holds the structure together.

Finally, we have the *synergistic*, cooperative action of the three round legs and the three square legs on their respective bases:

- Pieces 1, 2, 3, and 4 give strength to one another. These are the basic principles of the free market.
- Pieces 5, 12, 13, and 14 provide interdependent support to one another. These define the ideology that is the soul of the anti-market.
- These AM and FM substructures oppose each other, thus defining the never-ending AM/FM conflict.

When the executive or manager first removes the model from its shipping carton, he should handle all the pieces. As he does so—recalling the number and name of each—he will grow more confident that his memory can indeed retain the basic nomenclature.

His next step is to put flesh on the bones of the skeletal structure—to become comfortable with the meanings of the pieces. This step is best taken with a friend or peer *who has also completed the book*. The atmosphere should be mutually supportive. This is a learning process. Critiques should be saved for later! Within an hour, the two will feel their enthusiasm building! Both are on their way to becoming "free-market teachers."

When the "teacher" is with one "student," one Philomod model will serve the purpose for illustration and discussion. *Both* persons should have completed the book *Structures*. Both persons should handle the model. With a group of ten—an ideal number for good conference communication—three or four models work quite well. Best results will be obtained if each person has his own model to handle. *All, of course, should have completed reading the book beforehand.*

Perhaps the most useful function of the Philomod model is that it keeps attention focused on basics. The model is indispensible in maintaining "classroom control." The teacher uses the model to establish the boundaries for discussion. The model is used to keep discussion from wandering too far afield.

In particular, the model—with its newer, more precise nomenclature—helps control political discussion. Political matters can become emotionally charged. Our model reduces the chances of the disruptiveness of "conservative or liberal" labels, or "partisan" or "ism" labels. This book has deliberately avoided the use of all such labels.

By doing the same, the teacher will be able to *lead his class, maintain his impartiality*, and *increase his credibility*.

Appendix C Five Mentors Upon Whose Ideas These Structures Are Built

FOR POLITICAL PRINCIPLES

Thomas Jefferson (1743—1826)

Born in Shadwell, Virginia. College of William and Mary, 1762. Governor of Virginia, minister to France, first secretary of state, second vice president, third president. Author of the Declaration of Independence and the Virginia Statute for Religious Freedom. Founder of the University of Virginia.

James Madison (1751—1836)

Born in Port Conway, Virginia. Princeton University, 1771. Chief recorder, Constitutional Convention, 1787, thus often called "Father of the Constitution." House of Representatives, 1789. Secretary of State under Jefferson. Fourth president.

FOR ECONOMIC PRINCIPLES

Friedrich A. Hayek (1899—   )

Born in Vienna, Austria. University of Vienna, doctor of law, 1921. Doctor of political science, 1926. First Austrian minister of economics.

Professor of social and moral sciences, University of Chicago, 1950. Professor emeritus, University of Freiburg and the University of Chicago. Nobel laureate in Economics, 1974. Head of the "Austrian School." Author of: *The Road to Serfdom,* 1944. *The Constitution of Liberty,* 1960. *Studies in Philosophy, Politics and Economics,* 1967. *Law, Legislation and Liberty,* in three volumes, 1973, 1976, and 1980. Currently resides in Salzburg, Austria.

Milton Friedman (1912–   )

Born in Brooklyn, New York. Rutgers University, 1936; Ph.D. in Economics, Columbia University, 1946. Professor of economics, University of Chicago for thirty years until 1977. Nobel laureate in Economics, 1976. Head of the "Chicago School." Senior research fellow, Stanford University's Hoover Institute. Author of (with Rose Friedman): *Capitalism and Freedom,* 1962. *Free to Choose,* 1979. Currently resides in San Francisco and Ely, Vermont.

FOR MANAGEMENT PRINCIPLES

Peter F. Drucker (1909–   )

Born in Vienna, Austria. Economist, educated in Austria and England. Professor of management, Graduate Business School, New York University, 1950-1972. Since 1971, Clarke Professor of social science, Claremont Graduate School, Claremont, California. "The dean of American business management consultants." Frequent editorial contributor, *The Wall Street Journal.* Author of twenty-five books, among which: *The Practice of Management,* 1954. *Management: Tasks, Responsibilities, Practices,* 1973. Currently resides in Claremont, California.

In our first mail-order catalog, we want to include only the products you want most. Assuming our prices will be competitive, please help us by ranking your choice of the top five items. Place a "5" by your first choice, a "4" by your second choice, and so on through your fifth choice, which would be a "1". As soon as our catalog is ready, we will send you a free copy, along with a free supply of Freepod decals.

___ Our book, *Structures*, hard cover
___ Wooden Philomod, 8-inch diameter
___ Custom leather attache case for the 8-inch Philomod
___ Our vest-pocket sterling silver Philomod, 2-inch diameter
___ Our introductory 128-page *Structures* comic book
___ Program, 5¼-inch disk, How To Develop An AM/FM Database
___ Our movie-length *Structures* videocassette
___ Our audio-cassette *Structures*
___ Our enlarged CC/CP Grid, 17 by 22 inches
___ Men's Freepod neckties (navy, maroon, green, or gold)
___ Ladies' silk scarves, same color options plus others
___ Postcards and Christmas cards
___ Window decals and bumper stickers
___ Lapel pin, gold-filled or silver
___ Our Freepod front-license tag for your car
___ Our durable Freepod flags, 8 by 12 inches or 3 by 5 feet
___ Personalized address labels with the Freepod
___ Personalized memo pads with the Freepod
___ Our first-quality knit sport shirts, many colors and sizes
___ Our hats, caps and visors for sports, men's and ladies'
___ Embroidered Freepod patch, gold on navy, 3-inch diameter
___ *Structures* jigsaw puzzle
___ *Structures* board game
___ Video game, Invasion of the Forcemodes!

As we produce our videotape version of *Structures*, we want to clarify concepts that may have been unclear in the book. Any suggestions?

FOR AN EXCLUSIVE DISTRIBUTORSHIP

Would you like information on, and an application for a PHILOMOD CORPORATION DISTRIBUTORSHIP? If yes, please describe the territory you would be interested in. The territory should have a population of approximately 1 million. (Applicants for territories outside the states of Florida and California should not expect to be contacted prior to 1987.)

City:____

State:____

Number of Counties in Area Desired:______________________________

Approximate Population of Total Area Desired:_______________________

First Three Digits of Zip Codes of Area:___________________________

FOR A LICENSING AGREEMENT

If you are a manufacturer, would you be interested in receiving information on, and an application for, a PHILOMOD CORPORATION LICENSING AGREEMENT? If yes, please describe products of your manufacture that you believe would fit into and support our product line.

THANK YOU!

Please mail to:
PHILOMOD CORPORATION
P.O. Box 31339, Yukon Station
Jacksonville, Florida 32230

Your Name:____

Company:____

Address:____

City, State, Zip:____

Appendix D   This is a Questionnaire, Not an Order Form

In our first mail-order catalog, we want to include only the products you want most. Assuming our prices will be competitive, please help us by ranking your choice of the top five items. Place a "5" by your first choice, a "4" by your second choice, and so on through your fifth choice, which would be a "1". As soon as our catalog is ready, we will send you a free copy, along with a free supply of Freepod decals.

__ Our book, *Structures*, hard cover
__ Wooden Philomod, 8-inch diameter
__ Custom leather attache case for the 8-inch Philomod
__ Our vest-pocket sterling silver Philomod, 2-inch diameter
__ Our introductory 128-page *Structures* comic book
__ Program, 5¼-inch disk, How To Develop An AM/FM Database
__ Our movie-length *Structures* videocassette
__ Our audio-cassette *Structures*
__ Our enlarged CC/CP Grid, 17 by 22 inches
__ Men's Freepod neckties (navy, maroon, green, or gold)
__ Ladies' silk scarves, same color options plus others
__ Postcards and Christmas cards
__ Window decals and bumper stickers
__ Lapel pin, gold-filled or silver
__ Our Freepod front-license tag for your car
__ Our durable Freepod flags, 8 by 12 inches or 3 by 5 feet
__ Personalized address labels with the Freepod
__ Personalized memo pads with the Freepod
__ Our first-quality knit sport shirts, many colors and sizes
__ Our hats, caps and visors for sports, men's and ladies'
__ Embroidered Freepod patch, gold on navy, 3-inch diameter
__ *Structures* jigsaw puzzle
__ *Structures* board game
__ Video game, Invasion of the Forcemodes!

As we produce our videotape version of *Structures*, we want to clarify concepts that may have been unclear in the book. Any suggestions?

FOR AN EXCLUSIVE DISTRIBUTORSHIP

Would you like information on, and an application for a PHILOMOD CORPORATION DISTRIBUTORSHIP? If yes, please describe the territory you would be interested in. The territory should have a population of approximately 1 million. (Applicants for territories outside the states of Florida and California should not expect to be contacted prior to 1987.)

City:____

State:____

Number of Counties in Area Desired:_________________________

Approximate Population of Total Area Desired:_________________

First Three Digits of Zip Codes of Area:_____________________

FOR A LICENSING AGREEMENT

If you are a manufacturer, would you be interested in receiving information on, and an application for, a PHILOMOD CORPORATION LICENSING AGREEMENT? If yes, please describe products of your manufacture that you believe would fit into and support our product line.

THANK YOU!

Please mail to:
PHILOMOD CORPORATION
P.O. Box 31339, Yukon Station
Jacksonville, Florida 32230

Your Name:____

Company:____

Address:____

City, State, Zip:____

Notes

CHAPTER 1

p. 12   (CC-1) von Mises, Ludwig. *Human Action*. (Chicago: Henry Regnery Company, 1963), p. 13.

p. 12   (CC-1) Drucker, Peter F. *The Practice of Management*. (New York: Harper & Brothers, 1954), p. 60.

p. 13   (CC-2) Drucker, Peter F. *Management Tasks, Responsibilities, Practices*. (New York: Harper & Row, 1973), p. 473: "A decision without an alternative is a desperate gambler's throw ... Without such an alternative, one is likely to flounder dismally when reality proves a decision to be inoperative."

p. 15   (CC-3) Greenberg, Dr. Herbert M. A study, Marketing Survey and Research Corporation, Princeton, N.J.

p. 16   (CC-3) Biracree, Tom. *How You Rate. For Women*. (New York: Dell Publishing Co., Inc., 1984).

p. 16   (CC-3) Brown, Rex V., et al. *Decision Analysis, An Overview*. (New York: Holt, Rinehart and Winston, 1974), p. 4.

p. 17   (CC-4) See also: von Mises. *Human Action*. p. 97: "What gratifies less is abandoned in order to attain something that pleases more. That which is abandoned is called the price paid for the attainment of the end sought. The value of the price paid is called costs. Costs are equal to the value attached to the satisfaction which one must forego in order to attain the end aimed at."

p. 20   (CC-5) See Hayek, Friedrich A. *The Constitution of Liberty*. (Chicago: Henry Regnery Co., 1960), p. 13. Our freedom to act according to our subjective value preferences is basic. Hayek writes: "Whether he is free or not does not depend on the range of choice but on whether he can expect to shape his course of action in accordance with his present intentions, or whether somebody else has power so to manipulate the conditions as to make him act according to that person's will rather than his own."

p. 20   (CC-5) Ibid, p. 79. "The recognition that each person has his own scale of values which we ought to respect, even if we do not approve of it, is part of the conception of the value of the individual personality."

p. 20   (CC-5) von Mises. *Human Action*. p. 19: "Since nobody is in a position to substitute his own value judgments for those of the acting individual, it is vain to pass judgement on other people's aims and volitions. No man is qualified to declare what would make another man happier or less discontented."

p. 20   (CC-5) And this from Harper, F.A. *An Introduction to Value Theory*. (Menlo Park, CA: Institute for Humane Studies, 1974), p. 7. "The first step in understanding the Austrian concept is to realize that value is entirely subjective, rather than something objective. Value, therefore, is something that each individual person weighs on purely private, not a public, set of scales .... To illustrate, age in cheese or in eggs adds value for some persons in the world and detracts from their value for others."

p. 20   (CC-6) Drucker. *Practice of Management*. p. 359.

p. 21   (CC-6) See Williams, Roger J. *You Are Extra-Ordinary*. (New York: Pyramid Books, 1967), p. 235: "A nationally prominent businessman with many diverse successes to his credit told me, 'When you are fifty-five per cent sure, it is time to act. If you wait until you are ninety-five per cent sure, the show is all over.'"

p. 21   (CC-6) Downs, Anthony. *Inside Bureaucracy*. (Boston: Little, Brown & Company, 1967), p. 3.

p. 22   (CC-7) Viscott, David, M.D. *Risking*. (New York: Simon and Shuster, 1977), p. 56.

p. 23   (CC-7) See Hayek. *Constitution of Liberty.* p. 18: "Liberty does not mean all good things or the absence of all evils. It is true that to be free may mean freedom to starve, to make costly mistakes or to run mortal risks."

p. 23   (CC-7) See Hayek. *Constitution of Liberty.* p. 29: "Liberty is esssential in order to leave room for the unforseeable and unpredictable ..." and "Our necessary ignorance of so much means that we have to deal largely with probabilities and chances."

p. 24   (CC-7) Knight, Frank H. *Risk, Uncertainty and Profit.* (Chicago: University of Chicago Press, 1971), p. 47.

Ibid, p. 282: "Most decisions calling for the exercise of judgment in business or responsible life in any field involve factors not subject to estimate and which no one makes any pretense of estimating."

Knight also believed that the entrepreneurial system is best equipped to handle risks: "It is fundamental to the entrepreneur system that it tends to promote better management in addition to consolidating risks and throwing them into the hands of those most disposed to assume them." p. 260.

p. 24   (CC-7) I have not touched upon the risks in various forms of gambling. See Bowyer, J. Barton. *Cheating.* (New York: St. Martin's Press, 1982), pp. 273-279: "When one gambles against the 'house' at casinos, fairgrounds, carnivals, race tracks, public club houses, with bookies, or at charity bazaars, one must pay the edge." Here are house percentages on a few of the popular forms: Money Craps: 1 percent, Blackjack: 2 percent, Bingo: 10 to 30 percent, Harness Racing: 13 to 20 percent, Horse Racing: 18 percent, The Numbers: 51 to 61 percent, Football Pools: 60 percent, Baseball Pool Cards: 80 percent, and Three-Card Monte: 100 percent.

p. 24   (CC-8) Hazlitt, Henry. *Economics In One Lesson.* (New York: Harper and Brothers, 1946), p.5.

p. 26   (CC-9) Hayek. *Constitution.* p. 71.

p. 26   (CC-9) Ibid, p. 77. "The complementarity of liberty and responsibility means that the argument for liberty can apply only to those who can be held responsible. It cannot apply to infants, idiots, or the insane. It presupposes that a person is capable of learning from experience and of guiding his actions by knowledge thus acquired; it is invalid for those who have not yet learned enough or are incapable of learning."

p. 26   (CC-9) Viscott. *Risking.* p. 123.

p. 27   (CC-10) is closely related to (CC-8). The secondary consequences of an action which was taken years earlier may make it very difficult to reverse the process. Social security, for example, enacted in the 1930s as supplemental income in old age, has become the sole source for many fifty years later. A reversible decision early on, now a virtually irreversible one.

p. 28   Hayek, Friedrich A. *Law, Legislation and Liberty,* Vol. 1. (Chicago: University of Chicago Press, 1973), p. 18.

p. 29   Drucker. *Practice of Management.*

p. 29   Mises. *Human Action.* p. 14: "In colloquial speech we call a man 'happy' who has succeeded in attaining his ends. A more adequate description of his state would be that he is happier than he was before."

p. 29   For an instructive book on adult decision making: Rubin, Theodore Isaac, M.D. *The Eight Stages of Effective Decision-Making.* (New York: Harper & Row, 1984).

p. 31   Clabby, John and Elias, Maurice. *Teach Your Child Decision Making.* (New York: Doubleday Publishing, 1986) For children ages 4 and up, a fine book on decision making.

p. 32   Drucker. *Practice.* p. 359 and 362

p. 32   Drucker. *Practice.* p.364

p. 32   Drucker. *Management.* p. 480.

p. 33   Drucker. *Practice.* p. 361.

CHAPTER 2

p. 37   Lippmann, Walter. *Public Opinion.* (New York: The Free Press, The MacMillan Company, 1922). p. 11.

p. 42   *Forbes Magazine,* Dec. 3, 1984.

p. 44   See de Bono, Edward. *New Think.* (New York: Avon Books, 1967), p. 115: "One technique for avoiding the rigidity of words is to think in terms of visual images and not use words at all. It is perfectly possible to think coherently in this way and difficulty only arises when it is necessary to express what has been thought. Unfortunately not many people are good at thinking visually and not all situations can be examined in terms of visual images. Nevertheless it is a habit well worth acquiring for visual images have a fluidity and plasticity that words can never achieve."

p. 45   Peters, Thomas J. and Waterman, Robert H., Jr. *In Search of Excellence.* (New York: Warner Books, 1982), p. 106-107: "We need new language. We need to consider adding terms to our management vocabulary… More important still, we need new metaphors and models to stitch these terms together into a single, coherent, memorable whole."

CHAPTER 3

p. 49   Friedman, Milton. *Capitalism and Freedom.* (Chicago: University of Chicago Press, 1962), p. 15.

p. 55   Kohr, Leopold. Essay, "Property and Freedom." from *Property In A Humane Economy.* Blumenfeld, Samuel L., Editor. (LaSalle, IL: Open Court Publishing, 1974), p. 51.

p. 55   See also: Dietze, Gottfried. *In Defense of Property.* (Baltimore: Johns Hopkins University Press, 1971), for the clerical defenses of property: in the Catholic church by St. Thomas and other theologians who followed; in the Protestant thinking after the Reformation; in the Lutheran creed and, of course, Calvin: "The protection of private property was supported by other groups, such as Baptists, Mennonites, Quakers, Pietists, and Methodists."

p. 56   LeFevre, Robert, *The Philosophy of Ownership.* (Santa Ana, CA: Rampart College, 1966). I have quoted generously from this well-written book, and I recommend it highly. It is available from Rampart College, 104 W. Fourth Street, Santa Ana, CA 92701.

p. 58   Rothbard, Murray. Essay, "Justice and Property Rights." *Property In A Humane Economy.* p.109.

p. 62   Nozick, Robert. *Anarchy, State and Utopia.* (New York: Basic Books, 1974), p. 281-282.

p. 63   Kohr. *Property and Freedom.* p. 49.

p. 63   Ibid, p. 50

p. 64   Friedman, Milton. *Capitalism and Freedom.* p. 15.

p. 65   Hayek, Friedrich A. *The Road to Serfdom.* (Chicago: University of Chicago Press, 1944), p. 103.

p. 67   See Friedman, Milton. *Capitalism and Freedom*. pp. 14-15: "So long as effective freedom of exchange is maintained, the central feature of the market organization of economic activity is that it prevents one person from interfering with another in respect of most of his activities. The consumer is protected from coercion by the seller because of the presence of other sellers with whom he can deal. The seller is protected from coercion by the consumer because of other consumers to whom he can sell ... Indeed, a major source of objection to a free economy is precisely that it does this task so well. It gives people what they want instead of what a particular group thinks they ought to want. Underlying most arguments against the free market is a lack of belief in freedom itself."

p. 68   See Rothbard, Murray N. *Power and Market*. (Menlo Park, CA: Institute for Humane Studies, 1970), p. 12: "Before the development of economic science, people thought of exchange and the market as always benefiting one party at the expense of the other. This was the root of the mercantilist view of the market. Economics has shown that this is a fallacy, for on the market both parties to any exchange benefit."

p. 68   See Harper. *An Introduction to Value Theory*. p. 10. "In economic terms, an exchange yields a profit to both exchangers ... The other side of that coin— that value, being the person's subjective appraisal, cannot be objectively determined— is that it is not the proper concern of any other person ... By the same reasoning, every compulsory or involuntary exchange, where one person confiscates the goods or services of another or dictates the terms of the exchange under force or the threat of force, entails an economic loss for the unwilling participant. Economically as well as morally, all such transactions are the same as outright theft."

p. 73   For a crisp definition of competition, see Kirzner, Israel M. *Competition and Entrepreneurship*. (Chicago: University of Chicago Press, 1973), p. 122: "Competition, in this process, consists of perceiving possibilities of offering opportunities to other market participants which are more attractive than those currently being made available. It is an essentially 'rivalrous' process (to adopt Kuenne's term); it consists not of market participants' reacting passively to given conditions, but of their actively grasping profit opportunities by positively changing the existing conditions."

p. 73   See Hayek. *Constitution*. p. 37. "The competition upon which the process of selection rests must be understood in the widest sense. It involves competition between organized and unorganized groups no less than competition between individuals."

p. 73   Kirzner. *Competition and Entrepreneurship*. Chapter Three: Competition and Monopoly. pp. 88-134.

p. 76   Nozick. *Anarchy, State and Utopia*. p. 256.

CHAPTER 4

p. 81   "A whole," Aristotle wrote, "consists of a beginning, a middle, and an end." Piece 7 is the beginning. Pieces 8, 9 and 10 are the middle. Piece 11 is the end.

p. 85   Downs. *Inside Bureaucracy*. p.23.

p. 87   Wright, David McCord. *Capitalism*. (Chicago: Henry Regnery Co., 1962), p. 44.

p. 87   Ibid, p. 80.

p. 87   Ibid, p. 43.

p. 87   Ibid, p. 53.

p. 87   de Bono. *New Think*. pp. 210-212.

p. 87   Professor Israel Kirzner is particularly attuned to the mind of the entrepreneur. See his chapter on "Equilibrium vs. Market Process," in Dolan, Edwin G. *The Foundations of Modern Austrian Economics*. (Mission, KS: Sheed and Ward, Inc., 1976), pp. 120-124: "Entrepreneurial knowledge is a rarefied, abstract type of knowledge—the knowledge of where to obtain information (or other resources) and how to deploy it. This entrepreneurial alertness is crucial to the market process. Disequilibrium represents a situation of widespread market ignorance. This ignorance is responsible for the emergence of profitable opportunities. Entrepreneurial alertness exploits these opportunities when other pass them by... We do not clearly understand how entrepreneurs get their flashes of superior foresight. We cannot explain how some men discover what is around the corner before others do .... (It is) perceiving an opportunity waiting to be noticed."

p. 88   Russell, Peter. *The Brain Book*. (New York: Hawthorn Books, Inc., 1979), p. 55.

p. 88   Boorstin, Daniel J. *The Americans, The Democratic Experience*. (New York: Vintage Books, Div. of Random House, 1973), p. 539.

p. 88   McMurray, Robert N. *The Maverick Executive*. (New York: American Management Association, 1974) pp. 26-27, p.71.

p. 91   de Bono. *New Think*. p. 44.

p. 92   Hayek. *Constitution*. p. 33.

p. 94   Williams. *You Are Extra-ordinary*. (New York: Pyramid Books, 1967).

p. 95   Hutchinson, Eliot D. *How to Think Creatively*. (Nashville: Abingdon Press, 1949), pp. 38-40.

p. 96   Russell. *The Brain Book*. p. 56.

p. 96   Another recent and readable book on the brain: Wonder, Jacquelyn, and Donovan, Priscilla. *Whole-Brain Thinking*. (New York: William Morrow & Co., 1984).

p. 96   Barron, Frank. *Creativity and Personal Freedom*. (New York: D. Van Nostrand Company, 1968), p. 208.

p. 96   Ibid, p. 228.

p. 98   Lippmann, Walter. *Public Opinion*. p. 47.

p. 98   Ogilvy, David. *Confessions of An Advertising Man*. (New York: Atheneum, 1963), p. 20.

p. 98   Heinlein, Robert A. *Time Enough For Love*. (New York: G.P. Putnam's Sons, 1973), p. 251.

p. 98   de Bono. *New Think*. p. 139.

p. 99   Sibson, Robert E. *Increasing Employee Productivity*. (New York: American Management Association, 1976), pp. 170-173.

p. 100   Wallechinsky, David, et al. *The Book of Lists*. (New York: Bantam Books, 1978), pp. 241-243.

p. 104   Peters, Thomas J. and Waterman, Robert H., Jr. *In Search of Excellence*. (New York: Warner Books, 1982), p. 206.

p. 105   Ogilvy. *Confessions of An Advertising Man*. p. 21.

p. 105   Robert Fulton is given credit for the first steamboat, but Henry Adams, in his *History of the United States* (Chicago: University of Chicago Press, 1967) pp. 51-52, tells the sad tale of one John Fitch, whose discovery preceded Fulton's by twenty years:

"In 1789, John Fitch—a mechanic, without education or wealth, but with
the energy of genius—invented engine and paddles of his own, with so
much success that during a whole summer Philadelphia watched his ferry-
boat playing daily against the river current. No one denied that his boat
was rapidly, steadily, and regularly moved against wind and tide, with as
much certainty and convenience as could be expected in a first experiment;
yet Fitch's company failed. He could raise no more money; the public
refused to use his boat or help him build a better; they did not want it,
would not believe in it, and broke his heart by their contempt. Fitch strug-
gled against failure, and invented another boat moved by a screw. The
Eastern public still proving indifferent, he wandered to Kentucky, to try
his fortune on the Western waters. Disappointed there, as in Philadelphia
and New York, he made a deliberate attempt to end his life by drink; but
the process proving too slow, he saved twelve opium pills from the physi-
cian's prescription, and was found one morning dead."

p. 106   Wallechinsky. *The Book of Lists.* p. 260.

p. 107   Drucker. *Management.* p. 782.

p. 107   Peters et al. *In Search of Excellence.* p. 206.

p. 107   Ibid, p. 208

p. 108   Ibid, p. 238

p. 109   Downs. *Inside Bureaucracy.*

p. 109   Sibson. *Increasing Employee Productivity.* p. 84.

p. 110   Lipper, Arthur III. *Guide to Investing in Private Companies.* (Home-
wood, Illinois: Dow Jones-Irwin, 1984) p. 8.

p. 110   Drucker recently lent support to this observation. Interviewed by
U.S. News and World Report, "How Entrepreneurs Are Changing U.S. Business," March 28, 1984, he said, "Money is coming out of the woodwork.
Anybody with a track record today of having started two successful new
ventures can get all the money needed in maybe two telephone calls."

p. 112   Lipper. *Guide.* p. 155.

CHAPTER 5

p. 115   Read, Leonard E., editor. *The Free Man's Almanac.* (Irvington-on-
Hudson, N.Y.: Foundation for Economic Education, 1974). p. 199.

p. 115   Forbes, Malcolm, editor. *The Forbes Scrapbook of Thoughts on the
Business of Life.* (New York: B. C. Forbes and Sons Publishing Co., 1968).
p. 465.

p. 116   Adams, Henry. *The History of the United States During the Administrations of Jefferson and Madison.* Abridged and edited by Ernest Samuels. (Chicago: University of Chicago Press, 1967) pp. 106-108.

p. 117   Wright, Esmond. *Fabric of Freedom 1763-1800,* Revised Edition. (New York: Hill and Wang, 1978), pp. 133-135.

p. 118   Koch, Adrienne. *Jefferson.* (Englewood Cliffs, N.J.: Spectrum Books, Prentice-Hall, 1971). p. 68.

p. 118   Adams, Henry. *The History of the United States.* p. 65.

p. 123   Rand, Ayn. *Capitalism: The Unknown Ideal.* (New York: Signet Books, The New American Library, 1967). pp. 322-323. "The concept of individual rights is so new in human history that most men have not grasped it fully to this day.. The Declaration of Independence laid down the principle that 'to secure these rights, governments are instituted among men.' This provided the only valid justification of a government and defined its only proper purpose: to protect man's rights by protecting him from physical violence."

"Thus the government's function was changed from the role of ruler to the role of servant. The government was set to protect man from criminals— and the Constitution was written to protect man from the government. The Bill of Rights was not directed against private citizens, but against the government—as an explicit declaration that individual rights supersede any public or social power."

p. 124   Wright. *Fabric of Freedom.* p. 218.

p. 124   White, Morton. *The Philosophy of the American Revolution.* (New York: Oxford University Press, 1978), p. 8.

p. 124   See also Rand. *Capitalism.* p. 325. "Observe, in this context, the intellectual precision of the Founding Fathers; they spoke of the right to the pursuit of happiness—not of the right of happiness. It means that a man has the right to take the actions he deems necessary to achieve his happiness; it does not mean that others must make him happy."

p. 125   Becker, Carl L. *The Declaration of Independence.* (New York: Vintage Books, Random House, 1958). pp. 62-66.

p. 126   Rossiter, Clinton. 1787, *The Grand Convention.* (New York: Mentor Books, 1966), pp. 53-54.

p. 127   Schlesinger, Arthur M., Jr. *The Almanac of American History.* (New York: Bison Books, G. P. Putnam, 1983).

p. 128   From Wright. *Fabric of Freedom*. Abstracted from Chapter Three, "Riot and Resistance 1764-1774."

p. 128   Adams, Henry. *The History of the United States*. Chapter on "Physical and Economical Conditions."

p. 129   Koch. *Jefferson*. p.42-46.

CHAPTER 6

p. 131   Friedman, Milton. *Capitalism and Freedom*. (Chicago: University of Chicago Press, 1962), p. 201.

p. 131   See Hayek. *The Constitution of Liberty*. p. 13. "This conception of liberty can be made more precise only after we have examined the related concept of coercion."

p. 133   Roche, George Charles III. *Legacy of Freedom*. (Hillsdale, Michigan: Hillsdale College Press, 1973), p. 4.

p. 137   Hayek. *Law, Legislation and Liberty*. p. 62.

p. 137   See von Mises, Ludwig. *Planned Chaos*. (Irvington-on-Hudson, N.Y.: Foundation for Economic Education, 1947). p. 48. "Russia is a comparatively underpopulated country. Its soil is much better endowed by nature than that of any other nation. It offers the most advantageous conditions for the growing of all kinds of cereals, fruits, seeds and plants. Russia owns immense pastures and almost inexhaustible forests. It has the richest resources for the production of gold, silver, platinum, iron, copper, nickel, manganese and all other metals and of oil. But for the despotism of the Czars and the lamentable inadequacy of the communist system its population could long since have enjoyed the highest standard of living. It is certainly not lack of natural resources that pushes Russia toward conquest."

p. 137   Kaiser, Robert G. *Russia, the People and the Power*. (New York: Atheneum, 1976) pp. 350-351

p. 138   Ibid, p. 316, "The Russians also squander their enormous natural wealth. A Soviet newspaper once admitted that of all the timber cut down in the forests, only 30 percent was actually converted into useful products."

p. 138   Mises. *Planned Chaos*. p.81. "If history could prove and teach us anything, it would be that private ownership of the means of production is a necessary requisite of civilization and material well-being. All civilizations have up to now been based on private property. Only nations committed to the principle of private property have risen above penury and produced science, art and literature. There is no experience to show that any other social system could provide mankind with any of the achievements of civilization. Nevertheless, only few people consider this as a sufficient and incontestable refutation of the socialist program."

p. 139   The charts on this page and on p. 154 are based upon data in: *World Military Expenditures and Arms Transfers*, 1972-1982. U.S. Arms Control & Disarmament Agency, Department of State, 1984.

p. 139   *Wall Street Journal*, July 31, 1985. Article on the editorial page, entitled: 19/20 or Swelter: "Until the Carter and Reagan years, federal receipts (taxes) has been roughly 19 percent of GNP, and outlays had been roughly 20 percent of GNP ... During the Carter presidency, spending broke loose from its traditional 20 percent, hitting 23 percent of GNP in Mr. Carter's last fiscal year. By the third year of Mr. Reagan's presidency, with previously legislated entitlements rolling on and the decline in the defense share reversed, spending stood at an astounding 25 percent of GNP."

p. 141   The Department of Energy, formed in 1977 when the squeeze of the OPEC cartel was at its height, can now be dissolved. The oil shortage of 1973 has become the glut of 1986. This is typical of the nature of cartels. They never last. One member gets greedy and breaks the agreed price. From that point, the end of the cartel is a certainty.

p. 144   See Hayek. *Constitution of Liberty*. p. 37. "The argument for liberty is not an argument against organization, which is one of the most powerful means that human reason can employ, but against all exclusive, privileged, monopolistic organization, against the use of coercion to prevent others from trying to do better."

p. 145   Sennholz, Hans F. *Age of Inflation*. (Belmont, Massachusetts: Western Islands, 1979), p.131.

p. 145   See von Mises. *Planned Chaos*. p. 29: "What those who call themselves planners advocate is not the substitution of planned action for letting things go. It is the substitution of the planner's own plan for the plans of his fellow men. The planner is a potential dictator who wants to deprive all other people of the power to plan and act according to their own plans. He aims at one thing only: the exclusive absolute preeminence of his own plan."

p. 145   See Rothbard, Murray N. *Power and Market*. (Menlo Park, California: Institute for Humane Studies, 1970), pp. 154-155. "Mises states, quite rightly, that anyone who advocates governmental dictation over one area of individual consumption must logically come to advocate complete totalitarian dictation over all choices. This follows if the dictators have any set of valuational principles whatever. Thus, if the members of the ruling group like Bach and hate Mozart, and they believe strongly that Mozartian music is immoral, they are just as right in prohibiting the playing of Mozart as they are in prohibiting drug addiction or liquor consumption."

p. 146   See Rothbard, *Power and Market*, p. 31, for fourteen types of monopolistic grants. Briefly, the fourteen are (1) governmentally enforced cartels, (2) virtual cartels, (3) licenses, (4) "quality" standards, (5) tariffs, (6) immigration restrictions, (7) child labor laws, (8) minimum wage laws, (9) maximum hour laws, (10) compulsory unionism, (11) conscription, (12) governmental penalties, i.e., antitrust laws, (13) conservation laws, and (14) patents.

p. 147   See "Dress Codes," *The Boston Globe*, June 26, 1986, p. 77.

p. 147   For a short, clear definition of monopoly, see Kirzner, Israel M. *Competition and Entrepreneurship*. (Chicago: University of Chicago Press, 1973), p. 106: "For us monopoly means the position of a producer who is immune from the threat of other entrepreneurs' doing what he does."

p. 148   Kahn, Herbert L., "State Lotteries: The Only Legal Swindle," *The Wall Street Journal*, April 14, 1984.

p. 148   Bastiat, Frederic. *The Law*. (Irvington-on-Hudson, N.Y.: Foundation for Economic Education, 1977), p. 21.

p. 153   Rothbard calls this the "fatal flaw." See *Man, Economy, and State*, pp. 821-822: "What is this fatal flaw? It is the fact that government can obtain virtually unlimited resources by means of the coercive tax power (i.e., limited only by the total resources of society). Private businesses must obtain their funds from private investors .... Government, however, has no checkrein on itself, i.e., no requirement of meeting a test of profit-and-loss or valued service to consumers, to permit it to obtain funds. Private enterprise can get funds only from satisfied, valuing consumers and from investors guided by present and expected future profits and losses. Government gets more funds at it own whim."

p. 153   Friedman. *Free to Choose*, p.233: "The difference is that a private firm that makes a serious blunder may go out of business. A government agency is likely to get a bigger budget."

p. 155   Rothbard, Murray N. *America's Great Depression*. (Kansas City: Sheed and Ward, Inc., Subsidiary of Universal Press Syndicate, 1975), pp. 303-304.

p. 155   Chart is based upon data from *Historical Statistics of the United States, Colonial Times to 1970*. U.S. Department of Commerce, Bureau of the Census, Vol. 1, p. 244 and Vol. 2, pp. 1114-1115.

p. 156   Chart is based upon data from *Historical Statistics of the United States, Colonial Times to 1970*. U.S. Department of Commerce, Bureau of the Census. Tabular material entitled: "Federal, State, and Local Government Expediture and Governmental Debt: 1902 to 1970," Vol. 2, pp. 1119-1120.

p. 156   As *Structures* was about to go to the publisher, I had the pleasure of seeing the motion picture, *Brazil* (screenplay by Tom Stoppard, et al, directed by Terry Gilliam, released by Universal City Studios, Inc., 1986). *Brazil* is a terrifying update of George Orwell's *1984*, which was written in 1951. The story line shows clearly how terrorism might well be used as the excuse for totalitarian interference with our personal freedoms.

p. 156   Hayek. *Serfdom.* p. 61.

CHAPTER 7

p. 157   Hayek. *Law, Legislation and Liberty.* pp. 56-57.

p. 172   Friedman. *Free to Choose.* p.296.

p. 174   Sennholz, Hans F. *Age of Inflation.* p. 26.

p. 174   Our list, "Preludes to Power" was developed from: von Mises, Ludwig. *The Anti-Capitalistic Mentality.* (South Holland, Illinois: Libertarian Press, 1972).

p. 175   Hayek. *Constitution of Liberty.* p. 21.

p. 175   *Wall Street Journal*, May 9, 1985, "Keeping Our Nation's Streets Safe: Palm Beach Fights Topless Joggers."

p. 177   Downs. *Inside Bureaucracy.* p. 5.

p. 177   Durant, Will. *The Pleasures of Philosophy.* (New York: Simon and Schuster, 1929), p. 282.

p. 178   LeFevre. *The Philosophy of Ownership.* p. 84.

p. 180   *U.S. News & World Report*, March 9, 1981, p. 73. "Half of All Americans Now Depend on Government."

p. 180   Padover, Saul K., editor. *The Complete Madison—His Basic Writings.* (New York: Harper & Brothers, 1953).

p. 180   Durant. *The Pleasures of Philosophy.* p. 293.

CHAPTER 8

p. 181   Forbes. *The Forbes Scrapbook.* p. 67.

p. 182   *U.S. News & World Report,* April 17, 1978: "Uncle Sam's Liabilities: Topping $7 Trillion."

p. 185   Downs. *Inside Bureaucracy.* pp. 5-23.

p. 185   Ibid, pp. 77-78.

p. 192   Friedman. *Free to Choose.* p. 145: "When the law interferes with people's pursuit of their own values, they will try to find a way around. They will evade the law, they will break the law, or they will leave the country. Few of us believe in a moral code that justifies forcing people to give up much of what they produce to finance payments to persons they do not know for purposes they may not approve of." See also pp. 289-290. Friedman gives examples of what the British and Swedes do as a result of their high tax systems.

p. 192   *U.S. News & World Report,* June 30, 1975, p. 24, "The 'Regulators.' They Cost You $130 Billion a Year."

CHAPTER 9

p. 193   Read. *The Free Man's Almanac.* p. 104.

p. 194   See Naisbett, John. *Megatrends.* (New York: Warner Books, 1982), p. 181-194. Naisbett says we have important political machineries already in place—initiatives and referenda. Decentralization is already replacing centralization. "Citizen initiatives frequently tackle the tough sensitive issues that legislators avoid to protect their popularity. Citizens do not. After all, the electorate need not concern itself with staying in office; it must only live with the results of it own decisions."

p. 196   *U.S. News & World Report,* July 16, 1984, p. 85: "Voting Blocs— Can A Candidate Pile Them Up?"

p. 197   Wright. *Capitalism.* p. 38: "Any civilization, then, will decline which fails to transmit to its younger members the key ideas of its culture."

p. 201   Davidson, John Wells. *A Crossroads of Freedom.* (New Haven: Yale University Press, 1956). Woodrow Wilson's speech to the New York Press Club, Sept. 9, 1912.

p. 201   See Naisbitt's newer work: *The Year Ahead 1986* (New York: Warner Books, Inc., 1985). pp. 104-117, Chapter Eight, entitled: "Private Enterprise Takes A Chunk Out of Government. Discovering Profit in Schools, Transit Systems, Prisons." That which he saw as a minor trend in *Megatrends*, Naisbett now sees as one of the "ten powerful trends shaping your future."

p. 201   See Friedman. *Free to Choose.* p. 299: "Our founding fathers have shown us a more promising way to proceed: by package deals, as it were. We should adopt self-denying ordinances that limited the objectives we try to pursue through political channels. We should not consider each case on its merits, but lay down broad rules limiting what government may do.

"We need, in our opinion, the equivalent of the First Amendment to limit governmental power in the economic and social area—an economic Bill of Rights to complement and reinforce the original Bill of Rights."

p. 201   See Hayek. *Constitution of Liberty.* p. 83: "Responsibility, to be effective, must be individual responsibility. In a free society there cannot be any collective repsonsibility of members of a group as such, unless they have, by concerted action, all made themselves individually and severally responsible."

p. 201   I will never cease to wonder about corporate naivete with regards to the free market. Corporation executives give great sums of money, in their own names and in the names of their businesses, to foundations and universities with the most questionable credentials. The next time you go to your college reunion, for example, and before you write them your annual check, take an hour to go to your alma mater's library and to its card file. You will have little difficulty finding the works of Chairman Mao and Marx and Engels. Then, try to locate copies of the works of Hayek, von Mises, or Milton Friedman!

The Wall Street Journal has run several editorial-page articles on this phenomenom in the past several years. Two that I thought were notable were: Kristol, Irving, "On Corporate Philanthropy," WSJ, March 21, 1977; and Olasky, Marvin, "Corporate Giver Beware," WSJ, June 28, 1985.

p. 201   See Sennholz, Hans F. *Age of Inflation*, p.171: "To spearhead a rebirth of our free society, let us rededicate ourselves to a new covenant of redemption, which is a simple restatement of public morality. In the setting of our age of economic redistribution and social conflict it may be stated as follows:

No matter how the transfer state may vicitimize me, I shall seek no transfer payments, nor accept any.

I shall seek no government grants, loans, or other redistributive favors, nor accept any.

I shall seek no government orders on behalf of redistribution, nor accept any.

I shall seek no employment in the government apparatus of redistribution, nor accept any.

I shall seek no favors from the regulatory agencies of government, nor accept any.

I shall seek no protection from tariff barriers or any other institutional restrictions on trade and commerce.

I shall seek no services from, nor lend support to, institutions that are creatures of redistribution.

I shall seek no support from, nor give support to, associations that advocate or practice coercion and restraint."

p. 203   Rand, Ayn. *Capitalism: The Unknown Ideal.* (New York: Signet Books, 1967). p. 250.

p. 204   *U.S. News & World Report*, March 10, 1986, p. 60, "When A Generation Turns 40."

p. 205   *U.S. News & World Report*, July 2, 1984, p. 51, "Today's Senior Citizens: Pioneers of New Golden Era." Interview with Dr. Robert Butler, Geriatric Specialist, Mt. Sinai Medical Center: "We used to think that if people lived long enough that they would become senile. That's not true. There is increasing evidence that intellectual growth continues through the later years. Quality of life is critical. If you don't keep learning, you don't keep growing; then it looks less exciting to stay alive."

p. 205   See Yankelovich, Daniel. *New Rules.* (New York: Random House, 1981), p. 57. He found that "73 percent of Americans feel they have 'more freedom of choice' on how to live their lives than their parents did. Only 8 percent believe they have fewer choices; 17 percent report the same level of choice as their parents; 2 percent are not sure ... 75 percent claim that they are at least as happy as their parents or happier (only 20 percent say they are unhappier)."

But, Yankelovich also reports, "people in the strong-form group hold both an upbeat and downbeat view of their future at the same time—the paradox expressed by Abby as a feeling that 'all doors are open to me ... and yet at the same time they are closing.' Exuberance is shot through with anxiety. Willfulness is coupled with a crippling sense of powerlessness. Decisiveness is undercut by confusion. And the warmth of self-acceptance is muted by an odd feeling of estrangement from the world. They are not sure how to choose and they are reluctant to risk freedom by making committments that may prove irrevocable. They seek to preserve their freedom by failing to risk it." [Emphasis is mine.] pp. 61-62.

CHAPTER 10

p. 207   Lippmann, Walter. An *Inquiry into the Principles of a Good Society*. (Boston, 1937), p. 267.

p. 207   According to a May 10, 1985 article in *The Wall Street Journal*, by Ed Bean, "Riddle: Why Won't a Typical Millionaire Take You for a Ride in His Fancy Car?" ... there are actually "833,000 households in the U.S. with a net worth of $1 million or more. The average millionaire's age is 57. Most are from blue-collar or middle-class backgrounds and graduated from a state university."

p. 208   Feinberg, Andrew. "Inside the Entrepreneur," *Venture Magazine*, May 1984, p. 80. and "Probing the Entrepreneurial Psyche," a Venture survey summarized by Nancy Madlin, May, 1985,

p. 209   *Reason Magazine*, July, 1980, pp. 48-53, Interview with Robert Ringer, author of *Restoring the American Dream*.

p. 209   See Jung, Carl G. *The Undiscovered Self*. (New York: American Library, 1959). "Resistance to the organizaed mass can be effected only by the man who is as well organized in his individuality as the mass itself."

p. 218   See "Why America's Got So Many Jobs," editorial by Peter F. Drucker, *The Wall Street Journal*, Jan. 24, 1984: "For 10 years now, the U.S. economy's dynamics have been shifting to entrepreneurial and innovative businesses—mostly low-tech or no-tech. In economics 10 years is a long time—long enough to talk of a 'structural change'."

p. 218   See "The New Entrepreneurs," *The Economist*, Dec. 23, 1983, p. 61: "Entrepreneurs are in fashion."

p. 218   Jefferson. *Notes on Virginia*, 1782.

p. 219   Durant. *Pleasures of Philosophy*. p. 76

p. 219 According to Gumpert, David E. and Timmons, Jeffrey A., *The Insider's Guide to Small Business Resources*, (New York: Doubleday, 1982), there are now over 200 colleges in the United States offering courses in entrepreneurship.

evaluation, <u>see</u> choice; values
excellence, <u>see</u> Peters and Waterman
exchange, freedoms and restrictions of,
  <u>see</u> Piece 3: Freedom to Exchange;
    Piece 13: Controlled Markets
executive government power, <u>see</u> Piece
  6; United States government,
    balance of power

F-
factors of production, <u>see</u> Philomod,
  Substructures
farm price supports, <u>see</u> United States
  government, price policies
Fear of Unknowns and Uncertainties
  (PP-11),23,179-180
feelings, human, <u>see</u> Preludes to Power
  (PP's)
fires, creative <u>see</u> creativity
Five Universals of Liberty, 200-202,216
Florida, 89,139ff.,158-170,190-191
FM Organizations, <u>see</u> Free-Market (FM)
  organizations and societies
Force, A Choice Of One Is, (CC-2), 13-14
Forcemodes and Forcepods, <u>see</u>
  Philomods
forms, <u>see</u> Philomod Corporation, 239-
  242
formulas,
  AM/FM national profile ratios cal-
    culation, 138
  "CC + CP = Optimal Outcome" grid
    of Choice Characteristics and
    Phases, 34-35(ill.)
  liberty/tyranny theorems, 201-202
Founding Fathers, <u>see</u> mentors; United
  States government, founding of
France, 125,127ff.,139ff.,154
Franklin, Benjamin, 116ff.,132,170
Free Choice, the Structure of, <u>see</u> Choice;
  Piece 1: Freedom to Choose
freedom
  Five Characteristics of, 58-66
  political, 64
  vulnerability of, 56,79
Freedom to Choose, <u>see</u> Piece 1
Freedom to Exchange, <u>see</u> Piece 3
Freedom to Fund, <u>see</u> Piece 4
Freedom to Own, <u>see</u> Piece 2
Free-Market (FM) organizations and
  societies, 65,181,186
  antithesis of, 131-180
  databank and strategies, 189-190
  economy, competitive, 33,68,73-74
  international symbol need, 41-42
  models of, 46,53-54,134
  political-economic base of, 33,86,115-
    130

products, typical symbols of, 40-43
stocks and bonds, 140-141
  survival and self-destruction as-
    pects, 113,152,254n.
The Three-Questions Test, 78-80
trade organizations and government
  licensing, 147-148
<u>see also</u> entrepreneurs and
  entrepreneurship
Freemodes and Freepods, <u>see</u> Philomods
Friedman, Milton, <u>see</u> mentors
Friedman, Rose, 238
funding freedom, reasons for, <u>see</u> Pieces
  1, 4

G-
Galileo, 103
Gentle Flames, <u>see</u> creativity
Germany, 138-139,154
  National Socialist Party (Nazi party),
    40,100,156
glossaries, visual, 50,54,134
  <u>see also</u> mechanical drawings of
    Philomods
GNP (Gross National Product), <u>see</u> Anti-
  Market (AM) structures
gold standard, the, 61
goods and services, profitable, <u>see</u> Piece
  11; products; The Three Test
  Questions
governments
  and property
    ownership laws, examples, 61
    privatization, 258n.
    public ownership, 59-66,140
    tax-supported projects, 190
  assistance and grants, renunciations
    of, 259n.
  bureaucracies
    character of, 115-130
    impact of Anti-market growth on,
      181,184-186
    size of, "the Dinosaur effect," 179
  economic powers and fiscal policies,
    64-66
    insurance costs, 24
    licensing of enterprises, 147-
      148,164
    monopoly privileges, 74,255n.
    lotteries, 147-148
  funding of (the "fatal flaw"), 141,255n.
  policy consequences and mistakes,
    141,145,190,246n.,255n
  powers of, symbolic rings, 53-54
    protection from uncertainty, 24
  <u>see also</u> Pieces 5, 6, 12, 13, 14; United
    States government

PHILOMOD SUBSTRUCTURES: Related Mutually-Dependent Concepts

The Free-Market (FM) Principles Group

① Freedom to Choose
② Freedom to Own (Private Ownership of Property)
③ Freedom to Exchange (Competitive Markets)
④ Freedom to Fund (Voluntary Funding)

The Anti-Market (AM) Ideologies Group

⑤ Centralized Governmental Power
⑫ Public Ownership of Productive Property
⑬ Controlled Markets (Restricted Exchange)
⑭ Mandatory Funding (Taxation and Inflation)

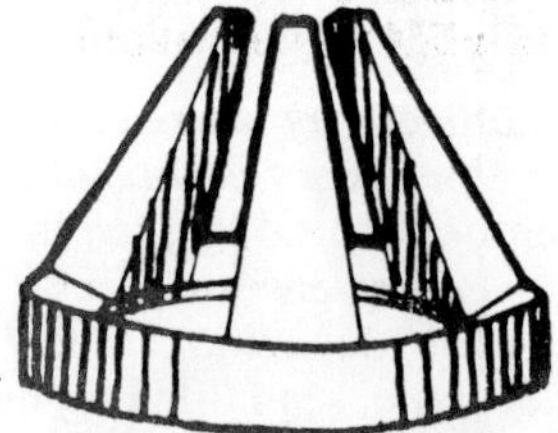

The Operating Organization Group

⑦ Creativity and Innovation
⑧ Management
⑨ People Resources
⑩ Property Resources
⑪ The Product or Service

The Entrepreneurial Function Sub-Group

⑦ Creativity and Innovation
⑧ Management

The Productive Resources Sub-Group

⑨ People Resources
⑩ Property Resources

The Constitutional Balance of Governmental Power

⑤ Centralized Governmental Power
⑥ Limitation & Dispersion of Government Power
① Powers Reserved to the Individual

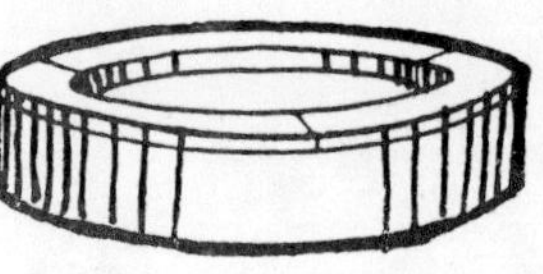

Below is our visual/verbal glossary. These are the six new words and the five new visual concepts that are basic to this book and its accompanying models.

Freepod

The structure of liberty.
The tripod of economic freedom.
The three legs upon their base,
taking their strength from the base.

**Freemode
(An FM Organization)**

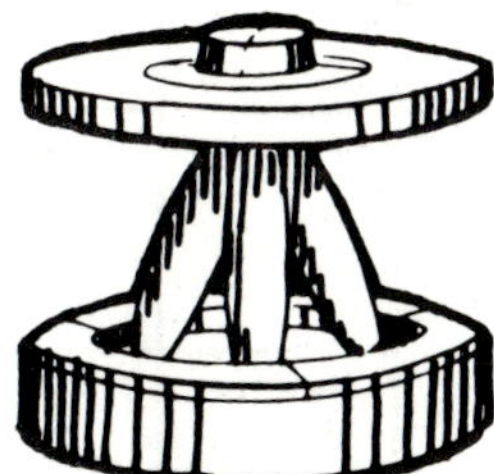

The model of a productive private enterprise based upon economic freedom and protected by a political policy of limited government. This organization is a member of the free-market (FM) community.

Forcepod

The tripod representing the anti-market (AM) economic ideology. Governmental power is the base. The three legs get their strength from this power.

**Forcemode
(An AM Organization)**

The model of an anti-market (AM) organization based upon the economic philosophy of controlled markets and the political policy of unlimited governmental power. This organization is a member of the anti-market (AM) community.

Hybrimode

The model of a hybrid organization, based in part on economic freedom but also dependent upon the political policy of centralized governmental power.

Philomods   All of the above. Philomods are visible, tangible, three-dimensional models of philosophies. Each piece stands for something of substance. Each piece in each structure represents a specific concept. Each structure illustrates the relationships and mutual dependencies of the concepts involved.

CC + CP = Optimal Outcome

Process

8 Evaluation	7 Action	6 Communication	5 Decision	4 Collection	3 Analysis	2 Definition	1 Awareness	**Characteristics**
								1 Purpose: Improve the situation
								2 Choices come in two's or more
								3 Best outcome, best inputs
								4 Every choice has a cost
								5 Individual value preferences
								6 Limited time, information
								7 Unknowns, uncertainties & risks
								8 Primary & secondary consequences
								9 You are responsible
								10 Big choices hard to change

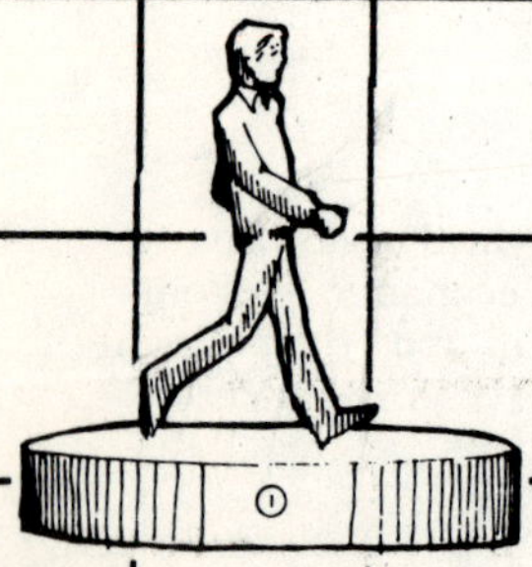